Dragon Professional – A Step Further

Michael Shepherd

Dragon Professional – A Step Further

First published in 2019 by Michael Shepherd: ASPA MEDIA

Published in London, United Kingdom

ISBN: 978-1-9160450-4-0

A catalogue record for this book is available from the British Library.

Trademarks

Dragon, Dragon Professional Individual, Dragon Professional Group, Dragon NaturallySpeaking, MouseGrid, NaturallySpeaking, DragonPad, DragonBar and Vocabulary Editor are registered trademarks of Nuance Inc.

Windows 8, Windows 10, MS-DOS, Command Prompt (cmd.exe), MSOffice 2010, Office 365, Microsoft 365, Excel, MS Excel, Excel 2010, Excel 365, Outlook, MS Outlook, Outlook 365, PowerPoint, MS PowerPoint, PowerPoint 2010, PowerPoint 365, Publisher, MS Publisher, Publisher 2010, Publisher 365, Visual Basic, Word, MS Word, Word 2010, and Word 365 are trademarks or registered trademarks of Microsoft Corporation.

Mindjet, MindManager, Mindjet MindManager are registered trademarks of Mindjet LLC.

Sonocent, Audio Notetaker, Sonocent Audio Notetaker are registered trademarks of Sonocent Ltd.

All other product names and services identified throughout this book are used in editorial fashion only and for the benefit of such companies with no intention of infringement of the trademark. No such use, or the use of any trade name, is intended to convey endorsement or other affiliation with this book.

Warning and Disclaimer

The author and publisher have made every effort to make this book as complete and as accurate as possible, but no warranty or fitness is implied. The information provided is on an "as is" basis. The information contained in this book is sold without warranty, either express or implied.

The author and the publisher disclaim all responsibility for errors or omissions, including without limitation responsibility for damages resulting from the use of or reliance on this work.

Neither the authors nor the publisher (or any of their employees, agents, subcontractors, distributors or assigns) has any responsibility for any loss of any kind, including lost profits, arising from your use of any of these code examples.

Use of the information and instructions contained in this book is at your own risk. If any code samples or other technology this work contains or describes is subject to open source licenses or the intellectual property rights of others, it is your responsibility to ensure that your use thereof complies with such licenses and/or rights.

The example macros contained in this book are designed to illustrate the potential of how Dragon Professional and Dragon NaturallySpeaking can interact with various applications. Each macro will only work with the stated application and are not designed to work impeccably under all conditions; therefore, you should treat them with caution if you decide to use them on anything other than the stated application.

Although every effort has been made to test the macros for errors and eliminate them, errors may unknowingly occur. I strongly suggest that you trial the macros using test documents and re-test, especially if there has been an update to any of the applications.

For macros that contain Object Referencing, make sure that you have selected the correct Object Library for your version of the application. Be aware that an application update can sometimes change the Object Library required.

Acknowledgments

Firstly, thanks go to the people at Nuance for their continued efforts to improve the Dragon software application over the years; to my students, many of whom overcome adversities and inspire me; to my family and friends, for providing me with their continued encouragement and support.

Finally, this book is the result of the hard work of Patricia Shepherd, David White and Yvette Newton. Patricia in particular, never fails to impress me with her meticulous attention to detail and editorial skills, David equally for providing editorial support and Yvette for providing me with countless hours of her design and layout skills and commitment to quality. Without all your efforts, this book would not have seen the light of day and I am forever grateful.

In loving memory of the late Yvette Michelle Newton,
whose spirit and guidance are with me every day.

About the Author

Michael Shepherd is a Dragon accredited trainer and freelance assistive technology (AT) tutor with more than 30 years of IT experience. He has created and delivered training courses for educational establishments in the UK and abroad. His roles have also included: systems analyst, software developer and business consultant.

For the last 10 years he has been teaching university students how to utilise their assistive technology software to aid them in their studies. It is his enthusiasm for the Dragon software and the benefits that it offers, not only to his students but also to a wider audience of businesses and organisations, which has encouraged him to share his passion for the product.

In his spare time, he runs a start-up tech company that specialises in developing educational apps.

Contents

Introduction

Dragon Professional (formerly known as Dragon NaturallySpeaking) is a fully-fledged application that will allow the end user to perform dictation, automation as well as enabling virtually full control over their PCs, all by voice. For several years Dragon has been the leading worldwide application for speech to text. Many people who own/use Dragon don't utilise the many fantastic features that the application can provide for them.

My ultimate goal for this book is to make Dragon more accessible for everyone who uses this application; to encourage users to explore its powerful features that enable integration with popular software, incorporation of VBA macros, the creation of amazing Dialog forms to gather and manipulate data and so much more.

Whether you are a student, professional or enterprise user, working with Dragon will without doubt boost your efficiency, save you time and make you more productive.

Which Version of Dragon is Required?

If you have a copy of Dragon NaturallySpeaking Version 13 or below, you will need either the professional, medical or legal versions to take full advantage of inputting, exporting and creating Dragon macros. Regarding Version 14 and above, Nuance reduced the number of versions of the product down to two i.e. Dragon Professional Individual (DPI) and Dragon Professional Group (DPG), both of which allow for full and Advanced Scripting.

Screenshots are from the Dragon Professional Group version.

Who is This Book For?

If you are a beginner/intermediate user of Dragon its more than likely you are dictating successfully, using commands to open, save and format your documents and perhaps inserting your email signatures and performing shortcut keys by dictating commands.

But, how about filling in a large form over several pages without having to scroll up and down to find specific fields, or copying all charts within a spreadsheet to a report you are working on in MS Word, or, if you are using custom macros within office documents, wouldn't you like to run these as voice commands?

Then this book is for you - All of the above and much more can be done automatically by dictating a made-up phrase of your choice.

Regardless of your programming background, in no time, you will get to grips with how Dragon can perform complex and tedious procedures by simple voice commands, as well as the ability to build custom user interfaces that allow users to interact with their PCs in ways not thought possible.

For the advanced user, this book can be used as a point of reference. It includes sample macros to demonstrate Dragon script functions and has ready to use commands that can be manipulated and adjusted to suit your needs.

"Dragon Professional - A Step Further" as the name suggests, is designed to develop, enhance and realise the potential and capabilities of using the Dragon application. You will find lots of example code and in addition there are several practical example macros, where I discuss the code in detail and provide links to chapters and topics within the book for more reading, if you wish.

I have endeavoured to make this book as clear and concise as possible and hopefully, by exploring the content you will be inspired to create your own Dragon commands that will automate repetitive tasks, saving you time and consequently improving productivity in your work, study and personal environment.

Essentially, anyone wanting to take Dragon Professional or Dragon NaturallySpeaking a step further will find this book a valuable resource.

What Does This Book Cover?

This book shows you how to create Dragon voice commands that will automate your work in Microsoft Office, MS Windows and other applications. You will learn how to create your own Bespoke Dialog Forms that can work as standalone user interfaces to gather and manipulate data, and before you know it, you'll be on your way to creating effective and powerful solutions for your work environment.

The book is divided into seven main sections, and to give you an overall picture, here is a summary:

Section 1, "Let's Get Started" - The chapters in this section introduce you to the various types of Dragon commands and how to determine which type is suitable for the task you wish your command to perform, as well as, learning how to create, edit and train the Dragon commands. You will be shown how to record a macro using the Macro Recorder, (available in MS Word and MS Excel) in order to create your own VBA scripts and then use these created scripts to produce Dragon voice commands. You'll also be made aware of the importance of Object Library References and the role they play when creating Dragon commands that incorporate application VBA.

Section 2, "Creating Dragon Lists" – In this section you will become familiar with creating commands that include Lists. The chapters highlight how to create macros that can be run by dictating multiple phrases; create macros that will perform different actions depending on what has been dictated; as well as how to create your own bespoke Dragon Lists. In addition, you will also be shown how to take advantage of the most powerful of all Dragon Lists - "<dictation>".

Section 3, "The Dialog Form Editor" - This section explores the under used (in my opinion) UserDialog Form Editor. You will learn how to create unique custom Dialog Forms from scratch, that works independently of other applications and interact with the user to gather data and produce results. Each aspect of the Dialog Form Editor is explained in detail, with lots of example code for you to experiment with.

Section 4, "Distributing and Encrypting Dragon Macros" – The chapters in this section focuses on importing & exporting your created Dragon commands, as well as details on how to apply protection and encryption to your macros for distribution to colleagues or friends.

Section 5, "Dragon Script Functions" - Here we take a look at the vast array of Dragon built-in commands, functions and statements that can be used when writing your scripts. There is a comprehensive list of SendDragonKeys, SendKeys & SendSystemKeys examples (very useful when creating your own keyboard shortcut macros). There is an explanation for each of the commands, the majority of which have example code to show how they can be used. This section is ideal as a point of reference.

Section 6, "Ready to use Dragon commands" – In this section you will find a number of example commands that will work with and automate popular Office applications, Mindjet MindManager, the Windows operating system, Command Prompt and others. These macros are ready to use and represent real-life scenarios.

Section 7, "Appendix" - The Appendix includes examples of Send Keys Step Dialog box codes; a list of popular ASCII character codes; some useful Dragon In-Built Commands and an Index.

How to Use This Book

This book is not written in the standard format of most technical books. It's designed as a reference guide with tutorials and examples that are easy to follow, with the addition of a personal touch of how to get more out of Dragon.

I have organised the book in such a way that users who are familiar with Dragon and its scripting language can go directly to a chapter for more information, detailed explanations and examples on a specific topic. However, for those who are totally unfamiliar with Dragon scripting, application VBA and macro creation, the temptation may be to dive in, but I would suggest that the earlier chapters are a good starting point.

In my attempt to avoid repetition of information, examples and explanations build on each other within chapters and topics. Therefore, at times, discussions within this book will generally assume that you have read earlier sections.

Conventions Used in This Book

Below you will find the typographical conventions used in this book.

The steps to follow using menu commands are written using the following format:

The ">>" is used to show the path for choosing an item from the DragonBar. For example, the line "Tools >> Command Browser" means that you should click on the "Tools" icon in the DragonBar and then select the option "Command Browser" from the list of available options. Figure 0-1 shows the DragonBar with the Tools icon selected.

Figure 0-1

The use of an apostrophe (') usually at the beginning of a line of code will turn the text following it to the colour green in the MyCommands Editor window. This text is ignored when the command is run and serves as a comment to assist in the understanding of the code (often referred to as commented code). You do not need to type in any of the comments.

Some of the example macros contain lines of commented code. These lines are included for you to experiment with the command, you can un-comment the examples individually by removing the apostrophe (') at the beginning of each line of code or alternatively un-comment them all and run the command.

The plus sign (+) is used to indicate the pressing of keyboard keys combinations, here are some examples:

- Pressing **Ctrl+Shift+F5** means that you should hold down the *Ctrl* key, *Shift* key and then press the *F5* key.
- Pressing **Alt+PrtSc** means you should hold down the *Alt* key and then press the *PrtSc* key.
- A line with **Ctrl+V, W** means you should press and hold down the *Ctrl* key and then press the *V* key, release the *Ctrl* key and then press the *W* key once.

Also, at times keyboard combinations will be represented without the plus sign (+). For example, **Alt, N, H** means to press the *Alt* key once, press the *N* key once, press the *H* key once (not simultaneously).

"*text written in italics and within quotes*" is used to represent something you should say.

You will come across lines that end with " _". This means that the line of code that follows is a continuation of the previous line. These have been placed merely for readability purposes and you can remove the underscore if you don't mind having long lines of code.

Below is an example of how one long line of code would be written out:

```
SendKeys WeekdayName(Weekday(Yesterday)) & " " _

MonthName(Month(Yesterday)) & " " _

Day(Yesterday) & " " & Year(Yesterday)
```

Actual Dragon scripting code is represented in the font style "A line of code"

Straight quotes are and must be used within Dragon scripting code (" ").

Curly and single quotes are used elsewhere for descriptive purposes (' ') (" ").

The terms 'macro', 'command', 'custom command', 'recipe', 'script', 'code' and 'voice command' are all interchangeable.

The terms 'Dragon', 'Dragon Professional', 'Dragon Professional Individual (DPI)', 'Dragon Professional Group (DPG)', 'Dragon NaturallySpeaking (DNS)' are all interchangeable.

The terms 'Visual Basic for Applications', 'Application Visual Basic', 'Visual Basic', 'VBA' are all interchangeable.

Throughout this book you will often see additional note sections, these provide extra information such as warnings, pitfalls, alternatives and what can and cannot be done in relation to the topic being discussed.

Creating and Testing the Macros for Yourself

As you delve into the book, I am sure there will come a point when you will want to try out some of these macro recipes for yourself.

The quickest way to get started is by having Dragon open and saying the command "*add a new command*" or alternatively go to the DragonBar Tools menu and select Add New Command. This will reveal the MyCommands Editor window (see Figure 0-2) with a prompt ready for you to give your new command a name.

Figure 0-2

A new Advanced Scripting type command in the MyCommands Editor.

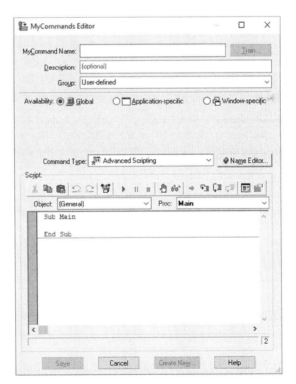

MyCommands Editor options:

MyCommand Name: Is the actual name you give to a command. It is also the words you say in order to execute the command, for example, "*Insert my signature*". The exception being where the command you have created includes Lists shown by the use of <...> in the MyCommand Name.

For example, if a MyCommand Name is "Please open <app>" and within the List <app> are the titles "Sublime Text" & "MS Paint". Then in order to run this command, you can either say "*Please open Sublime Text*" or "*Please open MS Paint*". If you were to say "*Please open Notepad*" or anything else that is not in the List, the command would not be executed. Refer to Chapter 4: Dragon List Commands for more information.

Description: Although not compulsory, it is good practice to insert text here that describes the function you wish the macro to perform.

Group: Organise your commands into groups to make them easy to find in the Command Browser. You can choose a group from the list or create a new group by typing a new name into the Group field.

Availability: Make a choice as to whether your macro will be Global (can be run from any environment), Application-specific (only runs when a specific application is active) or Window-specific (only runs when a specific window of an application is active).

Command Type: Select the type of command you wish to create.

Content: Insert the contents of the macro into this field.

Throughout this book I have displayed my recommended text and choices for you to use, however, please feel free to change the command name, add to the description or change the group name if you wish. Changing the Availability may produce undesired results as some commands are created to only work with a specific application.

Most of the recipes in this book will be of the Advanced Scripting command type.

Here is an example:

MyCommand Name: print screen directly to file

Description: Take a screenshot of the whole screen and save to a file

Group: Chapter 01

Availability: Global

Command Type: Advanced Scripting

Content:

```
Sub Main

  . . .

  . . . . .

End Sub
```

Try it by saying:
"print screen directly to file"

There will be times when perhaps it is more appropriate not to go through the whole process of creating and naming a command from scratch. As you go through the book you will come across code examples where all that is supplied is just the code that sits between the Sub Main and End Sub area. In order to quickly observe how such code works, you can right-click on an existing command and select **New Copy** (be sure to bear in mind the Availability option), rename the MyCommand Name and then copy and paste the new code to replace the existing code.

Running commands without performing the voice command.

At times it is more convenient and appropriate to test scripts by not having to perform a voice command. To do this, when editing your script in the MyCommands Editor window either click on the "Start/Resume" icon or press (F5) to run the command (see Figure 0-3).

Figure 0-3

Using the Code Examples

This book serves as a guide, a source of reference and a vehicle which allows you to experiment with pushing Dragon much further than you have done before. As such, I encourage you to try out the macro examples and make changes to suit your needs. You do not need to contact me for permission unless you're reproducing a significant portion of the code. For example, writing a program that uses several chunks of code from this book does not require permission. The selling or distributing of a CD-ROM, memory stick or downloadable file does require permission. Answering a question by citing this book and quoting an example code does not require permission. Incorporating a significant amount of the example code from this book into your products documentation does require permission.

Obtaining the Example Code

To avoid the time-consuming task of creating the example macros manually, the macros in this book can be downloaded from the book's companion site at www.dragonspeechtips.com/dp-further/

Once imported, the macros can be viewed and edited.

Where necessary, downloaded zip files (when unzipped) will include example documents and images.

Section 1: Let's Get Started

Chapter 1: Introduction to Macros, Dragon Commands and Dragon Command Types

What are Macros?

A macro can be described as a list of tasks that you want a program to perform in order to carry out an action; we could interpret it as being somewhat like a recipe, whereby we have the instructions, follow the instructions and the outcome is a dish of some sort.

Macros consists of a set of instructions that when put together into a single script can be invoked by a shortcut key combination; an additional button placed onto a menu system or by voice command, which is the focus of this book.

We have all at some point whilst working on our PCs found ourselves carrying out a particular task that we have performed countless times before. It may be a task that is time consuming and needs to be carried out in a strict set of steps where accuracy is paramount and by its very nature demands one's full attention. I have found myself in this position many times; whether it's making sure that the signature text in my emails are all formatted precisely in the same way; struggling to remember how to perform a complex calculation in a spreadsheet or meticulously navigating through an application's menu system in order to carry out a specific task.

Thankfully, this is where creating macros can make all the difference to your workflow, time and often sanity. They enable us to automate complicated sequences that may be difficult; prone to human error; time-consuming or tedious to perform. They will carry out your instructions to the letter; perform repetitive tasks flawlessly and in almost all cases will execute tasks a lot faster than is humanly possible.

 Macros are often created and used within applications such as MS Word and MS Excel.

Working with Dragon Commands

When Dragon listens to, and interprets your voice, it either recognises it as dictation, whereby what you say is actually being written/typed out (when using MS Word for instance) or as a command, where you want Dragon to perform a particular action, such as saying "*goto sleep*" in order to send the microphone into standby.

The commands can also be referred to as macros and Dragon by default, comes with lots of them. Some of these commands/macros you may already be using on a regular basis, "*goto end of line*", "*bold that*", "*mouse left click*" are just a tiny fraction of the commands available. Some commands only work when working within specific applications, others work no matter what environment you are currently working in.

You will notice that on the right-hand side of the DragonBar is the Full Text Control indicator (a green indicator light, also referred to as the circle indicator), which will be on or off depending on the application (environment) you are working in. Figure 1-1 shows the DragonBar with the Full Text Control Indicator light on and off.

Figure 1-1

The DragonBar with the Full Text Control indicator
(small green indicator light) on.

The DragonBar with the Full Text Control indicator light off.

The green indicator light when on, indicates that Dragon has full text control within the application and will respond to commands that act on specific text, such as "*correct <text>*" and "*select <text>*". Basically, there are a larger number of built-in commands available to you.

The green indicator light when off, indicates that Dragon has basic text control within the application. You will be limited in the amount of built-in commands at your disposal, and as such, may have to use the Dictation Box if you want more control over your dictation within the application.

Although Dragon has hundreds of built-in commands, there is no way the team at Nuance can meet the personal needs of all users. Thankfully, Dragon allows us to create our own personalised voice commands/macros by writing our own scripts.

If you haven't done so already, you will find that creating your own personalised macros can be extremely beneficial and satisfying and here are just a few reasons why:

- They can perform complicated sequences that may be difficult to remember; prone to human error; time-consuming or tedious.
- Sufferers of RSI who struggle with using the keyboard and mouse can use Dragon macros to control and automate their PCs in multiple ways.
- For those who struggle with remembering keyboard shortcuts, creating a memorable voice command is far easier than having to remember the keystrokes required.
- They will carry out your instructions to the letter; perform repetitive tasks flawlessly and in most cases execute tasks a lot faster than a human can.

There is no doubt that creating your own Dragon commands will allow you to accomplish more in less time, enable you to carry out tasks efficiently, turn Dragon into an automation tool and have more control over your PC, all by voice.

I have created Dragon voice command macros for countless scenarios, and it has become second nature to look for ways to automate my work processes. In fact, when it comes to using shortcut keys within applications (to perform tasks), I will often create voice commands as an alternative method, thus eliminating the need for me to remember the keystroke combinations required, very handy!

What type of Dragon Macro (Command) can, or should I create?

Dragon allows us to create four types of Macros:

- Auto-Text(Text and Graphics)
- Macro Recorder
- Step-by-Step
- Advanced Scripting

The type of macro you create is dependent on what you want it to do. Table 1-1 provides a basic guide.

Table 1-1

What you want it to do:	Appropriate Macro to create:
Insert a large amount of text such as a business letter template. Produce some text and/or graphics, such as an email signature with a logo.	Auto-Text(Text and Graphics)
Perform a set of keyboard keystroke actions. Open a specific application and carry out keyboard shortcuts. Open a specific website page in the browser.	Step-by-Step Advanced Scripting
Fully manipulate an application to perform several tasks. Perform a created application VBA macro. Create a custom user interface or Dialog form.	Advanced Scripting
Move the mouse, click and perform keystrokes.	Advanced Scripting Macro Recorder

In addition, when creating your Dragon commands, you should consider the environment in which you wish them to work. This is determined by the Availability option (found in the myCommands Editor window) selected at the point of building your commands. Here are the options:

- **Global:** The macro can be run at any time; it does not matter what environment or software application you are working in.
- **Application-Specific:** The macro will only run when you are working within a specific application. When selected, Dragon will reveal further options within the MyCommands Editor, most importantly it needs to know the application the macro is to work with.
- **Window-specific:** The macro will only run when you are working within a specified window within a specified application. When selected, Dragon will reveal further options within the MyCommands Editor.

Although many of the example commands used throughout this book could quite easily be made by creating Step-by-Step commands, the preferred method will be to use Advanced Scripting.

Creating an Auto-Text(Text and Graphics) Command

Auto-Text(Text and Graphics) commands are the preferred method for essentially inserting unlimited formatted text (with or without images) into your documents.

In a business setting you can use a created Auto-Text command to create email signatures, letter templates and fillable forms and by dictating the command name, have the entire text appear in your documents. Other uses include the ability to quickly insert often used repeated paragraphs, phrases or sentences.

Let's have a go at creating an Auto-Text command; which when run within a word processing application, generates a paragraph of formatted text and image.

To get started we need to create a new command: Click on the DragonBar; Click the Tools option and select Add New Command or do the same by saying "*add new command*", both methods will reveal the MyCommands Editor window.

Figure 1-2

An example of an Auto-Text(Text and Graphics) command, consisting of formatted text and an image.

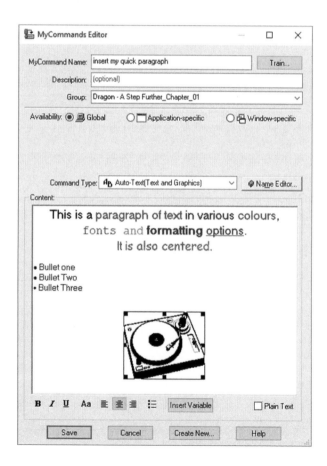

Figure 1-2 shows the intended text and image to be generated; fill in the fields as can be seen and attempt to format the text in the Content area in the same way.

Below is an explanation of the options available when creating an Auto-Text(Text and Graphics) command:

In the field **MyCommand Name**, we type in the command name ("insert my quick paragraph") for this command. This is also the phrase we will dictate in order to make Dragon execute the command.

The field **Description** is optional and allows us to insert a brief description of what our command does.

The **Group** option enables us to either have this command as part of an existing set of commands or create a new group name for the command. For now, let's leave it in the default "User-defined" group of commands.

In the **Availability** section of the window, we select the **Global** radio button option. Global is selected as we wish this command to be available to us regardless of the word processing application used.

The command type is selected by clicking on the down arrow within the **Command Type** drop-down menu and selecting Auto-Text(Text and Graphics).

The **Content** area is where we will place the text and image to be generated when running the command. When placing the text into the Content area we have two options, we can either:

- Format the intended text in a word processing application, copy the text and then paste it into the Content area.
- Type the intended text in the Content area and then use the Dragon options to format/style the text.

Should you decide to go for the latter option, you will need to use the formatting icons and make the necessary changes to any selected text. Further options, such as font selection, font size etc. are made available by clicking on the (**Aa**) icon, which when clicked, reveals the Font window as can be seen in Figure 1-3.

Figure 1-3

Clicking on the (Aa) icon reveals the Font window. The Font window enables you to format your text.

Inserting an Image

To place an image into the Content area, the image file must first be opened in another application such as MS Paint or MS Word. Select the image and then use the Copy command within the application; switch back to the MyCommands Editor window; place the cursor in the required position; right-click and select Paste. Once pasted the image can be selected and resized.

Click the Save button to save your new command, open a word processing application and try it by saying: "*insert my quick paragraph*".

 Tab indents can be made in the Content area; however, to achieve this, you need to press Ctrl+Tab, as Tab on its own will move you out of the Content area.

Inserting Variables (Fields) into Auto-Text(Text and Graphics) Commands

The **Insert Variable** button.

Adding Fields to your Auto-Text commands will add a degree of flexibility to how you work with generated text. They also enable you to take advantage of a number of Dragon built-in commands that will prove useful when navigating around or filling in your generated letters or forms.

Let's look at the benefits of inserting Fields by opening the previous macro ("insert my quick paragraph") in the MyCommands Editor window.

- To open the command, go to the DragonBar >> Tools >> Command Browser
- Select the User-defined group and double click the macro "insert my quick paragraph"

Place your cursor at the top line in the Content area and press Enter four times to insert four blank lines.

Now, on the first blank line type in the text "Date"; Click on the Dragon button "Insert Variable"; select "Date[default value]" and click on the right-justification icon.

On the second blank line type in the text "Dear"; Click on the Dragon button "Insert Variable"; replace the words "default value" with the word "user"; then after the "]" insert a comma.

On the third blank line type in the text "Do you require the "; Click on the Dragon button "Insert Variable"; replace the words "default value" with the words "English/German"; then after the "]" type in the text " version of our manual".

We will leave the fourth line blank for readability.

Figure 1-4 shows how the top of the Content area should now look.

Figure 1-4

The Auto-Text(Text and Graphics) command is updated by including fields. These fields provide the end user with a more interactive result.

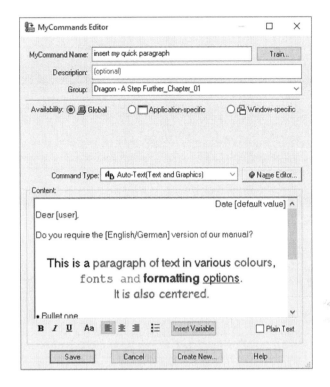

As you have just seen, a Field is created by placing the cursor in the required position and clicking on the "Insert Variable" button. By default, Dragon will produce a Field that has the words "default value" within it ([default value]).

Now that these Fields have been inserted, when the command is run it will enable us to insert a specific value for each of them or accept their default values.

Click the Save button to save your updated command, open a word processing application and try it by saying: "*insert my quick paragraph*".

Once the text (including Fields) is generated within a document, we are then able to take advantage of the following built-in Dragon commands:

- If we say, "*next field*" Dragon will move the focus to the next Field ready for us to dictate a value.
- By saying "*previous field*" focus will be moved to the previous Field.

Once a Field is focused, we can dictate a new value over the existing name (notice how the delimiters ([and]) are automatically removed). Or, if you have dictated your new values and only have the default field names remaining, we can say either "*accept defaults*" or "*clear variable delimiters*". These commands will automatically remove all remaining delimiters throughout the document.

The left ([) and right (]) square brackets that surround a Field name are referred to as "Delimiters" and they mark the beginning and end of each Field.

Inserting Multiple Variables (Fields)

Whenever you have to produce a form, a letter or a large amount of text that contains many Fields, it may seem easier to create all the Fields and leave them as default value. However, when it comes to running the command it could be confusing as to which Field should contain which information. Therefore, I would suggest that you replace the [default value] Fields with a name appropriate to the data you want to fill it with, as can be seen with the Fields [user] and [English/German].

It is a good idea to think about the name you wish to use for your Fields and to name them according to either of these circumstances:

- Do I want the Field name to serve as a reminder of the values I may dictate when the focus is on this Field? e.g. Do you require the [English/German].
- Do I want the Field name to be a default value? As more often than not, this will be the value inserted. e.g. Dear [user].

All Fields can be overwritten when the text has been generated.

The Plain Text CheckBox Option

When creating or editing an Auto-Text(Text and Graphics) command, you will notice in the bottom right-hand corner of the MyCommands Editor window a CheckBox labelled "Plain Text".

If the CheckBox is checked (and the command is saved), it will have the following effect on the text, images and Fields within the Content area:

- All formatted text will become plain text and the styling will be removed.
- All images will be removed.
- All inserted Fields will remain.

When an Auto-Text command containing text (with the CheckBox checked) is run in a word processing application, the text generated will be in the style (font, colour, size, etc.) determined by the format set in the application and also where the cursor is positioned when the command is run.

Auto-Text(Text and Graphics) commands can include Dragon Lists.

Refer to:

Chapter 4: Dragon List & Written\Spoken words Lists in Auto-Text(Text and Graphics) Dragon Commands

Creating a Macro Recorder Command

The Macro Recorder command provides us with ability to record all the manual steps, including mouse actions that one would undertake to perform a specific task.

To create a Macro Recorder command type to perform a task, press the Record button. Dragon will then record all your mouse movements, mouse clicks and keyboard entries. The information gathered is then used to populate the Actions area in the MyCommands Editor window (see Figure 1-5) with a list of instructions, which Dragon will carry out to perform the task when the command is run.

Figure 1-5

An example of a Macro Recorder type command. It will perform the clicking of the left mouse button and perform cursor movement around the screen.

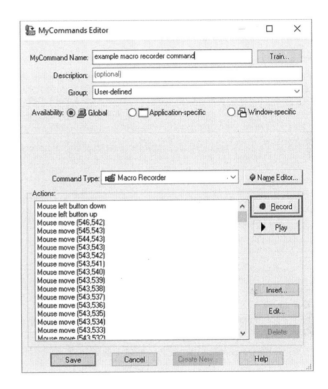

Often these types of commands contain a large amount of detail, as the information will include the precise screen coordinate values of the mouse position throughout the process.

In this book I do not go into detail about Dragon Macro Recorder commands because they are the slowest of the command types, and often do not provide reliable results, especially when sharing your commands with others.

Creating a Step-by-Step Command

Step-by-Step commands are an ideal way to get started in creating your own Dragon commands. You can quickly create effective commands with no coding experience that will instruct your applications to perform a vast range of useful functionalities.

A Step-by-Step command as the name suggests is a macro that consists of a number of sequenced instructions (steps) that Dragon will perform one after the other. Consequently, for some, Step-by-Step commands are an ideal way to create voice commands that reproduce shortcut keystrokes within applications; create commands that will open the browser at a specific web page (URL); open documents ready for editing and a lot more.

Step-by-Step commands are efficient and does work well. However, when creating macros, a more experienced user may prefer to create the same macro as an Advanced Scripting type command, as these are much faster in the execution of a command.

In this section of the book, I will walk you through the thinking and processes required to create Step-by-Step commands; and trust me! There is no greater feeling than that sense of achievement when producing your own commands which will perform the tasks you require, all by voice.

Let's start by creating a command that when we say, "*go back*", will emulate the pressing of the back button (as can be seen in Figure 1-6) when browsing web pages within the Google Chrome browser.

Figure 1-6

The Google Chrome back button; used to return to the previous web page.

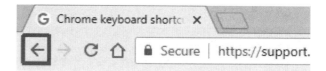

Our approach to this scenario would be to think about and answer the following questions:

1. Is there a shortcut keystroke or sequence of keystrokes that will carry out this action when using Chrome? Yes (**Alt+Left arrow**)
2. Do I want this voice command to only work when I am using Google Chrome? Yes
3. Is creating a Step-by-Step type of Dragon command suitable for performing the task? Yes

 The answer to question 1 is found by searching the Internet with the question "what is the keyboard shortcut for the back button in Google Chrome?"

Now that we have answered "Yes" to all our questions, let's go through the process of how we put our command together:

First, on the DragonBar; click the Tools option and select Add New Command or do the same by saying "*add new command*", both methods will reveal the MyCommands Editor window.

Now let's fill in the fields, here is an explanation for each of the options available:

In the field **MyCommand Name**, we type in the command name ("go back"). This is also the phrase that we will dictate to make Dragon carry out the command.

 Command names should be written in lowercase.

The field **Description** is optional and allows us to insert a brief description of what our command does.

The **Group** option enables us to either have this command as part of an existing set of commands or create a new group name for the command. For now, let's leave it in the default "User-defined" group of commands.

 A command can be moved to another group at any time.

Next, in the **Availability** section of the window, we select the **Application-specific** radio button option. This is in answer to our second question, where we want this command to only work and be available when we are browsing within Google Chrome.

By selecting the Application-specific option, you will notice that Dragon has also revealed a number of other options for us to address.

The revealed **Application** drop-down menu is where, by clicking on the down arrow, reveals several application options, select the Google Chrome option.

 If you do not see Google Chrome in your list, you will need to click on the Browse button and navigate to the folder containing the Google Chrome executable file (Chrome.exe). Most likely the file can be found in the following path: C:\Program Files (x86)\Google\Chrome\Application. Select it and click the Open button. Figure 1-7 shows the path to the file in the Choose Application window.

Figure 1-7

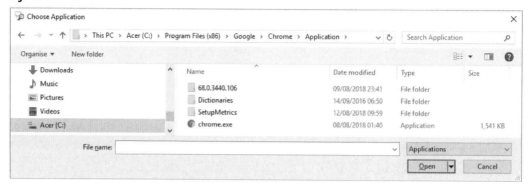

Next, by clicking on the down arrow within the **Command Type** drop-down menu, we are able to select the type of command we wish to create, as shown in Figure 1-8.

Figure 1-8

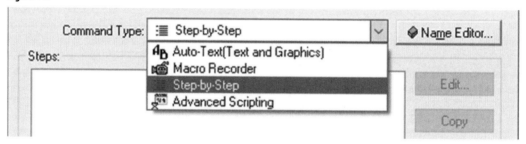

Now, within the **Steps** area, we need to add the Steps that will perform the action we require. To do this, click on the **New Step** drop-down menu to reveal several options (see Figure 1-9).

Figure 1-9

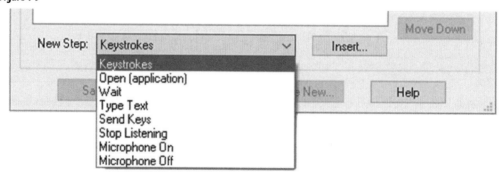

As we know, to perform our action requires the pressing of Alt+Left arrow keys; therefore, we will select **Keystrokes** from the list and then press the **Insert** button.

This now presents us with the Send Keystrokes window (see Figure 1-10). Click inside the field and perform the keystroke Alt+Left Arrow Key. The result should look as shown in Figure 1-10.

Figure 1-10

Perform the required keystroke in the Send Keystrokes window. If you make a mistake, perform the keystroke again and it will overwrite the mistake. Press the OK button to confirm the Step.

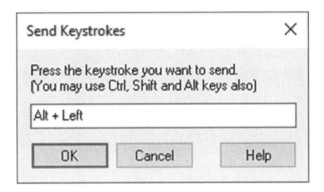

Click the OK button to close the Send Keystrokes window.

That's it! your MyCommands Editor window should now look as shown in Figure 1-11.

Figure 1-11

The MyCommands Editor with an Application-specific Step-by-Step command. A created Step is shown in the Steps area.

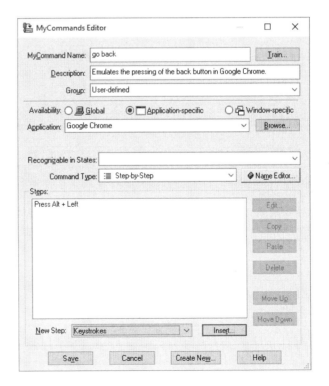

Click the Save button to save your new command.

Now, to test our new command, open Google Chrome, search through a number of web pages and when you are ready, try your new command by saying "*go back*".

Discuss

In this scenario we only needed one set of keystrokes to achieve our objective. There will be times when you might need two or more keystrokes to perform an action, in such instances, the same procedure applies. However, once you have inserted your first keystroke, you will then need to click on the Insert button again to insert your second keystroke and so on. This will eventually build a list of keystrokes in the Steps area.

Let's now look at a second example that involves more Steps. Below, albeit not the most efficient way of achieving this, is a Step-by-Step macro that will select all the text in a MS Word document, open the Font window and change the font.

Try it by creating a new Step-by-Step Dragon command and populating the MyCommand Editor with the following:

To insert the `Wait 1000 milliseconds` **Step, click on the New Step drop-down menu and select Wait, click on the Insert button, adjust the timescale to 1000 in the revealed Wait Step window and click OK.**

The Steps `Press Down` **and** `Press Up` **are achieved by pressing the keyboard down/up arrows keys in the Send Keystrokes window.**
The Step `Press Enter` **is achieved by pressing Enter in the Send Keystrokes window.**

The order of the Steps is important to achieve the desired result. To rearrange the order of the Steps, select a Step and click either the Move Up or Move Down buttons to rearrange the order.

MyCommand Name: make a change to my font

Description:

Group: Dragon - A Step Further_Chapter_01

Availability: Application-specific

Application: Microsoft Word

Command Type: Step-by-Step

Steps:

```
Press Ctrl + A
Wait 1000 milliseconds
Press Ctrl + D
Wait 1000 milliseconds
```

```
Press Down
Press Down
Press Down
Press Up
Press Down
Press Enter
```

Now try the command by opening MS Word, type in some text and then say, "*make a change to my font*".

Discuss

In this scenario, the first step is Press Ctrl-A, which is the keyboard shortcut to select everything in the Word document.

The Wait 1000 milliseconds Step is used to pause the command for one second before moving onto the next Step.

The Step Press Ctrl-D within MS Word will open the Font window.

The second **Wait** Step is used to allow time for the Font window to open before moving onto the Keystroke Steps of Press Down and Press Up. These emulate the pressing of the up and down keyboard arrow keys.

Finally Press Enter is the Step which tells Dragon to press the Enter key, which will close the Font window and change the font of the text within the document.

 When creating Step-by-Step commands, think about the logical order of keyboard sequences needed to achieve a task. Practice the steps by keyboard first; sometimes you will need to use a Wait step to slow down the speed of the command, to allow an application to keep up.

Below is an overview of the various **New Step** options available to you when creating Step-by-Step commands:

Keystrokes:

Figure 1-12

An example keystroke combination in the Send Keystrokes window.

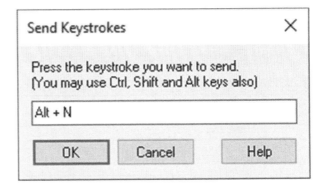

The Keystroke option is used when we want Dragon to perform the pressing of a specific keystroke or keystrokes combination. Once you have selected Keystrokes and clicked on the Insert button, the Send Keystrokes window will appear. Place the cursor in the blank field and carry out the keystroke. If you make a mistake, just carry out the keystroke again and it will overwrite the mistake. Figure 1-12 shows an example keystroke combination in the Send Keystrokes window.

Example keystrokes include: `Press Alt+B, Press Ctrl+B, Press Enter, Press Escape, Press Tab.`

Open (application):

Figure 1-13

The Open Application / Document Step window. Inserted in the Target field is the directory path to the file to be opened.

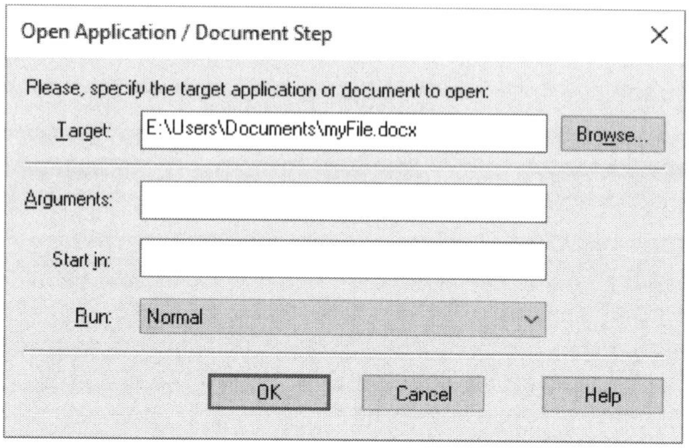

The Open (application) step tells Dragon to open a specific application/document. If a document/application is already open it switches to that document or application.

The Open Application / Document Step window (see Figure 1-13) has several parameters:

Target field: Click on the Browse button to reveal the Choose Application or Document window. Navigate to the folder containing either your document or application executable file and click the Open button.

Arguments: This field is used where additional information may be needed. As an example, if you require a specific web page to be opened, then you would insert the full URL into this field.

Start in: Usually Dragon will automatically supply this information. It refers to the Directory in which the application or document should open.

Run: Determines the mode in which the application should be run, either:

- Normal
- Minimised
- Maximised

Wait:

Figure 1-14

You can pause the flow of a macro by adjusting the wait time in the Wait Step window.

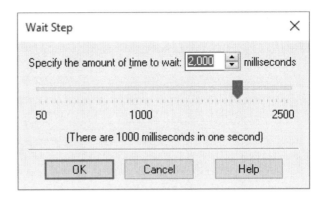

Use the Wait command to pause the running of a command for a specific amount of time. This will delay the command process from moving onto the next line in the order of Steps. As an example, your previous line might be to open a specific application or document; and as such, it would be a good idea to include a Wait Step on the next line. This would give time for the application or document to open before moving onto the next step, which might be to populate that application or document with data. Figure 1-14 shows the Wait Step window.

Type Text:

Figure 1-15

The Type Text Step window. Insert the text you want Dragon to type out.

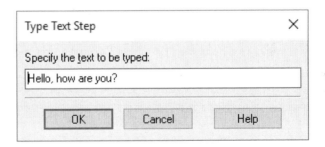

Use the option Type Text to have Dragon type out the text you specify in the field (see Figure 1-15).

Send Keys:

Figure 1-16

The Send Keys Step window. Specify the key sequence you want Dragon to perform.

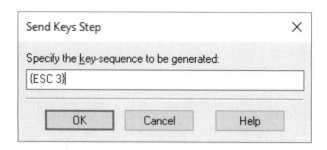

The Send Keys step is used to send a sequence of keys (see Figure 1-16); for example, if you want your command to press the Tab button 5 times, this can be done by inserting {Tab 5}. There are a number of Send Keys codes available; such as {LBUTTON} to press the left mouse button and {RBUTTON} to press the right mouse button.

 There must be a space between the word Tab and the number 5.

The CTRL, ALT and SHIFT key sequences can also be included; therefore, in order to achieve the pressing of the Shift+Tab 2 times, we would insert +{Tab 2}. Table 1-2 shows the symbols used to include Ctrl, Shift and Alt in a Step.

Table 1-2

Ctrl+Tab is written as:	^{TAB}
Shift+Tab is written as:	+{TAB}
Alt+Tab is written as:	%{TAB}

For a list of the Send Keys codes, see the Appendix, *Send Keys Step Dialog Box Table*.

Stop Listening:

By including the Stop Listening Step, Dragon will place the microphone into standby mode when it reaches this line.

Microphone On:

By including the Microphone On Step, Dragon will turn on the microphone when it reaches this line in the order of steps.

Microphone Off:

By including the Microphone Off Step, Dragon will turn off the microphone when it reaches this line in the order of steps. It is sometimes useful to use this step when you want to make sure that the command is carried out without any interruptions, which may occur as a result of a user speaking during the process.

 Step-by-Step commands can include Dragon Lists.

Refer to:

Chapter 4: Dragon List & Written\Spoken words Lists in Step-by-Step Commands

Creating Advanced Scripting Commands

Advanced Scripting commands are the most powerful and effective of all the command types. Here are just a few reasons why:

- Dragon will carry out an Advanced Scripting type command many times faster than an equivalent command made by using the Step-by-Step type.
- Advanced Scripting commands can be made up of Dragon script and/or VBA code. This enables us to create commands that can control and automate our PCs far more than other command types.
- Advanced Scripting commands enable us to automate and manipulate applications such as MS Word and MS Excel by incorporating application VBA into Dragon commands.
- Standalone (separate from any applications) Dialog forms which enable user interaction are created within Advanced Scripting type commands. These forms can be used to gather and process information in multiple ways.

To create an Advanced Scripting command: Click on the DragonBar, Click the Tools option and select Add New Command or do the same by saying "*add new command*", both methods will reveal the MyCommands Editor window.

In the MyCommands Editor window click on the Command Type drop-down menu and select the option Advanced Scripting.

Any Dragon script or VBA code required to perform the command is inserted between the lines Sub Main and End Sub. Figure 1-17 shows an example of an Advanced Scripting command containing Dragon Script, which when run, produces a simple Dialog Form.

Figure 1-17

An example of an Advanced Scripting command. It is made up of Dragon script and produces a Dialog Form when run.

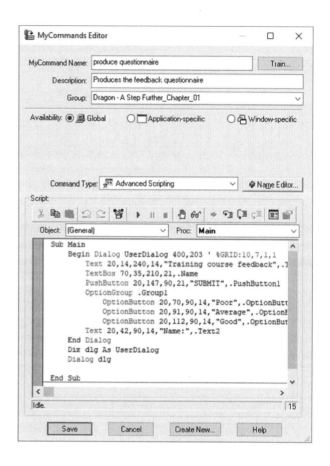

Chapter 2: Dragon Script and Visual Basic for Applications (VBA)

As you explore the recipes in this book and start to think of ideas of your own, you may find yourself wanting to seek information on how you can push the boundaries of writing advanced Dragon commands.

Dragon has its own programming language, "Dragon Script", which in some ways can be described as a combination of portions of the Basic programming language and a dialect of the Visual Basic programming language. Having said that, it's more than powerful enough to enable you to perform calculations, read and write files and virtually program anything within a voice command.

There is no doubt that those with an understanding of Visual Basic (VB) or Visual Basic for applications (VBA) will have an advantage when it comes to creating Dragon scripts. There are some differences, so you will need to learn the Dragon extensions to effectively write scripts in the Dragon scripting language. As you start to create advanced commands it will become apparent how you can use some Visual Basic commands directly in your Dragon scripts. You will also notice how close some Visual Basic commands are to the Dragon scripting language.

To help you on your way, I would advise you to make use of the Help files within Dragon NaturallySpeaking, be aware that they only show a limited portion of the functions available, more functions are available by way of MS Office, Windows, Visual Basic, Word VBA, Excel VBA and other applications.

I would highly recommend reading books and searching the web for further information which will enable you to learn more about VB and VBA. They will definitely help.

For more information on specific commands and Dragon Language extensions refer to **Chapter 8:** Overview of Dragon Script Commands and Functions.

Using VBA Macros in Dragon Advanced Scripting Commands

Within applications such as MS Word and MS Excel, macros are often created to perform complicated tasks, speed up workflow and allow us to automate tedious or repetitive tasks. These macros are created using the VBA scripting language, which differs in places from the Dragon Script language and are stored within the applications they are created for. Often, users will run these macros either by pressing created shortcut keys or additional buttons placed onto the ribbon of MS Word for example.

Dragon can run these macros by voice commands created with Advanced Scripting provided you have the relevant application and document open. For instance, if you have created a Word VBA macro named "testMacro", this can be run from a Dragon script by using the following script within a Dragon Advanced Scripting command:

```
Sub Main
Word.Application.Run "testMacro"
End Sub
```

This is all well and good, but what if you want to distribute your Dragon command to another user on another computer? There is no guarantee that they will have the same macro, named the same or shortcut keys setup exactly as yours.

To overcome this issue, we need to incorporate the Word VBA script into our Dragon Advanced script and carry out a process called Referencing.

 An Advanced Scripting command that includes application VBA code will need the application Object Library to be added to the macro in order to work (refer to Chapter 2: Object Library References).

Create the above Dragon command script and attempt to save it. Oops! We have an error, as shown in Figure 2-1.

Figure 2-1

A Message Box activates when you attempt to save a command that contains an error.

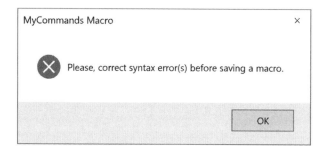

I can assure you that the command above is correct in syntax and should save, even if you do not have a Word VBA macro called "testMacro". However, Dragon displays this message because at this moment in time, this command needs a Reference to the Microsoft Word Object Library.

To do this:

- Place your cursor over the code between the lines Sub Main and End Sub
- Right-click your mouse and select "References" from the menu (see Figure 2-2). The "References - mycommand" window (see Figure 2-3) will appear.

Figure 2-2

Right click on the Advanced Scripting code to reveal a
menu, click on the References option.

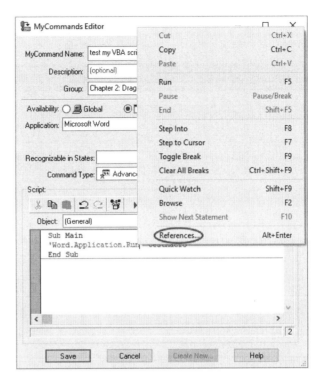

Figure 2-3

Selecting the Microsoft Word Object Library from the
References list.

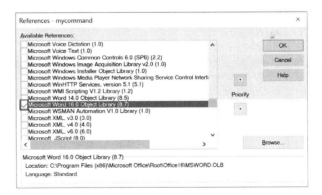

- Look for the "Microsoft Word (x) Object Library (for Word (x)", where (x) is the version of Word you
  have installed on your computer (an example is Microsoft Word 14.0 Object Library (8.5)).
- Check the box next to your Microsoft Object Library and Click "Save" again.

If you do not have MS Word installed on your computer, you might not find this Object Library. You will also need to carry out the same process to select other Object Libraries for other applications.

Why incorporate VBA Scripts into Dragon Commands?

Sometimes when writing a Dragon script, it may at first seem easier to take a step by step approach to carrying out a task and write the script accordingly.

For example, in MS Word if we wanted a voice command that inserts page numbers and position them in the center of the footer, we could easily create a script using the *SendDragonKeys* instruction.

MyCommand Name: insert page numbers the long way

Description:

Group: Dragon - A Step Further_Chapter_02

Availability: Application-specific

Application: Microsoft Word

Command Type: Advanced Scripting

Content:

```
Sub Main
SendDragonKeys "{Alt}" 'Press the Alt key
SendDragonKeys "{n}" 'Press the n key
SendDragonKeys "{n}" 'Press the n key
SendDragonKeys "{u}" 'Press the u key
SendDragonKeys "{b}" 'Press the b key
SendDragonKeys "{Down}" 'Press the down arrow key
SendDragonKeys "{Enter}" 'Press the Enter key
SendDragonKeys "{Alt}" 'Press Alt key
SendDragonKeys "{j}" 'Press the j key
SendDragonKeys "{h}" 'Press the h key
SendDragonKeys "{c}" 'Press the c key
End Sub
```

This will work perfectly fine, however, when we run this voice command, we see on the screen the menus drop down and accessed. Imagine how it would look if this was a longer script that accessed many menus.

For a more professional outcome we could use Word VBA to carry out the same task:

MyCommand Name: insert page numbers the short way

Description:

Group: Dragon - A Step Further_Chapter_02

Availability: Application-specific

Application: Microsoft Word

Command Type: Advanced Scripting

Content:

```
Sub Main
With ActiveDocument.Sections(1)
    .Footers(wdHeaderFooterPrimary).PageNumbers.Add _
    PageNumberAlignment:=wdAlignPageNumberCenter, _
    FirstPage:=True
End With
End Sub
```

For this to work, you will need to apply Reference to the Microsoft Word (x) Object Library.

When we run this type of command, no menus appear to be accessed; the task is executed straight away.

VBA code comes in handy when the task you wish to carry out cannot be achieved by accessing application menus. Also, by incorporating VBA into your scripts you can create complex/powerful commands that will execute tasks significantly quicker than any other means of Dragon scripting.

Dragon Commands with Incorporated VBA Scripts

Throughout this book, commands that use VBA script to perform tasks are represented by having the headings such as:

<Word VBA Solution>, <Excel VBA Solution> etc.,

I will not explain in detail the VBA code used, as that goes beyond the realms of this book. I would suggest using the internet for resources on the subject of VBA.

In order for these recipes to work you may need to firstly Reference the specific application Object Library.

Below is an example of a voice command recipe to perform a task in MS Word that was created by using Word VBA:

<Word VBA Solution: Needs Microsoft Word Object Library>

MyCommand Name: insert my page numbering style

Description: Insert page numbers in a specific style

Group: Dragon - A Step Further_Chapter_02

Availability: Microsoft Word

Command Type: Advanced Scripting

Content:

```
Sub Main
With ActiveDocument.Sections(1)
    .Footers(wdHeaderFooterPrimary).PageNumbers.Add _
```

```
        PageNumberAlignment:=wdAlignPageNumberRight, _
        FirstPage:=True
End With
With ActiveDocument.Sections(1)
    .Footers(wdHeaderFooterPrimary).PageNumbers.NumberStyle =
wdPageNumberStyleNumberInCircle
End With
End Sub
```

Open an MS Word document and try it by saying:

"insert my page numbering style"

Refer to:

Chapter 2: Using VBA Macros in Dragon Advanced Scripting Commands

Creating your own Visual Basic for Applications (VBA) Scripts

As previously mentioned, this book does not go into detail about the various commands and parameters which make up the VBA scripts used throughout this book.

Some of you may be curious as to how the VBA commands are put together and may want to learn more in order to create your own variations, such as applying a specific page margin, inserting a customised bulleted list, or inserting a complex styled table etc. For many, the creation of these scripts can seem like a daunting task, involving countless hours of precious time studying and comprehending the VBA scripting language.

However, whilst it is true that VBA experts have indeed spent vast amounts of time learning their craft, it is not true to say that an absolute beginner cannot be up and running within a very short time, and thankfully there are tools out there that can help to easily produce a detailed script for someone with no coding experience.

 Dragon allows us to create Advanced Scripting commands that incorporate Application VBA scripts and with a little tweaking, we can perform existing VBA macros by voice commands.

In this section, I will show step by step how with no coding experience, one would go about creating a detailed VBA Script within MS Word and how we can then take that script and incorporate it into our own Dragon voice command.

Our objective will be to create a macro that will insert a custom styled, two-column "For and against" table. Now, in order to achieve this, we will record the manual steps necessary to create the styled table and have MS Word automatically generate the required VBA script/code for us. How cool is that!

 In this example I am working with Microsoft Word version Office 365 (32 bit), however, the same steps and procedures, albeit slightly different, will work for other versions of MS Word.

Step 1. Show the Developer Menu Ribbon

The Developer menu is the designated ribbon that contains commands for working with macros. By default, it is hidden from view and the following instructions will reveal it to you:

- In Word, click File menu >> Select New and click Blank document.
- Click on the File menu >> Select Options to reveal the "Word Options" window (see Figure 2-4).
- In the Word options window, on the left-hand side, select the option Customize Ribbon.
- On the right-hand side, click the CheckBox next to the word Developer.

Figure 2-4

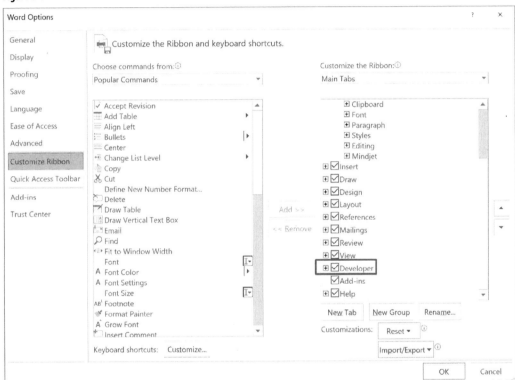

- Click OK to return to your blank document.

You should now see that there is an additional menu option ("Developer"), as shown in Figure 2-5. Click on the Developer menu to reveal the contents in the ribbon.

Figure 2-5

Step 2. Assign a Keyboard Shortcut to the Macro

Before we begin recording our macro, you will notice that we have the option to assign it to a keyboard shortcut. We will do this as it allows us to quickly test and run our macro in MS Word once it has been created.

On the Developer tab, in the code section, click the Record Macro option (see Figure 2-6) to reveal the Record Macro window (see Figure 2-7).

Figure 2-6

Press the Record Macro option on the Ribbon of the Developer menu to start the recording process.

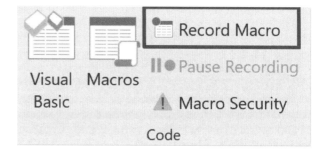

In the Macro name field, type in "myStyledTable", and then click the Keyboard option to reveal the Customize Keyboard window (see Figure 2-8).

 Feel free to give the macro an alternative name. However, the use of spaces and special characters such as: ?, @, ! etc. are not permitted.

Figure 2-7

In the Record Macro window, enter a name for the macro you're about to record.

Record Macro	? ×
Macro name:	
myStyledTable	
Assign macro to	

Button   Keyboard

Store macro in:

All Documents (Normal.dotm)

Description:

OK   Cancel

Place the cursor within the Press new shortcut key field and then press CTRL+SHIFT+T. This is the keyboard shortcut we will use to run our macro and generate our styled table.

Figure 2-8

Place the cursor in the Press new shortcut key field and perform the shortcut key combination to be used to run the macro.

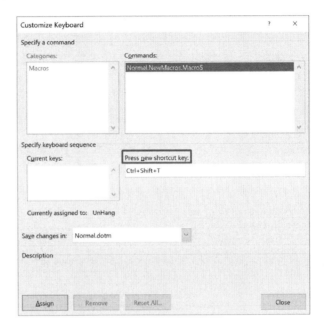

- Click the Assign button.
- Click the Close button.

On the Developer tab, you will notice that the "Record Macro" option has now changed to a "Stop Recording" option (see Figure 2-9) and your mouse pointer has changed in design to show that MS Word is currently recording your actions and is in the macro recording mode.

Figure 2-9

The Record Macro option is changed to the Stop Recording option while the recording process is taking place.

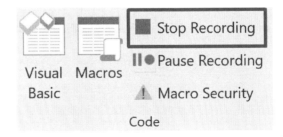

Step 3. Record the Macro

To record the macro, we now need to manually proceed through the task to achieve our objective. As you perform the necessary steps, MS Word will be recording each click, keystroke, and any text typed. The result being a VBA script that can be edited later.

Make sure you are in macro recording mode and perform the following:

- Click on the Insert menu.
- Click the Add a table icon, then drag to create a 2 x 5 table, as shown in Figure 2-10.

Figure 2-10

Click the Table option and define the table size by dragging the mouse over the grid.

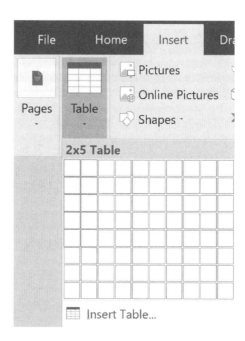

Hold down the SHIFT key and press the right arrow key on your keyboard until the table is selected as shown in Figure 2-11.

Figure 2-11

When recording a macro, you cannot use the mouse to select, copy, or drag content in the document. To record these actions, you must use the keyboard.

Click on the down arrow within the Table Styles section of the ribbon to reveal a selection of table styles (see Figure 2-12).

Figure 2-12

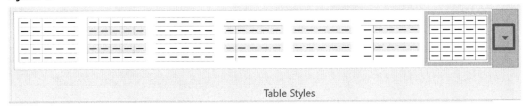

For this exercise I have selected the List Table 1 Light - Accent 4 style (of course feel free to choose an alternative).

Click on the down arrow underneath the Borders icon on the right, to reveal a list of border types (see Figure 2-13).

Figure 2-13

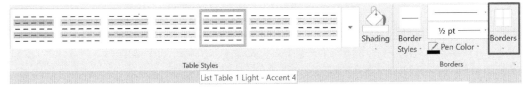

Select "All Borders" as the border style to be used (see Figure 2-14).

Figure 2-14

Click the Borders option and select the All Borders option from the list on show.

Type the word "*For*", press the Tab key and then type "*Against*", as shown in Figure 2-15.

Figure 2-15

For	Against

Finally, click on the "Developer" menu and click the "Stop recording" option (see Figure 2-16).

Figure 2-16

Press the Stop Recording option on the Ribbon of the Developer menu to stop the recording process.

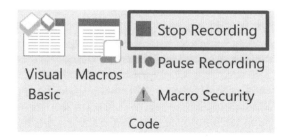

Step 4. Run and test the Macro

Now, to check if our macro is working as expected, open a new blank MS Word document.

Press the shortcut keys CTRL+SHIFT+T or if you have created an alternative keyboard shortcut, press that instead.

If all has gone well, you should now see our custom table in the document.

Step 5. Accessing the VBA Code produced

While we were going through the motions of creating our custom table, behind the scenes, MS Word has been putting together the VBA script needed to produce our table.

It is this code that we will use when we create our Dragon voice command.

To access the code, click on the "Developer" menu and select the icon "Macros" (see Figure 2-17)

Figure 2-17

Press the Macros option on the Ribbon of the Developer menu to reveal the list of available macros.

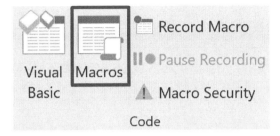

This will open the Macros window (see Figure 2-18) which is a list of macros created on your computer. You should be able to see your created macro ("myStyledTable").

Select the macro and click the Edit button to view the VBA code that MS Word has produced.

Figure 2-18

The Macros window displays a list of available macros. Select the macro and click the Edit button to view the code.

Figure 2-19 and Figure 2-20 shows a portion of the VBA code produced.

Figure 2-19

Shows a portion of the VBA code produced.

Figure 2-20

Shows a portion of the VBA code produced.

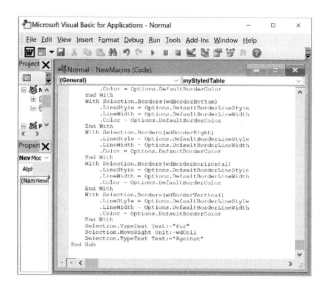

As you can see, MS Word has done a lot of work behind the scenes. All these lines of code when run produce our customised table.

Now, to move on to the next stage, we need to copy this script, from the line Sub myStyledTable() to End Sub.

Step 6. Create a Dragon Command that will produce our custom styled table

In order to use the copied VBA script, we need to create a Dragon Advanced Scripting type of command.

Go to the DragonBar Tools menu and select Add New Command in order to reveal the MyCommands Editor window.

Apply and populate the fields with the following:

MyCommand Name: insert my custom table

Description: inserts my custom table

Group: Dragon - A Step Further_Chapter_02

Availability: Application-specific

Application: Microsoft Word

Command Type: Advanced Scripting

Content:

```
Sub Main
End Sub
```

 Notice that we have the availability set to "Application-specific" and the application set to "Microsoft Word"; as this command will only work within MS Word.

Now, highlight in the main body of the window the lines "Sub Menu" to "End Sub", as shown in Figure 2-21.

Figure 2-21

Select the text Sub Main through End Sub in the MyCommands Editor window.

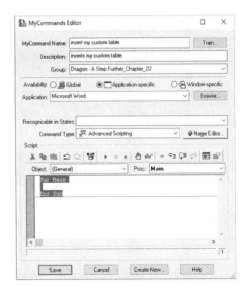

Then paste the code you copied from MS Word (see Figure 2-22).

Figure 2-22

Paste the copied VBA script into the script area of the MyCommands Editor window.

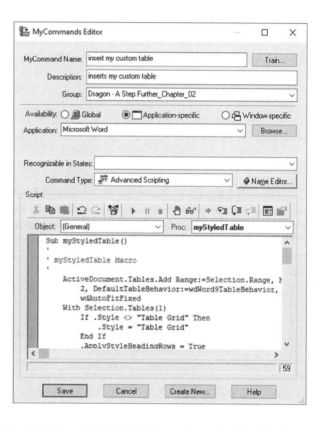

Next, we need to make a change to the script. The line `Sub myStyledTable()` must be replaced with the line `Sub Main`. Figure 2-23 shows how the top of your script should look.

Figure 2-23

```
Sub Main|
' myStyledTable Macro
'
'
'
```

We now need to reference the new command; right-click on any portion of the pasted code to reveal a menu of options and select the "References" option or alternatively press the keys Alt+Enter.

This will open the References - mycommand window, that shows a list of available references for various software which Dragon can work with, as shown in Figure 2-24.

Look for the Microsoft Word x.x Object Library in your list. As I am using MS Word Office 365 (32 bit), the Object Library I have chosen may have a different number to yours, if you happen to be using a different version of MS Word.

Select it by clicking the CheckBox next to it and click the OK button.

Figure 2-24

Selecting the Microsoft Word Object Library from the References list.

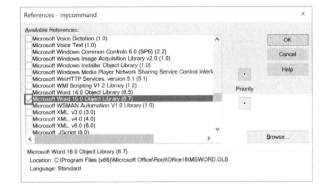

You will then be taken back to the MyCommands Editor window and can now click Save, to save your new command.

When inserting VBA Script into a command, you will need to set the Object Reference before attempting to save the command; otherwise Dragon will flag up an error.

That's it!

Open a new MS Word document and try the new VBA command by saying:
"insert my custom table"

Object Library References

Advanced Scripting type commands that consist of application VBA script need to have an application Object Library reference added to the command. If you fail to include the reference you may find that Dragon will not allow you to save the command.

For example, if you have a command that consists of MS Excel VBA code then you will need to include the Microsoft Excel Object Library reference. To do this, carry out the following:

- Place your cursor over the code between the lines Sub Main and End Sub
- Right-click your mouse and select "References" (see Figure 2-25) from the drop-down menu. As an alternative you can use the shortcut keystroke Alt+Enter.

Figure 2-25

Right click on the Advanced Scripting code to reveal a menu, click on the References option.

The References - mycommand window will appear (see Figure 2-26).

- Look for and check the box next to the Microsoft Excel Object Library.
- Click OK, you will now be able to save the command.

Figure 2-26

Selecting the Microsoft Excel Object Library from the References list.

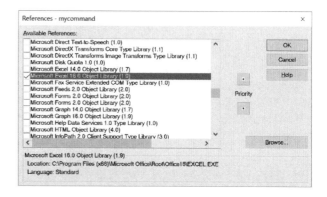

The version of the Object Library you will see is dependent on the version of the application installed on your PC. Figure 2-26 shows two Object Libraries for Microsoft Excel; this is because my machine has two versions of Microsoft Office installed.

If you do not have MS Excel installed on your computer, you might not find this Object Library. You will also need to carry out the same process to select other Object Libraries for other applications.

An application Object Library will often be updated and renamed by software companies for different versions of an application, for example.

The Object Library for Microsoft Excel:

- Version 2010 - Microsoft Excel 14.0 Object Library (1.7)
- Version 2016 - Microsoft Excel 16.0 Object Library (1.9)

The Object Library for Mindjet's MindManager:

- MindManager version 16 - MindManager 16 Type Library (10.0)
- MindManager version 18 - MindManager 18 Type Library (12.0)

When importing a command that contains a reference to an Object Library, if the version of the application on the end user's PC is different, then a bad reference may be created in the list of Object Libraries. This may result in the command not working. See the section "Importing and using sample macros" for a solution.

Chapter 3: Editing and Training your Dragon Commands

All your created macros (including imported ones) can be found by accessing the Command Browser – MyCommands window via the DragonBar >> Tools >> Command Browser, or by saying "*open command browser*".

Select your macro from the appropriate group and double click the macro to open it in the MyCommands Editor window.

Editing Auto-Text(Text and Graphics) Macros

To edit Auto-Text commands, place your cursor within the Content area section and make the necessary changes.

Editing Macro Recorder Macros

Changes can be made to the Actions within the Actions section of the MyCommands Editor window. Additional buttons such as Insert, Edit and Delete allows for the editing of specific Actions and the inclusion of new ones.

Editing Step-by-Step Macros

When editing Step-by-Step macros, Dragon makes available a number of additional button options within the MyCommands Editor:

Edit button: By selecting a Step and clicking on the Edit button, Dragon will reveal the pop-up window for that Step, which will enable you to change the settings, text or code.

Copy button: Use the Copy button to copy a selected Step and its properties.

Paste button: Use the Paste button to paste the copied Step(s) into another position in the order of Steps.

Delete button: The delete button will delete the selected Step.

Move Up / Move Down buttons: Use the Move Up and Move Down buttons to move the selected Step up or down in the order of Steps.

Editing Advanced Scripting Macros

Advanced Scripting macros are edited by making changes to the script within the script area.

Training Dragon to recognise how you pronounce your voice commands

Whether it's the macros you import or the commands you create, there will be times when Dragon does not recognise or is inconsistent with performing a voice command that you dictate.

In such circumstances it is a good idea to go through the process of training Dragon to recognise how you pronounce the voice command. By following the training process Dragon will not only improve in accuracy but will also update your user profile.

The process for training a voice command (of any type) is as follows:

- Open the command within the MyCommands Editor window (see Figure 3-1).
- Click on the "Train" button to reveal the Train Words window (see Figure 3-2).

Figure 3-1

Open a command in the MyCommands Editor window and click the Train button to begin the training process.

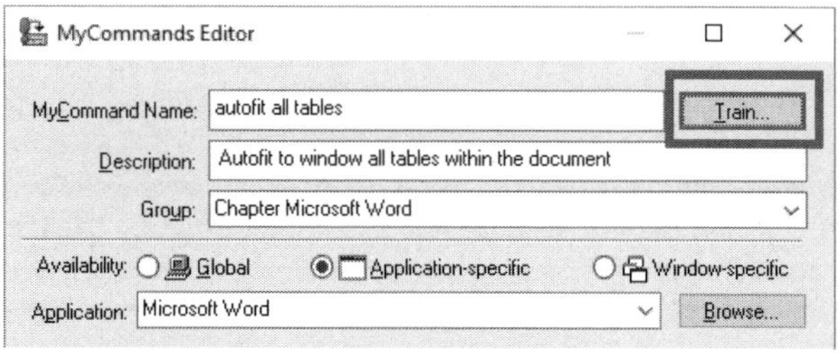

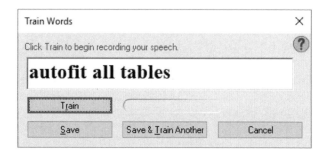

Figure 3-2

The Train Words window displays the word or phrase to be trained. Click the Train button to record your speech and then click the Save button.

- Click the Train button and dictate the voice command name.
- Click Save.

In cases where your voice command contains a Dragon List(s), as shown in Figure 3-3, the Train Words window will give you the opportunity to train Dragon for each variation (see Figure 3-4).

Figure 3-3

Open a command containing a Dragon List in the MyCommands Editor window and click the Train button to begin the training process.

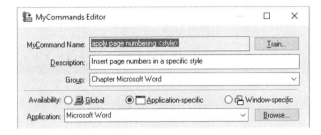

Figure 3-4

The Train Words window displays each word(s) or phrase(s) variations and enables the user to train each of them.

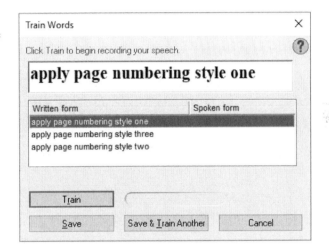

Training Locked (Protected, Encrypted) Dragon Commands

Unlike conventional commands, locked commands cannot be opened to reveal the "Train" button in the Command Browser. Therefore, to train a locked command you will need to:

- Click on the DragonBar.
- Click the Audio option.
- Select "Improve recognition of word or phrase" (see Figure 3-5).

Figure 3-5

To begin the training process, click the Audio icon on the DragonBar and select the Improve recognition of word or phrase option.

This will reveal the Training window (see Figure 3-6).

Figure 3-6

Insert the word or phrase (myCommand name) to be trained into the Enter the word or phrase you want to train field.

If required, you can insert an alternative phrase to run the command into the Spoken form (if different) field.

Click the Train button to begin the training process.

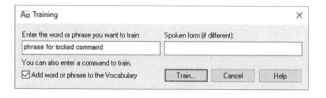

Insert the word or phrase (myCommand Name) required to run the locked command and click the "Train" button to carry out the training process.

Section 2: Creating Dragon Commands with List Variables

Chapter 4: Dragon List (List Variables) Commands

What are Dragon List Commands?

Dragon List commands are extremely useful for creating complex commands that perform actions dependent on what a user has dictated. They can be used where you want to allow a user to dictate multiple phrases to run the same command. They also allow us to reduce the length of our scripts, especially where we might require a lot of *If Then* statements.

Using Lists in your commands may seem complex at first, but I assure you, once you have got your head around how they work, you will be producing commands that you will be totally proud of.

When to consider creating a Dragon List command:

- If you find yourself creating a number of commands each of which have almost identical script.
- If you are creating a command script that will require a vast number of *If Then* statements.
- When you want to create a command that allows for multiple variations of the dictated phrase.

The following scenario demonstrates how incorporating a Dragon List is an effective way of creating a command:

A user has three documents that they regularly review throughout the day. These documents are named "Prices.docx", "Terms.docx" and "Suppliers.docx". The user wants to be able to say, "*Open Prices*" which will open the "Prices.docx" document; say "*Open Terms*" for the "Terms.docx" document and "*Open Suppliers*" for the "Suppliers.docx" to open.

Instinctively, you may think of creating three separate Advanced Scripting commands and name them accordingly, as shown in Table 4-1.

Table 4-1

MyCommand Name: open prices	MyCommand Name: open terms	MyCommand Name: open suppliers
Description: Open the prices.docx file	**Description:** Open the terms.docx file	**Description:** Open the suppliers.docx file
Group: Dragon - A Step Further_Chapter_04	**Group:** Dragon - A Step Further_Chapter_04	**Group:** Dragon - A Step Further_Chapter_04
Availability: Global	**Availability:** Global	**Availability:** Global
Command Type: Advanced Scripting	**Command Type:** Advanced Scripting	**Command Type:** Advanced Scripting
Content:	**Content:**	**Content:**

`Sub Main`
 	
`AppBringUp`
`"C:\...Path..to..file\prices.docx"`
 	
`End Sub`
	`Sub Main`
	
	`AppBringUp`
	`"C:\...Path..to..file\terms.docx"`
	
	`End Sub`
		`Sub Main`
		
		`AppBringUp`
		`"C:\...Path..to..file\suppliers.docx"`
		
		`End Sub`

Well, that might be fine, but what if the user wants the same approach for opening 5, 10 or more documents? You can quickly see how tedious a task this would become. This is where using a Dragon List command would be very useful.

Let's now create a Dragon List command to satisfy the requirements of our user:

First, we need to come up with a name for our list. As it relates to documents, we will call it <docs>. The less than (<) and more than (>) signs are important and tells Dragon we are creating a List variable.

It is this new variable that will be used in our new command name and as a result our command name will be "open <docs>".

 You can name your List variable as you see fit; letters, numbers and underscore (_) characters can be used. However, letters must be lowercase, and no spaces are allowed in the List name.

Open the MyCommands Editor window via the Tools menu >> Add New Command.

Select the option Advanced Scripting from the Command Type drop-down menu.

In the MyCommand Name field start typing slowly the name of the command (see Figure 4-1) **"open <docs>"**

Figure 4-1

A new Advanced Scripting type command in the MyCommands Editor window.

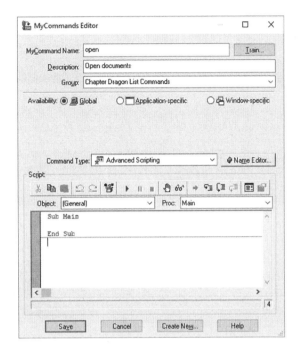

You will notice that as soon as you type the "<" sign a new window appears named MyCommands Name Editor with the prompt ready for you to finish typing the name of the List.

Once you have typed the ">" sign you will notice the word "docs" appears in the main body of the new window (see Figure 4-2).

Figure 4-2

The MyCommands Name Editor displays a list of the Dragon Lists used in the command.

To edit the items/variables of a Dragon List, select the Dragon List from the Lists used in this command field and click the Edit button.

Click on the newly created List called docs in the main body of the window, the Edit button will now become available.

Click on the Edit button which will open a new window named View List.

The View List window enables us to populate our List with options/items. In our case we want this command to run when the user says either "*open prices*", "*open terms*" or "*open suppliers*". Therefore, our List will contain the words **prices**, **terms** and **suppliers** all on separate lines.

The order in which the options/items are entered is not important.

Figure 4-3

The View List window displays the contents/items of a selected Dragon List. You can add, edit or delete items.

All items must be inserted on a separate line.

The order of the items is not important and will be sorted in alphabetical order automatically.

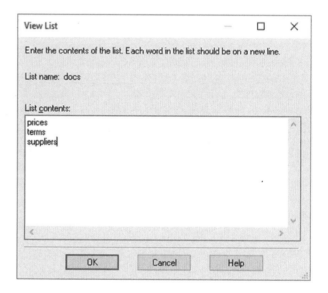

Insert the words into the View List window, as shown in Figure 4-3 and Click OK.

Next, click OK in the MyCommands Name Editor window and you will be returned to where we started, namely the MyCommands Editor window.

To edit or change the list of words we have created, you will need to do the following:

- In the MyCommands Editor window click and place the cursor after the "<docs>" in the MyCommand Name field, as shown in Figure 4-4.

Figure 4-4

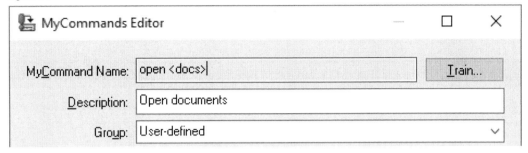

- Press the Backspace key and the MyCommands Name Editor window will automatically open.
- Select the docs List and Click the Edit button to reveal the View List window.
- Edit the list of options/items and Click OK.
- Click OK to close the MyCommands Name Editor window.

Now that we have created our List, we need the code that will enable this command to work. In the script section of the MyCommands Editor window enter the following code:

```
Sub Main
  If ListVar1 = "prices" Then AppBringUp "C:\...Path..to..file\prices.docx"
  If ListVar1 = "terms" Then AppBringUp "C:\...Path..to..file\terms.docx"
  If ListVar1 = "suppliers" Then AppBringUp "C:\...Path..to..file\suppliers.docx"
End Sub
```

Figure 4-5 shows how your MyCommands Editor should look.

Figure 4-5

In the MyCommands Editor window is an Advanced Scripting type command that contains a Dragon List.

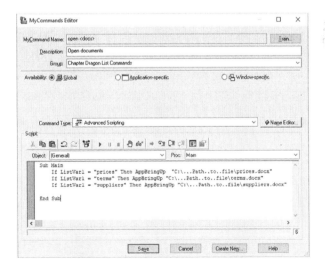

Create or choose three documents and adjust the Dragon script to match your own directory paths to the three files, then Save the command.

Try it by saying:
"open prices"
"open terms"

In our command we are only using one List variable (**<docs>**). Dragon refers to this List as ListVar1 and because of this we use `ListVar1` in the required script. In fact, the line `If ListVar1 = "prices" Then` `AppBringUp "C:\...Path..to..file\prices.docx` can be interpreted in the following way: If the user says, *"open prices"* it checks if the word said after the word "open" is "prices" and if the word "prices" is within our List then it will open the relevant document.

 If you have a command where you are using two lists for example open <xxx> and <yyy>. Dragon will refer to these lists as ListVar1 and ListVar2. The same formula applies for a command with three lists and so forth.

Refer to:
Chapter 8: If Then Statement

Dragon List Commands a step further

Let's take our created Dragon List command a step further.

Our user has decided that they would like to open any two of the three documents by a single voice command.

Let's look at how we can cater for these new requirements:

The good news is that we already have our List created (<docs>) and in fact we are going to use it twice in order to create our new command name which will be "**open <docs> and <docs>**".

This will enable our user to say, *"open terms and prices"* or *"open suppliers and prices"* or any of the other combinations.

Open the MyCommands Editor window via the Tools menu >> Add New Command.

Select the option Advanced Scripting from the Command Type drop-down menu.

In the MyCommand Name field start typing slowly the name of the command "open <docs>" as before, once you type the "<" sign the MyCommands Name Editor window will open. Continue to type the characters "docs>" to confirm that you wish to use the List <docs> in the command.

Click on the List docs and Click the Edit key, you will notice that our list of words is still there. Click OK to close the View List window.

Now place the cursor within the MyCommands Name field of the MyCommands Name Editor window and continue to type out the name of the command. Figure 4-6 shows how the MyCommands Name Editor should look.

Figure 4-6

The MyCommands Name Editor displays a list of the Dragon Lists used in the command.

To edit the items/variables of a Dragon List, select the Dragon List from the Lists used in this command field and click the Edit button.

Click OK to return to the MyCommands Editor window.

Now we will insert the code that will enable this command to work. In the script section of the MyCommands Editor window enter the following code:

```
Sub Main
  If ListVar1 = "prices" Then AppBringUp  "C:\...Path..to..file\prices.docx"
  If ListVar1 = "terms" Then AppBringUp "C:\...Path..to..file\terms.docx"
  If ListVar1 = "suppliers" Then AppBringUp "C:\...Path..to..file\suppliers.docx"
  If ListVar2 = "prices" Then AppBringUp  "C:\...Path..to..file\prices.docx"
  If ListVar2 = "terms" Then AppBringUp "C:\...Path..to..file\terms.docx"
  If ListVar2 = "suppliers" Then AppBringUp "C:\...Path..to..file\suppliers.docx"
End Sub
```

Figure 4-7 shows how your MyCommands Editor should look. Save the command.

Figure 4-7

In the MyCommands Editor window is an Advanced
Scripting type command that contains a Dragon List.

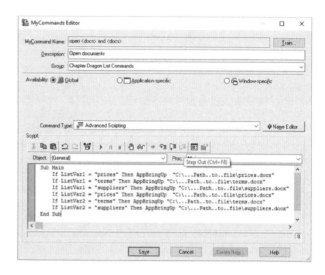

Create or choose three documents and adjust the Dragon script to match your directory paths to the file's
location.

Try it by saying:
"open prices and terms"
"open suppliers and prices"

Discuss
In our command we use the same List variable (<docs>) twice as we are keeping the choice of documents and
words allowed the same. All we are doing is giving the user the option to open any two of the three documents.

We could have made an alternative named List, but for the purposes of this scenario the contents of the List
would be the same so there is no point.

The command name is **open <docs> and <docs>**; therefore, Dragon will refer to the first instance of the
<docs> List as ListVar1 and the second <docs> as ListVar2.

Basically, if the user says, *"open terms and suppliers"* then ListVar1 becomes equal to the word "terms" and
ListVar2 becomes equal to the word "suppliers". Both the words "terms" and "suppliers" are in the list of
words found in the Dragon List variable <docs>, therefore, the command will run and the appropriate
documents will open.

This command will only work if the dictated phrase contains words which are in the Dragon List called <docs>.

Refer to:

Chapter 8: If Then Statement

Dragon Written\Spoken words List

Creating commands using Dragon Written\Spoken words Lists adds another dimension to the art of using Lists. You would create such a List where you want to make it possible for a user to say something and have something else typed out.

A scenario could be where a user works in the servicing department of a car dealership. He is responsible for contacting suppliers with the list of car parts required. Each car part has its own unique part code which is often made up of letters and numbers that are hard to remember. The user would like to create the list by dictating ordinary language and have Dragon write out the part codes instead. For example, he wants to be able to say, "Volvo spark plug" and for Dragon to write out "Part Code No. vsp0239".

The user has provided us with a list of car parts and their code numbers (see Table 4-2).

Table 4-2

ITEM	CODE
Volvo spark plug	vsp0239
Ford spark plug	fsp1390
Volvo front brake pads	fbpv71z
Volvo back brake pads	bbpv90y
Ford front brake pads	ffbp7213h
Ford back brake pads	fbbp2568z

Let's now create a Dragon Written\Spoken words List command to satisfy the requirements of our user:

Firstly, let's think of a name for our new List, I am going to suggest "<parts>"

Open the MyCommands Editor window via the Tools menu >> Add New Command.

Select the option Advanced Scripting from the Command Type drop-down menu.

In the MyCommand Name field, only insert **<parts>** as the command name. We do this because the user has requested that he wishes to dictate the item only, in order to run the command.

As we have seen before, as soon as you type the "<" sign, the MyCommands Name Editor window appears with the prompt ready for you to finish typing the name of the List. Once you have typed the ">" sign you will notice the word "parts" appears in the main body of the window.

Click on the newly created List called "parts" in the main body of the window, the Edit button will now become available.

Click on the Edit button which will open the View List window.

The View List window enables us to populate the List (<parts>) with options/items. In our case, and as an example we want this command to run when the user says, "*ford brake pads*" and have Dragon type out the code number. Therefore, it is important how we construct our List.

The format for writing Written\Spoken words Lists is as follows:

What we want Dragon to do or write is on the left-hand side of the backslash (\) character and the spoken form is on the right.

Written-form*Spoken-form*

e.g. `vsp0239\Volvo spark plug`

As before, all options/items are on separate lines and the order is not important.

Insert the options into the View List window.

Figure 4-8 shows how your View List window should look.

Figure 4-8

The View List window displays the contents/items of a selected Dragon List. You can add, edit or delete items.

All items must be inserted on a separate line.

The order of the items is not important and will automatically be sorted in alphabetical order.

Click OK to close the View List window.

Next, click OK in the MyCommands Name Editor window and you will be returned to where we started, namely, the MyCommands Editor window.

Having created our List, we now need the code that will enable this command to work. In the script section of the MyCommands Editor window enter the following code:

```
Sub Main
SendDragonKeys Mid(ListVar1, 1, InStr(ListVar1, "\")-1)
End Sub
```

Figure 4-9 shows how your MyCommands Editor should look.

Figure 4-9

In the MyCommands Editor window is an Advanced Scripting type command that contains a Dragon List.

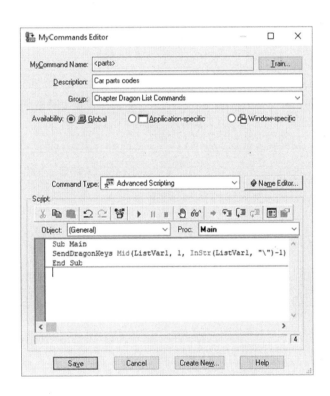

Open a word processing application and try it by saying:

"volvo spark plug"

"new line"

"ford back brake pads"

"new line"

"volvo back brake pads"

Discuss

As you may have noticed, we have introduced some new commands that will enable us to work with our created Dragon Written\Spoken words List.

Let me explain:

From our previous sections on the subject of using Dragon Lists, we know that Dragon refers to the first instance of a List as ListVar1.

In fact, in our scenario it is important to note that when Dragon recognises the spoken form of a phrase that is within our <parts> List, the ListVar1 variable will become equal to the entire Written\Spoken string.

For example, if the user says *"volvo spark plug"* then ListVar1 will in fact become equal to the string vsp0239\Volvo spark plug

Therefore, to satisfy our user requirements, we need to extract from the string, only the written form, which is in fact all the characters to the left of the "\". We then use the Dragon *SendDragonKeys* command to type out those characters.

This is achieved by the line in the script:

```
SendDragonKeys Mid(ListVar1, 1, InStr(ListVar1, "\")-1)
```

Let's look at this line of the script in more detail by breaking it down into three sections and using the example vsp0239\Volvo spark plug (where the user has said *"volvo spark plug"*).

1. InStr(ListVar1, "\")-1): The *InStr* function looks at the string of characters held within the variable ListVar1 and enables us to determine the character position of the "\" within the string. The inclusion of the -1 in the function, tells us how many characters there are before the "\".

Table 4-3 shows the string of characters held within the variable ListVar1 and their character position.

Table 4-3

v	s	p	0	2	3	9	\	V	o	l	v	o		s	p	a	r	k		p	l	u	g
1	2	3	4	5	6	7	8	9	10	11	12	13	14	15	16	17	18	19	20	21	22	23	24

The *InStr* function finds that the backslash "\" is in position 8 and therefore with the -1 returns a value of 7. The (7) now forms part of the *Mid* function.

2. Mid(ListVar1, 1, 7: The *Mid* function looks at the string of characters held within ListVar1 and provides us with all the characters from position 1 to 7.

Table 4-4 shows the string of characters that occupy position 1 to 7 within the variable ListVar1.

Table 4-4

v	s	p	0	2	3	9
1	2	3	4	5	6	7

3. SendDragonKeys: The *SendDragonKeys* command types out the text that is returned as a result of the *InStr* and *Mid* functions being executed (vsp0239).

Alternative

We could use an alternative piece of Dragon script to achieve the same result:

```
Sub Main
slash_position = InStr (Listvar1, "\")
part_code$ = Mid$ (ListVar1, 1, slash_position -1)
SendDragonKeys part_code$
End Sub
```

In this example we use two new variables to help us carry out the command.

- The variable slash_position will hold the numerical position of the slash.
- The variable part_code$ will hold all the characters from position 1 to the value within the slash_position variable -1

The *SendDragonKeys* command will type out the characters held within the part_code$ variable.

> Having only the List name "<parts>" as the name for the command, runs the risk that when the user is writing an ordinary letter and wants to actually dictate the item name, Dragon may instead write out the part code number. To overcome this, I would suggest naming the command "item <parts>", thereby, to perform the command the user would say "*item ford brake pads*" instead of just saying "*ford brake pads*".

Refer to:

Chapter 8: InStr Function, Mid Function

Performing Calculations with Dragon Lists

The scenario below shows how we can perform calculations when using Dragon Lists.

A Bricklayer who uses Dragon would like to have the quantity of bricks required for jobs calculated and the results typed out in a word processing application.

He has informed us that a one brick wide wall requires 120 bricks per square metre. Therefore, when he manually carries out his calculations, he measures the height and length of the intended wall and the result is then times by the constant 120.

He would like to have a command which, for example, if he was to dictate "number of bricks for a 6 by 5 metre wall" the result would then be typed out.

Solution

The command created will need to cater for alternative values that the Bricklayer may dictate. Therefore, a command which includes Dragon Written\Spoken words List would be the most suitable solution here, as this will provide flexibility.

As part of the command name, we will incorporate a Written\Spoken words List type named **<1..10>** that will consist of the following list of options:

0\oh

1\one

...

10\ten

 When incorporating numbers as options/items within your Written\Spoken words Lists. I would suggest that you stick with the same convention, as Dragon tends to interpret numbers better when using written forms of numbers in commands (2\two, 16\sixteen, 23\twenty three etc.).

The macro below will perform our Bricklayer's requirements:

MyCommand Name: number of bricks for a <1..10> by <1..10> meter wall

Name of List(s) used: <1..10>

List items:

1\one

2\two

...

10\ten

Description: Calculate number of bricks needed

Group: Dragon - A Step Further_Chapter_04

Availability: Global

Command Type: Advanced Scripting

Content:

```
Sub Main
'Declare our variables
bricksPerSqMetre = 120
numberOfBricks = 0
height = 0
width = 0
'Get the numbers for width and height
height = Mid(ListVar1, 1, InStr(ListVar1, "\")-1)
width = Mid(ListVar2, 1, InStr(ListVar2, "\")-1)
'convert and perform calculation
numberOfBricks = CStr(CLng(height) * _
```

```
   CLng(width) * _
   CLng(bricksPerSqMetre))
SendDragonKeys "You need "
SendDragonKeys numberOfBricks
SendDragonKeys " Bricks"
End Sub
```

Open a word processing application and try it by saying:

"number of bricks for a 6 by 5 metre wall"

"number of bricks for a 2 by 3 metre wall"

 The use of underscores (_) in our script tells Dragon that this is one line of code; it comes in handy for long statements.

Discuss

Firstly, we create four variables and assign values to them, the most important being the variable bricksPerSqMetre with a value of 120 which is the constant needed to perform our calculation.

The line height = Mid(ListVar1, 1, InStr(ListVar1, "\")-1) uses the *InStr* and *Mid* functions to populate the variable height with the numerical value extracted from ListVar1

The line width = Mid(ListVar2, 1, InStr(ListVar2, "\")-1) uses the *InStr* and *Mid* functions to populate the variable width with the numerical value extracted from ListVar2

The line numberOfBricks = CStr(CLng(height) * _

  CLng(width) * _

  CLng(bricksPerSqMetre)) is where we perform our calculation using the values within the variables height, width and bricksPerSqMetre and assign the result to the variable numberOfBricks.

Looking closely at this section, you will notice that we have included two new functions, CLng and CStr. As is the case with VBA coding, the asterisk (*) is used to multiply two variables by each other and you would be forgiven for thinking that "numberOfBricks = height * width * bricksPerSqMetre" as a command should work. However, this is not the case when we write Dragon script.

Dragon script demands that we convert string values to integers before we can perform any calculations. Furthermore, Dragon script does not allow us to use the *SendDragonKeys* command with integers and therefore these variables will need to be converted back to strings before we can display any results.

CLng(variable) converts a number or string value into an integer type variable, enabling us to perform calculations.

CStr(variable) converts a number or string value into a string type variable, thus enabling us to use the *SendDragonKeys* instruction to type out the results.

In our scenario we convert the variables height, width and bricksPerSqMetre into integers to perform the calculation. The result is then converted into a string and stored in the variable numberOfBricks.

The line SendDragonKeys "You need " types out the words within the quotes, notice the space after the word "need".

The line SendDragonKeys numberOfBricks types out the contents of the variable numberOfBricks. This works because when we performed our calculation we made the contents of the variable numberOfBricks a string type.

The line SendDragonKeys " Bricks" types out the word within the quotes, notice the space before the word "Bricks".

Alternative

As you become proficient in coding you will inevitably find numerous ways of achieving the same results. Below is an example of how we could have written the code for this scenario in a different way to achieve the same result. As a general rule; the less lines the better the code.

```
Sub Main
'Declare our variables
bricksPerSqMetre = 120
SendDragonKeys "You need "
SendDragonKeys CStr(CLng(Mid(ListVar1, 1, InStr(ListVar1, "\")-1)) * CLng(Mid(ListVar2,
1, InStr(ListVar2, "\")-1)) * CLng(bricksPerSqMetre))
SendDragonKeys " Bricks"
End Sub
```

Refer to:

Chapter 8: CLng Function, CStr Function, InStr Function, Mid Function

Working with multiple Dragon Lists in multiple Commands

As you become familiar with creating Dragon commands that include multiple Lists, you will find that your variations in Dragon scripts are often determined by the number of Lists within a command.

Good and efficient script writing involves the creation of scripts that where possible can be used for multiple commands and thankfully Dragon allows us to achieve this.

The scenario below shows an example:

A user who works in a record shop needs two Dragon commands to produce reports in a word processing application.

He wants to be able to input music album catalogue numbers; the format for the catalogue numbers remains constant in that they start with two capital letters followed by three digits. The numbers are to be dictated one letter or number at a time, e.g. by saying "catalogue Z A 5 4 2" or saying, "catalogue M J 1 9 0" and they will be typed out as "Catalogue-ZA542" or "Catalogue-MJ190".

He also wants to be able to input the genre and decade of albums, once again, the format remains constant in that they start with the genre followed by the decade. Examples of how these will be dictated are: "Genre Soul and Decade Eighties" or, "Genre Rock and Decade Sixties" and typed out as "Genre-SOUL 80s" or "Genre-ROCK 60s".

At this stage in the book I will presume that you are now familiar with the steps to create a command.

Let's first look at how we will construct the two commands.

Our required command names will be:

- **catalogue <capletter> <capletter> <digit> <digit> <digit>**
- **genre <genre> and decade <decades>**

The Lists that needs to be created are as follows:

The <capletter> List ensures that the letter dictated is typed out as a capital.

A\a

B\b

…

Z\z

The <digit> List ensures that numbers are interpreted as single numerical digits.

0\oh

1\one

…

9\nine

The <genre> List contains the list of capitalised genres.

SOUL\soul

ROCK\rock

…

DISCO\disco

The <decade> List contains the list of abbreviated decades.

30s\thirties

60s\sixties

…

80s\eighties

Now we are going to create a script that can satisfy both commands. As you can see from the command names, the first command contains five Lists and the second command contains two Lists. Our script needs a way of knowing how many Lists our commands contain.

This is where we introduce the use of **UtilityProvider.ContextValueCount** object.

A script that includes UtilityProvider.ContextValueCount when run, records the number of Lists within the command. Therefore, in our two intended commands UtilityProvider.ContextValueCount records that we have "5" Lists in command one and "2" Lists in command two.

By using `UtilityProvider.ContextValueCount` within a script we can now access the contents of our List variables. For example, in a command with 5 Lists we can access the contents of ListVar1, ListVar2… ListVar5 by the following commands:

```
SendDragonkeys UtilityProvider.ContextValueCount(0) 'ListVar1
```

```
SendDragonkeys UtilityProvider.ContextValueCount(1) 'ListVar2
```

...

```
SendDragonkeys UtilityProvider.ContextValueCount(4) 'ListVar5
```

Each of these commands will type out the contents of their respective ListVar numbers. For example, the command `SendDragonkeys UtilityProvider.ContextValueCount(2)` is the same as the command `SendDragonkeys ListVar3`.

 It is important to remember that numbering for UtilityProvider.ContextValueCount(x) starts at "0" which in turn refers to ListVar1.

Now, by using `UtilityProvider.ContextValueCount` we will create a script that can be used in both of our commands (see Table 4-5).

Table 4-5

MyCommand Name: catalogue <capletter> <capletter> <digit> <digit> <digit>	**MyCommand Name:** genre <genre> and decade <decades>
Group: Dragon - A Step Further_Chapter_04	**Group:** Dragon - A Step Further_Chapter_04
Availability: Global	**Availability:** Global
Command Type: Advanced Scripting	**Command Type:** Advanced Scripting

Content for both:

```
Sub Main

Dim outputString As String

outputString = ""

For i = 1 To (UtilityProvider.ContextValueCount)

outputString = outputString & Mid(UtilityProvider.ContextValue(i-1), 1, _

InStr(UtilityProvider.ContextValue(i-1), "\") -1)

Next i

SendDragonKeys outputString

End Sub
```

Create and save the two commands, open a word processing application and try it by saying:

"Catalogue A K 5 4 2"
"Catalogue J A 2 5 6"
"Genre Soul and Decade Sixties"
"Genre Disco and Decade Eighties"

Discuss

The line Dim outputString As String creates a variable called outputString that will hold string characters (alphabetical and numerical characters).

The line outputString = "" sets the value of the outputString variable to null.

The line For i = 1 to (UtilityProvider.ContextValueCount) is the start of a *For...Next Loop* whereby the script will perform *x* number of times all the statements between the line For i = 1 to (UtilityProvider.ContextValueCount) and the line Next i.

When running command one, `UtilityProvider.ContextValueCount` becomes equal to "5" as there are five Lists in command one. This would mean that the *For...Next Loop* would be interpreted as `For i = 1 to 5` and therefore the statements in between will be performed five times. If we were running the 2nd command this line would be interpreted as `For i = 1 to 2`.

The line `outputString = outputString & Mid(UtilityProvider.ContextValue(i-1), 1, _`

`InStr(UtilityProvider.ContextValue(i-1), "\") -1)` is the heart of our script and it is important to note that it lies within the *For...Next Loop*, so therefore, it will be executed *x* number of times.

Let's look at this line in more detail by breaking it down:

`InStr(UtilityProvider.ContextValue(i-1), "\") -1)`

Up until now, when we have used the *InStr* command it has had the appearance of `InStr(ListVar1, "\")-1)`, whereby the *InStr* command looks at the string of characters held within `ListVar1` which in turn enables us to determine the character position of the backslash "\" within the string and by including the `-1` in the command tells us how many characters there are before the backslash "\".

On this occasion we replace `ListVar1` with `UtilityProvider.ContextValue(i-1)`.

This works because `UtilityProvider.ContextValue(i-1)` is in fact a value, the value is achieved by using the value of the counter variable `i` which on the first time of entering the loop is equal to "1" (`For i = 1 to` ...) minus "1" which gives us a value of "0". Therefore, our line will be interpreted as `InStr(UtilityProvider.ContextValue(0), "\") -1)` or, in other words, look at the contents of `ListVar1` and provide the number of characters before the "\".

The portion of code `Mid(UtilityProvider.ContextValue(i-1), 1,` replaces our familiar *Mid* command `Mid(ListVar1, 1,` and works in the same way within the loop to provide us with all the characters from position 1 to *x* (i.e. *x* is the number of characters before the "\" as provided by the *InStr* portion of the line) in the contents of `ListVar1`.

`outputString = outputString &`

The string variable `outputString` will become equal to whatever is already in `outputString` and concatenate it with the results of performing the *InStr* and *Mid* commands. For example, if the content of the `outputString` variable is currently "Z" and the result of performing the *InStr* and *Mid* commands provide us with "R00". Then the variable `outputString` would become equal to "ZR00".

The line `Next i` increments the value of the counter variable `i` by one and will return the flow of the script back to the line `For i = 1 to (UtilityProvider.ContextValueCount)` (Hence, why we call it a *For...Next Loop*). However, it is important to note that this loop will only continue until the counter variable "i" is equal to the value of `UtilityProvider.ContextValueCount` and then it will come out of the loop.

As the script is run the counter variable "i" is being incremented by 1, therefore at the point of running the script "i" equals 1. When the script loops, "i" now becomes equal to "2" and so on. Because of this increment we are able to explore all the Lists in our commands.

The line SendDragonKeys outputString **tells Dragon to type out the contents of the variable** outputString

The SendDragonKeys outputString line is executed only when the For...Next Loop has finished looping.

Refer to:

Chapter 8: For...Next Loop, InStr Function, Mid Function

The unique Dragon List named <dictation>

Dragon has its own built in named Lists. The most useful of all is the **<dictation>** List.

Let's look at the <dictation> List in more detail:

- Open the MyCommands Editor window via the Tools menu >> Add New Command.
- In the MyCommand Name field type a less than sign "<" as usual, as soon as you type the "<" sign the MyCommands Name Editor window will appear.
- Delete the "<"
- Click on the Insert list... button, this will open the Insert List window.
- Click on the down arrow in the List name: field, this provides a drop-down menu showing your previously created Lists as well as some Dragon default Lists.
- Select the List called dictation and you will see in the main body "any phrase" (greyed out), as shown in Figure 4-10.

Figure 4-10

The dictation List does not show a list of items. The List contents field contains the word "any phrase" greyed out.

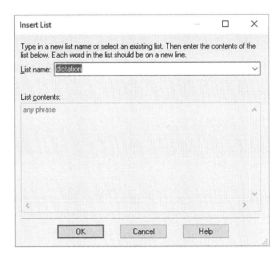

- Click the OK button, to go back to the MyCommands Name Editor window and you will notice unlike other Lists, that the Edit button is not available (see Figure 4-11).

Figure 4-11

Dragon does not allow you to edit the "dictation" Dragon List.

Up until now we have been able to look at, add to and edit the options/items of our created Lists. Our Lists have also contained a set number of items which force Dragon to carry out the commands only when it hears a word or phrase (item) contained in our Lists.

However, when we use this special <dictation> List, Dragon does not require any options/items. This is because the <dictation> List will work with any word or phrase and as a result, makes a command using it, much more flexible. Here is a scenario.

A Receptionist has the role of taking calls from potential customers to whom a standard email reply and accompanying questionnaire has to be sent out to them. The Receptionist notices that all the emails are the same except for the customer's name. The Receptionist would like to have a Dragon command that will enable her to produce the email replies by voice.

The following Dragon List command will do this:

MyCommand Name: produce questionnaire for <dictation>

Description: Produce questionnaire email

Group: Dragon - A Step Further_Chapter_04

Availability: Global

Command Type: Advanced Scripting

Content:

```
Sub Main
SendDragonKeys "Dear "
SendDragonKeys ListVar1
SendDragonKeys "{Enter}"
SendDragonKeys "Thank you for your enquiry and please find the questionnaire attached."
SendDragonKeys "{Enter}"
SendDragonKeys "We look forward to working with you "
SendDragonKeys ListVar1
SendDragonKeys "{Enter}"
SendDragonKeys "Kind regards"
End Sub
```

Figure 4-12 shows how your MyCommands Editor should look.

Figure 4-12

In the MyCommands Editor window is an Advanced Scripting type command that contains the "Dictation" Dragon List.

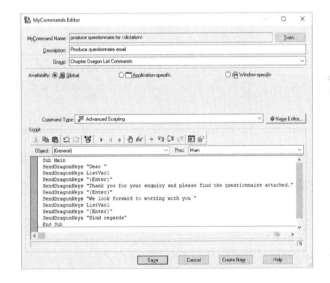

Open a word processing application and try it by saying:

"Produce a questionnaire for Michael"

"Produce a questionnaire for Mary Smith"

"Produce a questionnaire for Professor Peter Green"

Discuss

Because the Receptionist has no idea of the names of the potential customers who will call, this is an ideal opportunity for us to demonstrate how the <dictation> List can be used to create our command.

The power of using the <dictation> List is that we are not constrained to a set list of words or phrases in order for the command to work.

In our command, Dragon will populate the variable `ListVar1` with **whatever** is said after the Receptionist says, *"Produce a questionnaire for"*. We can then use the contents of the variable `ListVar1` to construct our email.

The line `SendDragonKeys ListVar1` will type out the contents of `ListVar1`.

The line `SendDragonKeys "{Enter}"` will press the Enter button in this case to produce a new line.

The line `SendDragonKeys "Thank y..."` will type out the text within the quotes.

The following is an overview for when creating commands that include the <dictation> List:

- You cannot have more than one <dictation> List in your command name.
- In a command containing multiple Lists, the <dictation> List must be the last List in the command name.

Valid and invalid command names using the <dictation> List:

- **MyCommand Name:** member of staff <dictation> job <tasks> **INVALID**
- **MyCommand Name:** member of staff <dictation> job <dictation> **INVALID**
- **MyCommand Name:** member of staff <staff> job <dictation> **VALID**
- **MyCommand Name:** member of staff <staff> job <tasks> notes <dictation> **VALID**

Dragon List & Written\Spoken words Lists in Auto-Text(Text and Graphics) Commands

When creating Dragon commands of the type Auto-Text(Text and Graphics), we are able to include both Dragon Lists and Dragon Written\Spoken words Lists.

The scenario below shows how we do this.

Imagine you are a comic shop owner who receives orders for comics. You want to quickly create a response to the orders by sending out a confirmation email or letter. The reply is to include a paragraph of text that is standard for all replies relating to comics ordered; you want the reply to include the comic's unique code number for the comic ordered as well as the name of the person who ordered it.

Figure 4-13 shows the intended format when replying to purchasers.

Figure 4-13

The required format for email responses to purchasers when a purchase has been made.

Item ordered: (comic code)

Dear: (name of purchaser),

Thank you for your order.

Your comic (comic code) will be dispatched within two working days and an invoice will be dispatched accordingly.

Yours sincerely,

My Comics Inc.

Tel: 00000 - 123456

E-mail: sales@mycomicsinc.com

Address:

123 Super Hero Avenue, London, E9

Please consider the environment before printing this email.

Can you imagine having to type or dictate all this out every time you receive an order!

To demonstrate this scenario, we will create a Written\Spoken words Dragon List called <comics> and make use of the powerful Dragon <dictation> List.

Let's now create the Auto-Text(Text and Graphics) command with the following specifications:

MyCommand Name: <comics> order by <dictation>

Name of List(s) used: <comics><dictation>

List items:

<comics>

Superman code: sup002\superman

Spiderman code: spi005\spiderman

Avengers code: ave222\avengers

Hulk

Description: Produces a reply confirmation body of text

Group: Dragon - A Step Further_Chapter_04

Availability: Global

Command Type: Auto-Text(Text and Graphics)

Content:

As can be seen in Figure 4-14.

Open a new Notepad or word processing application and try it by saying:

"spiderman order Mr Jones"

"superman order Peter Smith"

"hulk order Miss Green"

Figure 4-14

In the MyCommands Editor window is an Auto-Text(Text and Graphics) type command that contains the "Dictation" Dragon List.

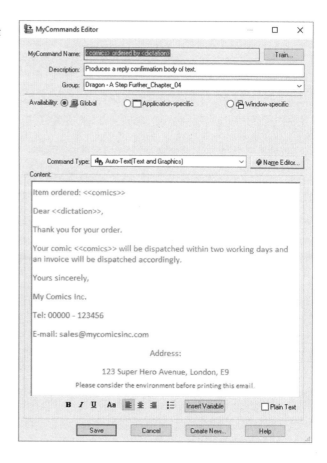

Discuss

The Content area within the MyCommands Editor window is where we insert the text to be typed out.

In order to change the font type or colour of the text, highlight the text and click on the (**Aa**) icon. This will in turn open the Fonts window enabling you to select from the options.

Because the command is of the type Auto-Text(Text and Graphics), Dragon also makes available a number of other icons that will enable you to apply justification, bold, italic and bullet point formatting if you require.

As an alternative you can create the customised text in a word processing application first and then copy and paste the text into the Content area. In fact, for some, it may be easier to create the formatted (styled) text in a word processing application, highlight the text and then run Dragon's built in command by saying "*make this a command*". This will automatically open the MyCommands Editor window with the text already placed in the Content area, ready for you to name your new command.

The CheckBox "Plain Text" must be un-checked to enable custom formatting of the text.

You will notice that the text within the Contents area also contains the Dragon List variables <<**comics**>> and <<**dictation**>>. These variables have been placed in specific positions so that when the command is run their value forms part of the generated text as well as providing readability to the overall confirmation email/letter.

There may be times where you may need to insert extra spaces within the text surrounding the variables to further improve readability.

The Dragon List names when inserted are surrounded by an extra less than (<) and more than (>) sign, for example <<dictation>> and is a requirement within Auto-Text(Text and Graphics) commands.

As we are using a Dragon Written\Spoken words List within an Auto-Text(Text and Graphics) command, Dragon automatically knows to, and will display the written text on the left side of the (\) items within the List. Also, as can be seen with the List item "Hulk", Dragon will automatically work **with** or **without** items that contain a backslash (\). Therefore, in this case it knows to display the word "Hulk" when that option is dictated.

Dragon List & Written\Spoken words Lists in Step-by-Step Commands

When creating Step-by-Step Dragon commands, we are able to include both Dragon Lists and Dragon Written\Spoken words Lists.

The only reason you would want to add a Dragon List to a Step-by-Step command is so that you can increase the dictation options to run the command. For example, say you have created a Step-by-Step command named "insert my address", that when run, types out your home address in full. A good idea might be to add a Dragon List which contains the following items:

- "insert my home address"
- "type my address"
- "insert where I live"

With the creation of the Dragon List, you will now be able to dictate any of the options/items in order to run the same command.

Dragon List Commands overview

Creating a macro that contains Lists enables us to carry out a single command using multiple utterances. It also allows us to carry out a variety of actions based upon the word or phrase that is recognised from the options/items in a List.

Points to consider when creating Dragon Lists:

- A command can have more than one List in the command name.
- Each List has a name and is represented by its enclosure within the less than and more than signs (<..name..>).
- A List must consist of 1 or more entries.
- Each entry within a List can be a single word or phrase.
- Each entry must be on a separate line.

Dragon has a number of built-in Lists to enable us to perform some of its default commands. For example, Dragon uses the <mouseaction> List, which responds to the dictated phrases, "*mouse left click*", "*mouse double click*" and other variations to control your mouse by voice.

The built-in command is named "mouse <mouseaction>" and the <mouseaction> List contains the following items:

click
double click
go
left click
mark
right click

Creating your own personal Dragon Lists

The creation of your own personal Lists can be a great asset to getting more out of Dragon and I would encourage you to do so. Here are some Advanced Scripting examples and suggestions:

Example 1

MyCommand Name: Insert the Roman Numeral for <romannumbers>

Entries for the List <romannumbers> **could be:**

I\one
IV\four
X\ten
XCIX\ninety nine
CXXI\one hundred and twenty one

...

Dragon script:

```
Sub Main
SendDragonKeys Mid(ListVar1, 1, InStr(ListVar1, "\")-1)
End Sub
```

Open a word processing application and try it by saying:

"Insert the Roman numeral for ten"

"Insert the Roman numeral for one hundred and twenty one"

...

 When working with commands, Dragon will interpret the written form of numbers ("one", "four") better than using values such as "1" or "4".

Example 2

MyCommand Name: insert the latin name for <latinplants>

Entries for the List <latinplants> **could be:**

Genus Rosa\roses

Bellis perennis\daises

Genus Tulipa\tulips

...

Dragon script:

```
Sub Main
SendDragonKeys Mid(ListVar1, 1, InStr(ListVar1, "\")-1)
End Sub
```

Open a word processing application and try it by saying:

"Insert the latin name for roses"

"Insert the latin name for tulips"

...

Example 3

MyCommand Name: show me the chemical symbol for <chemsymbols>

Entries for the List <chemsymbols> **could be:**

Au\gold

Ag\silver

Mg\magnesium

Sn\tin

...

Dragon script:

```
Sub Main
MsgBox Mid(ListVar1, 1, InStr(ListVar1, "\")-1)
End Sub
```

Try it by saying:

"Show me the chemical symbol for Gold"

"Show me the chemical symbol for Tin"

…

For the above example we use the *MsgBox* command to reveal a popup window containing the result.

Example 4

MyCommand Name: tweet<twitter_names>

Entries for the List <twitter_names> **could be:**

@theresa_may\theresa may

@jeremycorbyn\jeremy corbyn

@UKParliament\parliament

@UKLabour\labour party

@Conservatives\conservative party

…

Dragon script:

```
Sub Main
SendDragonKeys " "
SendDragonKeys Mid(ListVar1, 1, InStr(ListVar1, "\")-1)
SendDragonKeys " "
End Sub
```

Open a word processing application and try it by saying:

"tweet theresa may"

"tweet jeremy corbyn"

…

Refer to:

Chapter 8: MsgBox Function

Section 3: The Dragon Dialog Form Editor

Chapter 5: Working with the UserDialog (Form) Editor

What is the UserDialog Editor?

The UserDialog Editor (Dialog Form Editor) is a subject area that is often un-explored by users and at first glance can seem somewhat daunting. But if you take the time to at least get to grips with the basics of creating Dialog commands, you will value what this user interface brings to the table in assisting you to create customised forms.

The UserDialog Editor has two main purposes:

- Style our intended form.
- Generate the code to produce the form.

Creating Dialog Forms enable us to interact with users and gather information in multiple ways. The forms we create can contain fields that allow users to dictate or input text. They can also include Checkboxes, Drop-down menus and Option buttons (Radio buttons) that allows users to make choices. Furthermore, we can take these choices and inputs and use them to send information to applications, populate variables with data or perform and carry out specific tasks.

 Creating Dialog commands is no different to other Advanced Scripting macros in that you can make them Global, Application-specific or Window-specific.

Create a Simple Dialog Form

Let's start by creating a simple Dialog Form that will ask a user for their name and when the OK button is clicked, will then write out the name into a word processing application.

In order to create our Advanced Scripting Dialog command, let's open the MyCommands Editor window via the Tools menu >> Add New Command.

Fill in the other command information, such as name, description etc. as you would with other Advanced Scripting commands.

Feel free to follow my naming example:

MyCommand Name: example simple dialog form

Description: Shows a simple dialog form

Group: Dragon - A Step Further_Chapter_05

Availability: Global

Command Type: Advanced Scripting

Content:

```
Sub Main
 ...
End Sub
```

To produce the script necessary to create our simple Dialog Form, position and click your cursor between the lines Sub Main and End Sub. Next, click on the Edit UserDialog button (see Figure 5-1), which is positioned 2nd from the right in the row of buttons on show for Advanced Scripting (Pressing Ctrl+D is also an option).

Figure 5-1

A new Advanced Scripting type command in the MyCommands Editor window. Click on the Edit UserDialog icon to open the UserDialog Editor window.

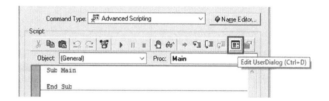

Either method will reveal the UserDialog Editor window (see Figure 5-2).

Figure 5-2

Use the UserDialog Editor window to create a Dialog Form.

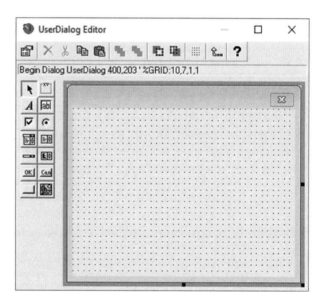

Look closely at the image above and take note of the line Begin Dialog UserDialog 400,203 ' %GRID:10,7,1,1 which is situated just below the top row of icons. Your numbers might be different as the 400,203 refers to the height and width dimensions of the form being created.

Let's now add a caption for our intended form by either double clicking on the grid dots or by clicking on the Edit Item Properties icon to reveal the Edit UserDialog Properties window (see Figure 5-3).

Figure 5-3

Use the Edit UserDialog Properties window to change the properties of a Dialog Form.

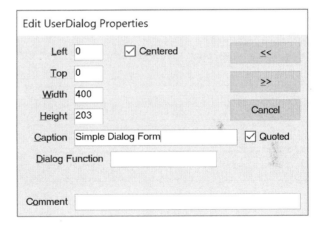

Figure 5-4

Use the Edit UserDialog Properties window to change the caption displayed in the title bar of a Dialog Form. Type the intended title into the **Caption** field.

In the Caption field insert the words "Simple Dialog Form" (see Figure 5-4).

Within this window you can also create a specific or same sized form by adjusting the values in the Width and Height fields.

Press the Enter key or click on the UserDialog Editor window to continue.

> **The form size can also be changed by dragging the border handles when viewing the UserDialog Editor window.**

Next, we are going to add the elements that will make up our form.

Let's add text to the form:

Click on the Add Text icon A, move the cursor to the main area and then click.

Figure 5-5

Once you have placed the Add Text item, you can move it by clicking and dragging it, you can resize it as necessary by dragging one of its selection handles.

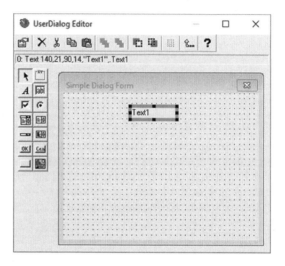

A Text item is produced, as shown in Figure 5-5, which you can resize by adjusting the border handles or move around by placing the mouse inside and dragging.

Double click or right-click inside the newly formed Text item to reveal the Edit Text Properties window (see Figure 5-6).

Figure 5-6

Use the Edit Text Properties window to change the properties of the Text item. Type the text to be displayed into the **Caption** field.

In the Caption field, type in "Enter your name".

Text Properties explained:

- **Left** field value: Refers to the position of the Text item from the left edge of the form.
- **Top** field value: Refers to the position of the Text item from the top edge of the form.
- **Width** field value: Refers to width of the Text item.
- **Height** field value: Refers to the height of the Text item.
- **Caption** field: Refers to the text that is to be displayed.
- **Quoted CheckBox:** By default, this is checked, when unchecked the text within the Caption field is treated as a variable name.
- **Field** field: Contains the name (also referred to as a label or variable) by which the Text item can be identified.
- **Drop-down menu:** Refers to the justification of the text to be displayed (options are Left, Right and Center).

Let's add a TextBox to the form:

We add a TextBox field in order to capture information and also enable the user to type or dictate their name into the form.

In the UserDialog Editor window, click on the Add TextBox icon [abl] , move the cursor to the main area and then click.

A TextBox item is produced, which you can resize by adjusting the border handles or move around by placing the mouse inside and dragging.

Double click or right-click inside the newly formed TextBox item to reveal the Edit TextBox Properties window.

Now, let's change the "Field" field value to "name" (see Figure 5-7), this will be the label/variable that will contain the name that the user types in, we will refer to this later on in the code.

TextBox Properties explained:

- **Left** field value: Refers to the position of the TextBox from the left edge of the form.
- **Top** field value: Refers to the position of the TextBox from the top edge of the form.
- **Width** field value: Refers to width of the TextBox.
- **Height** field value: Refers to the height of the TextBox.
- **Field** field: Refers to the label/variable or name by which this TextBox item can be identified. Its value becomes equal to what a user has typed or dictated into the TextBox.
- **Drop-down menu:** Allows us to set whether a user can enter a **Single** line of text, **Multiple** lines of text or for **Passwords**; any inserted text will be displayed as asterisk (***).

Figure 5-7

Use the Edit TextBox Properties window to change the properties of the TextBox item. Insert a label/variable name into the **Field** field.

The label name is how we refer to this TextBox in the code.

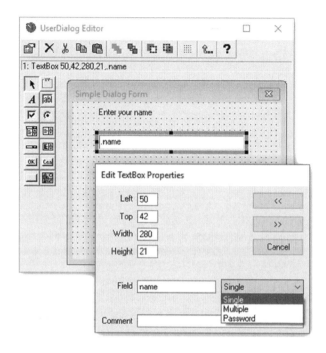

Let's add the action buttons "OK" and "Cancel" to the form

These action buttons are what a user clicks on in order for the form to process the information. In this example, when a user clicks on the OK button, Dragon will type out the name inserted into a word processing application.

In the UserDialog Editor window, click on the Add OKButton icon ![OK], position the cursor in the main area and then click, to add the OK button.

In the UserDialog Editor window, click on the Add CancelButton icon ![Can], position the cursor in the main area and then click, to add the Cancel button.

In both cases a button item is produced, which you can resize by adjusting the border handles or move around by placing the mouse inside and dragging (see Figure 5-8).

Figure 5-8

Once you have placed the OKButton and CancelButton items, you can move them by clicking and dragging, you can resize them as necessary by dragging one of their selection handles.

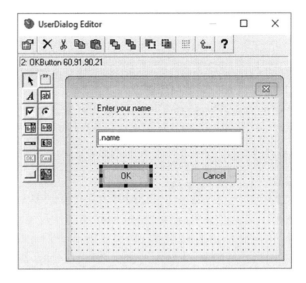

For a more precise sizing and placing of the buttons, double click or right-click inside either of the newly formed buttons to reveal the Edit OKButton Properties window (see Figure 5-9) or the Edit CancelButton Properties window.

Figure 5-9

Use the Edit OKButton Properties window to change the properties of the OKButton item. You can adjust the values in the **Left**, **Right**, **Top** and **Height** fields to size and position the item.

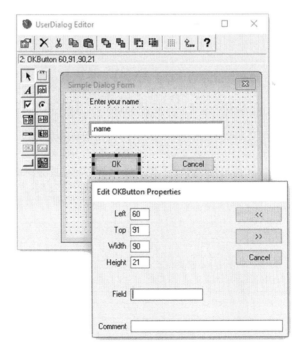

OKButton and CancelButton Properties explained:

- **Left/Top** field values: Refers to the position of the button from the left and top edges of the form.
- **Width/Height** field values: Refers to the width and height of the button.
- **Field** field: Refers to the label/variable or name by which this button can be identified.

Save the form to reveal the code

Now that we have our items in position, in the UserDialog Editor window, click on the Save and Exit icon  (2nd from the right in the top row of icons).

You will now notice that Dragon has produced some code in the MyCommands Editor (see Figure 5-10). It is this code that will produce our form when we run the command.

Figure 5-10

The MyCommands Editor window shows the generated script produced due to the work carried out in the UserDialog Editor window.

The make-up, the design of the form and the items it contains, are created by the following portion of the code:

```
Begin Dialog UserDialog 400,203 ' %GRID:10,7,1,1
    Text 50,7,220,14,"Enter your name",.Text1
    TextBox 50,42,280,21,.name
    OKButton 60,91,90,21
    CancelButton 230,91,90,21
End Dialog
```

To re-open and edit the Dialog Form, we highlight the portion of the code (From `Begin Dialog` to `End Dialog`) and click on the Edit UserDialog icon 🖼 or press Ctrl+D.

 The order of the lines is not important and may be different to what you see above; it is dependent on the order in which you placed the items.

Let's look at this code in more detail:

- The line `Begin Dialog UserDialog 400,203...` - Sets the Dialog Form size in width and height.
- The line `Text 50,7,220,14,"Enter your name",.Text1` - Places the text within the quotes in a specific position on the form and in a frame of a specific size.
- The line `TextBox 50,42,280,21,.name` - Places a TextBox of a specific size in a specific position. The variable `.name` will become equal to the content dictated or typed into the TextBox.
- The line `OKButton 60,91,90,21` - Places the OK button of a specific size in a specific position.
- The line `CancelButton 230,91,90,21` - Places the Cancel button of a specific size in a specific position.
- The line `End Dialog` - Concludes the Dialog Form. It lets Dragon know that every line between the `Begin Dialog...` line and the `End Dialog` line is what makes up the Dialog Form.

The last two lines of code perform the following:

- The line `Dim dlg As UserDialog` - Creates a variable called `dlg` which becomes equal to the Dialog Form credentials and the items it contains.
- The line `Dialog dlg` - Is what causes the form to be displayed. We will adjust this line of code to enable us to check for various values of the items within the Dialog Form. We will also add extra code to this line to enable an action to be carried out based upon certain values.

 When working with more than one Dialog Form, I would suggest that you change all occurrences of the variable name "dlg" to "dlg01" and increment for other forms accordingly.

 Refer to Chapter 5: An Advanced Dialog Form, for an example of a script with two Dialog Forms.

Let's add extra code to complete our simple Dialog Form

Finally, in order for our Dialog Form to work correctly, we need to remove the line `Dialog dlg` and replace it with the following:

```
If Dialog (dlg) = -1 then
    SendKeys dlg.name, True
End If
```

This new piece of code uses an *If Then* statement to firstly check if Dialog (dlg) is equal to the value of -1. This basically means, has the "OK" button been pressed?

> Dragon applies/returns the value of:
> "-1" to Dialog (dlg) if the "OK" button has been pressed.
> "0" to Dialog (dlg) if the "Cancel" button has been pressed.

Next, the line SendKeys dlg.name, True means, if the Dialog (dlg) is equal to -1 then type out the contents of the variable called name which is within the UserDialog Form called dlg.

The portion of code , True tells Dragon to perform the action of typing out the contents of the variable name before moving on to the next line in the script.

The final code and MyCommands Editor details should look similar to the following:

MyCommand Name: example simple dialog form

Description: Shows a simple dialog form

Group: Dragon - A Step Further_Chapter_05

Availability: Global

Command Type: Advanced Scripting

Content:

```
Sub Main
Begin Dialog UserDialog 400,203 ' %GRID:10,7,1,1
  Text 50,7,220,14,"Enter your name",.Text1
  TextBox 50,42,280,21,.name
  OKButton 60,91,90,21
  CancelButton 230,91,90,21
End Dialog
Dim dlg As UserDialog
  If Dialog (dlg) = -1 Then
  SendKeys dlg.name, True
  End If
End Sub
```

Open a word processing application and try it by saying:
"example simple dialog form"

Editing a Dialog Form

In order to edit an existing Dialog Form, double click the command to open it in the MyCommands Editor:

- Highlight all the lines of code between the lines Begin Dialog UserDialog... and End Dialog.
- Then click on the Edit UserDialog icon to reveal the UserDialog Editor, as shown in Figure 5-11 (pressing Ctrl + D is also an option).

Figure 5-11

The script produced reflects the settings of the items used in the UserDialog Editor window.

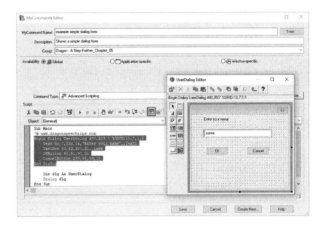

 You can have more than one Dialog Form within a command; each would have their own "Begin Dialog UserDialog..." & "End Dialog" lines.

Using OptionButtons (Radio buttons) in Dialog Forms

Figure 5-12

An example of a group of Option buttons (Radio buttons).

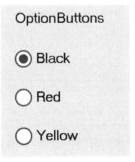

OptionButtons also referred to as Radio buttons, are an ideal way to force a user to make a single choice from a number of options. Figure 5-12 shows an example of a group of OptionButtons.

OptionButtons are created within the UserDialog Editor window by clicking on the Add OptionButton icon and then positioning the cursor and clicking in the main area. As you would expect, an OptionButton has several properties that can be accessed by either double clicking or right-clicking on it, which in turn reveals the Edit OptionButton Properties window (see Figure 5-13).

Figure 5-13

Use the Edit OptionButton Properties window to change the properties of an OptionButton.

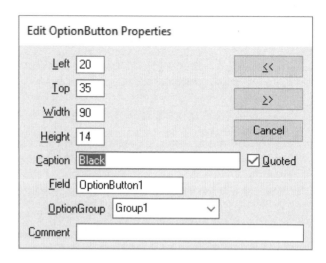

OptionButton Properties explained:

- **Left/Top** field values: Refers to the position of the OptionButton from the left and top edges of the form.
- **Width/Height** field values: Refers to the width and height of the frame surrounding the OptionButton.
- **Caption** field: Refers to the text (title) that is to be displayed next to the OptionButton.
- **Quoted CheckBox:** By default, this is checked, when unchecked the text within the Caption field is treated as a variable name.
- **Field** field: Contains the name (also referred to as a label or variable) by which the OptionButton item can be identified.
- **OptionGroup drop-down menu:** Refers to the name of the group that the OptionButton belongs to.
- **Comment** field: This may be used to write additional notes.

Each OptionButton you create will belong to a group, which is set by the OptionGroup value in the properties of each OptionButton, and when a form is presented to a user, the user is only able to select one of the OptionButtons within a group.

If you require two or more groups of OptionButtons, each group of OptionButtons will have their own OptionGroup named individually (for example, Group2, Group3 etc.).

To change the group name or group that an OptionButton belongs to, select the OptionButton and right-click on it to reveal the Edit OptionButton Properties window. Select the OptionGroup drop-down menu and either make a change or select another if there is one.

 There must be at least two OptionButtons in a group.

To demonstrate how we can include OptionButtons within a Dialog Form, the macro below when run, places three OptionButtons onto a form, which enables a user to select either of the OptionButtons and when the OK button is clicked, a Message Box will appear confirming the choice made by the user.

MyCommand Name: example option buttons dialog form

Description: Shows how we can use option buttons in Dialog forms

Group: Dragon - A Step Further_Chapter_05

Availability: Global

Command Type: Advanced Scripting

Content:

```
Sub Main
  Begin Dialog UserDialog 400,203,"OptionButtons" ' %GRID:10,7,1,1
    Text 50,7,220,14,"Select the colour you like.",.Text1
    OptionGroup .Group1
      OptionButton 20,35,90,14,"Black",.OptionButton1
      OptionButton 20,63,90,14,"Red",.OptionButton2
      OptionButton 20,91,90,14,"Yellow",.OptionButton3
    OKButton 60,154,90,21
    CancelButton 230,154,90,21
  End Dialog
  Dim dlg As UserDialog
  If Dialog(dlg) = -1 Then
    Select Case dlg.Group1
      Case 0 'black
        MsgBox ("You selected Black")
      Case 1 'red
        MsgBox ("You selected Red")
      Case 2 'yellow
        MsgBox ("You selected Yellow")
    End Select
  Else
  End If
End Sub
```

Try it by saying:

"example option buttons dialog form" or in the **MyCommands Editor window**, click on the **"Start/Resume"** **icon (F5)**

Discuss

The most relevant portion of this script is from the line Dim dlg As UserDialog to End If, as it is this portion of code that checks which of the OptionButtons is selected and carries out an action based upon the selected OptionButton.

The lines `Dim dlg As UserDialog` and `If Dialog(dlg) = -1 Then` as usual, makes the Dialog Form ready for when the OK button is pressed, once pressed, it will then carry out the instructions within the *If Then* statement.

In order to know which OptionButton has been selected, we use the *Select Case* function on the group name of the OptionButtons.

The line `Select Case dlg.Group1` is the start of the *Select Case* function, where, in this scenario the name of our group of OptionButtons is called `Group1`.

The line `Case 0` means that if the 1st OptionButton within this group (`Group1`) is selected, then carry out the line `MsgBox ("You selected Black")` which will display a Message Box with the words "You selected Black".

The line `Case 1` means that if the 2nd OptionButton within this group is selected then carry out the line `MsgBox ("You selected Red")`.

The line `Case 2` acts in exactly the same way as the previous cases (Do you get the picture?).

We wrap up this *Select Case* statement by including the line `End Select`.

When writing scripts that involve working with OptionButtons and their groups, the following applies:
- The value -1 is returned if No OptionButtons are selected within a group.
- The value 0 is returned if the first OptionButton within a group is selected.
- The value 1 is returned if the second OptionButton within a group is selected.
- The value 2 is returned for the third OptionButton and so on.

Within a Select Case statement, you cannot refer to the individual OptionButtons by their Field names such as OptionButton1, OptionButton2, Yellow etc. or a name you may have changed them to, as this will cause an error.

Refer to:

Chapter 8: If Then Statement, MsgBox Function, Select Case Function

Using CheckBoxes in Dialog Forms

Figure 5-14

An example of Check boxes.

Including CheckBoxes in your Dialog Forms, offers an alternative way of engaging with users. Users can select none, some or all of the CheckBoxes you make available. Figure 5-14 shows example Checkboxes.

CheckBoxes are created within the UserDialog Editor window by clicking on the Add CheckBox icon ☑ and then positioning the cursor and clicking in the main area.

To view the properties of a CheckBox, either double click or right-click on a CheckBox item to reveal the Edit CheckBox Properties window (see Figure 5-15).

Figure 5-15

Use the Edit CheckBox Properties window to change the properties of a CheckBox.

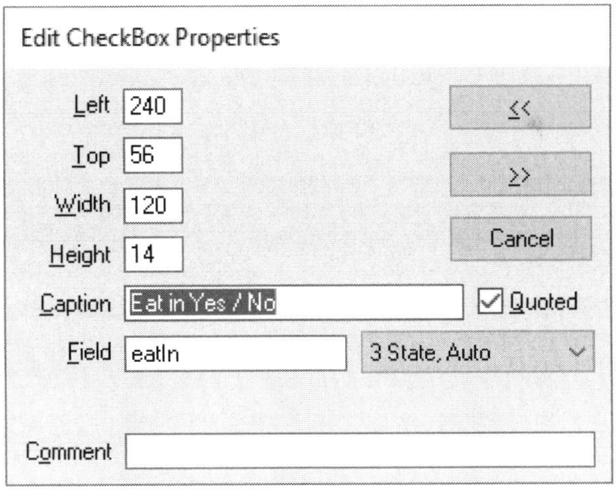

CheckBox Properties explained:

- **Left/Top** field values: Refers to the position of the CheckBox from the left and top edges of the form.
- **Width/Height** field values: Refers to the width and height of the frame surrounding the CheckBox.
- **Caption** field: Refers to the text (title) that is to be displayed next to the CheckBox.
- **Quoted CheckBox:** By default, this is checked, when unchecked the text within the Caption field is treated as a variable name.
- **Field** field: Contains the name (also referred to as a label or variable) by which the CheckBox item can be identified.
- **Comment** field: This may be used to write additional notes.
- **Drop-down menu:** Determines the type of CheckBox you wish to be displayed.
  - **2 State:** Produces a CheckBox that can either be checked or unchecked.
  - **3 State:** Produces a CheckBox that can either be checked, unchecked or greyed out (switches between checked and unchecked when clicked).
  - **3 State, Auto:** Produces a CheckBox that can either be checked, unchecked or greyed out (rotating through all three states as the button is clicked).

To demonstrate how we can include CheckBoxes within a Dialog Form, the macro below will create a form consisting of a Text field and four CheckBoxes. A user can select any number of the CheckBoxes and then press OK. The result is a written message (written out in a word processing application) stating the number of items selected and the choices made by the user.

MyCommand Name: example check box dialog form

Description: Shows an example of how Checkboxes are created in Dialog forms

Group: Dragon - A Step Further_Chapter_05

Availability: Global

Command Type: Advanced Scripting

Content:

```
Sub Main
  Begin Dialog UserDialog 400,203,"CheckBox" ' %GRID:10,7,1,1
    Text 70,14,270,21,"Select your order",.Text1
    CheckBox 70,56,110,14,"Fried chicken",.fried_chicken
    CheckBox 70,84,110,14,"Crispy Chips",.crispyChips
    CheckBox 70,112,90,14,"Drink",.drink
    CheckBox 240,56,120,14,"Eat in Yes / No",.eatIn,2
    OKButton 60,154,90,21
    CancelButton 220,154,90,21
  End Dialog
  Dim dlg As UserDialog
  If Dialog (dlg) = -1 Then
      number_of_items = 0
      If dlg.fried_chicken = 1 Then number_of_items = number_of_items + 1
```

```
            If dlg.crispyChips = 1 Then number_of_items = number_of_items + 1
            If dlg.drink = 1 Then number_of_items = number_of_items + 1
    End If
    SendKeys "Thank you, you have ordered " & number_of_items & " items:"
    SendKeys "~~~"
    If dlg.fried_chicken = 1 Then SendKeys "Fried chicken" & "~~"
    If dlg.crispyChips = 1 Then SendKeys "Chips" & "~~"
    If dlg.drink = 1 Then SendKeys "Drink" & "~~"
    If dlg.eatIn = 0 Then SendKeys "ORDERED BY PHONE"
    If dlg.eatIn = 1 Then SendKeys "AN EAT IN ORDER"
    If dlg.eatIn = 2 Then SendKeys "A TAKE AWAY ORDER"
End Sub
```

Open a word processing application and try it by saying:

"example check box dialog form"

Discuss

Let's examine the script in more detail.

Firstly, when creating each of the CheckBoxes, each one has its own unique Field name ("fried_chicken", "crispyChips", "drink" & "eatIn") which is achieved by editing the Field name in the Edit CheckBox Properties window of each CheckBox.

The CheckBox "eatIn" has had its state changed to "3 State, Auto", again achieved via the Edit CheckBox Properties window. This means that the CheckBox can be in one of three states.

We will use these field names later in the script to help us achieve our objective.

> **Good coding practice is to create field names that at least start in lowercase, make them relevant to the cause and replace any spaces you may have with underscores.**

The lines `Dim dlg As UserDialog` and `If Dialog(dlg) = -1 Then` as usual, makes the Dialog Form ready for when the OK button is pressed, once pressed, it will then carry out the instructions within the *If Then* statement.

The line `number_of_items = 0` creates a variable called `number_of_items` that at the start will hold a value of zero (0) and will be used to store the number of items selected.

The line `If dlg.fried_chicken = 1 Then number_of_items = number_of_items + 1` checks whether the CheckBox named "`fried_chicken`" has a value of 1 and if it does, it will add 1 to the value of the variable `number_of_items` (our counting system).

> **Dragon returns the number 1 if a CheckBox has been checked.**
> **If the CheckBox has not been checked, it will return the number 0.**

The next two lines work in the same way, in that they check to see whether the CheckBoxes named "crispyChips" & "drinks" have been checked or not.

The next portion of the script is to write out the information into an open word processing application to see the results. Applications such as Notepad and DragonPad works just as well.

Think of the line SendKeys "Thank you, you have ordered " & number_of_items & " items:" as three parts which are all joined together by the "&" symbol.

SendKeys *"The text "* **& variable &** *" The text"*

This line determines how we write out the text "Thank you...ordered ", followed by the value held in the variable number_of_items, followed by the text " items:"

Notice the deliberate space after the word ordered and before the word items:. We do this, so that the final outcome will look like a complete sentence - Rather than: "Thank you, you have ordered2items:".

The "&" is used to join text and the contents of a variable in the same SendKeys command line. The text to be written out is within quotes, the variable name is not within quotes.

The line SendKeys "~~~" is how we achieve three-line breaks (press the Enter key 3 times) in our outputted text. Each tilde (~) represents the pressing of the Enter key.

The line If dlg.fried_chicken = 1 Then SendKeys "Fried chicken" & "~~" asks the question, is the CheckBox called fried_chicken in the Dialog Form called dlg checked? (Is the value returned equal to 1?). If the returned value is equal to 1 (yes, it is checked) then the SendKeys "Fried chicken" portion of the line will type out the text "Fried chicken". The latter part of this line & "~~" uses the "&" to add "~~" (two tildes) which will insert two Line Feeds (as if the Enter key has been pressed twice).

The next two lines work in the same way, in that they check to see whether the CheckBoxes named "crispyChips" & "drinks" have been checked or not.

Finally, the last three lines starting with If dlg.eatIn... checks the CheckBox state (the value returned) of the CheckBox named eatIn and dependent on the state will write out the appropriate message.

A blank CheckBox returns a value of "0".
A Checked (ticked) CheckBox returns a value of "1".
A 3 State CheckBox returns a value of "2" when the CheckBox is neither blank nor checked.

Refer to:
Chapter 8: SendDragonKeys, SendKeys & SendSystemKeys

Using PushButtons (user defined buttons) in Dialog Forms

Figure 5-16

An example of a PushButton with the label name "MyButton".

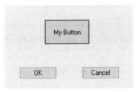

Adding PushButtons to your Dialog Forms is a way for you to add your own labelled/custom buttons, that when clicked, will carry out an action. Figure 5-16 shows an example PushButton.

PushButtons are created within the UserDialog Editor window by clicking on the Add PushButton icon ⌐⌐ and then positioning the cursor and clicking in the main area.

To view and edit the properties of a PushButton, either double click or right-click on a PushButton item to reveal the Edit PushButton Properties window (see Figure 5-17).

Figure 5-17

Use the Edit PushButton Properties window to change the properties of a PushButton. Insert the label name of the button into the **Caption** field.

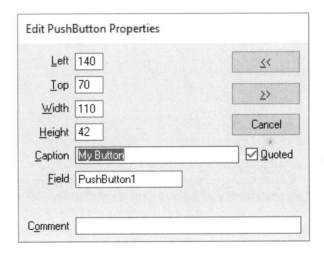

PushButton Properties explained:

- **Left/Top** field values: Refers to the position of the PushButton from the left and top edges of the form.
- **Width/Height** field values: Refers to the width and height of the PushButton.
- **Caption** field: Contains the title (My Button) to be given to the PushButton.
- **Quoted CheckBox:** By default, this is checked, when unchecked the text within the Caption field is treated as a variable name.
- **Field** field: Contains the name (also referred to as a label or variable) by which the PushButton item can be identified.

To demonstrate how we can include PushButtons within a Dialog Form, the macro below will create a form consisting of two PushButtons and the usual OK and Cancel buttons.

Once the command is run, and the form is displayed, a user will be able to click on any of the buttons. If a PushButton (custom button) is clicked, a Message Box will appear confirming the choice of button selected by the user.

MyCommand Name: example push buttons dialog form

Description: Shows how we can use PushButtons in Dialog forms

Group: Dragon - A Step Further_Chapter_05

Availability: Global

Command Type: Advanced Scripting

Content:

```
Sub Main
  Begin Dialog UserDialog 400,203,"PushButtons" ' %GRID:10,7,1,1
    PushButton 50,70,110,42,"Button 1",.PushButton1
    PushButton 240,70,110,42,"Button 2",.PushButton2
    OKButton 80,147,90,21
    CancelButton 230,147,90,21
  End Dialog
  Dim dlg As UserDialog
  button_pressed=Dialog (dlg)
  If button_pressed = 1 Then
    MsgBox("you pressed button one")
  End If
  If button_pressed = 2 Then
    MsgBox("you pressed button two")
  End If
     'MsgBox("you pressed button " & button_pressed)
End Sub
```

Try it by saying:

"example push buttons dialog form" or in the **MyCommands Editor window,** click on the **"Start/Resume" icon (F5)**

Discuss

When any of the buttons on the form are pressed a numerical value is returned and it is this value that we must first capture and then use, in order to carry out a specific action.

The line `button_pressed=Dialog (dlg)` makes the variable `button_pressed` become equal to the value of the button pressed.

If either of the two custom PushButtons is clicked, the values returned will be either 1 for the first PushButton or 2 for the second. Therefore, for these two custom buttons, the variable `button_pressed` can only become equal to either 1 or 2.

Each PushButton added to a Dialog Form, has its own value, values start at "1" for the first PushButton, "2" for the second, "3" for the third and so on.

In the case of where a user presses the OK button, the variable `button_pressed` will become equal to -1 (looks familiar? we use it a lot!). If the Cancel button is pressed, the variable `button_pressed` will become equal to 0.

Once we have that value, the line `If button_pressed = 1 Then` is where we use an *If Then* statement on the variable `button_pressed` to direct Dragon to display the correct Message Box.

Alternative

Un-comment the following line in order to produce a second Message Box that displays the numerical value returned, from any of the buttons pressed.

```
'MsgBox("you pressed button " & button_pressed)
```

Refer to:

Chapter 8: If Then Statement, MsgBox Function

Placing GroupBoxes and Images in Dialog Forms

Inserting GroupBoxes and Images into Dialog Forms enables us to jazz up the look of our forms.

GroupBoxes are created within the UserDialog Editor window by clicking on the Add GroupBox icon and then positioning the cursor and clicking in the main area.

To view the properties of a GroupBox, either double click or right-click on a GroupBox item to reveal the Edit GroupBox Properties window (see Figure 5-18).

Figure 5-18

Use the Edit GroupBox Properties window to change the properties of a GroupBox. Insert the title name for the GroupBox into the **Caption** field.

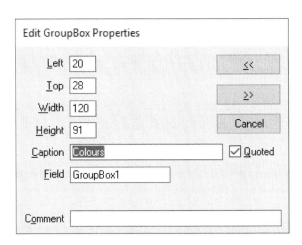

GroupBox Properties explained:

- **Left/Top** field values: Refers to the position of the GroupBox from the left and top edges of the form.
- **Width/Height** field values: Refers to the width and height of the GroupBox.
- **Caption** field: Contains the text that will be used as the title of the GroupBox.
- **Quoted CheckBox:** By default, this is checked, when unchecked the text within the Caption field is treated as a variable name.
- **Field** field: Contains the name (also referred to as a label or variable) by which the GroupBox item can be identified.

Adding Images to a Dialog Form.

To enable images to be displayed within your Dialog Forms, open the UserDialog Editor window and click on the Add Picture icon 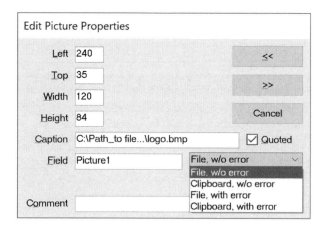, position the cursor and click in the main area.

To view the properties of a Picture item, either double click or right-click on a Picture item to reveal its Edit Picture Properties window (see Figure 5-19).

Figure 5-19

Use the Edit Picture Properties window to change the properties of an image.

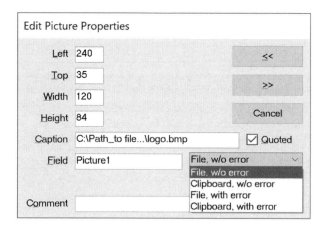

Picture Properties explained:

- **Left/Top** field values: Refers to the position of the Picture item from the left and top edges of the form.
- **Width/Height** field values: Refers to the width and height of the Picture item.
- **Caption** field: Contains the directory path to the bitmap (.bmp) image.
- **Quoted CheckBox:** By default, this is checked, when unchecked the text within the Caption field is treated as a variable name.
- **Field** field: Contains the name (also referred to as a label or variable) by which the Picture item can be identified.

When displaying images within a Dialog Form, you can either use an image that currently resides in the Clipboard or use an image that resides in a directory path/folder on the PC.

The **File, w/o error** drop-down menu enables us to select how we will access an image (whether it's via the Clipboard or a file within a Folder) and what type of error message will appear if Dragon cannot find the intended image. There are four options:

1. The default **File, w/o error** option will:

- Display the bitmap image (.bmp) file located at the directory path within the Caption field.
- Produce the line of code: `Picture 240,35,120,84,"C:\...Path..to..file\logo.bmp",0,.Picture1`
- Display the message "(missing picture)" if no image is found or the image is not in a .bmp format.

2. The **Clipboard, w/o error** option will:

- Display the bitmap image (.bmp) file copied to the Clipboard.
- Produce the line of code: `Picture 240,35,120,84,"C:\...Path..to..file\logo.bmp",3,.Picture1`
- Display the message "(missing picture)" if no image is found or the image is not in a .bmp format.

3. The **File, with error** option will:

- Display the bitmap image (.bmp) file located at the directory path within the Caption field.
- Produce the line of code: `Picture 240,35,120,84,"C:\...Path..to..file\logo.bmp",16,.Picture1`
- Cause a run-time error to occur if no image is found or the image is not in a .bmp format.

4. The **Clipboard, with error** option will:

- Display the bitmap image (.bmp) file copied to the Clipboard.
- Produce the line of code: `Picture 240,35,120,84,"C:\...Path..to..file\logo.bmp",19,.Picture1`
- Cause a run-time error to occur if no image is found or the image is not in a .bmp format.

The following macro shows how we can use a GroupBox to form a rectangle around a group of OptionButtons and include a logo on a Dialog Form. When the macro is run, the Dialog Form is created and if the user clicks on the OK button a Message Box is revealed.

 You will need to change the portion of code `C:\...Path..to..file\logo.bmp` **to the directory path and name of your bitmap file.**

MyCommand Name: example group box and images

Description: Shows how we can include GroupBoxes and Images in Dialog forms

Group: Dragon - A Step Further_Chapter_05

Availability: Global

Command Type: Advanced Scripting

Content:

```
Sub Main
  Begin Dialog UserDialog 400,203,"GroupBox and Images" ' %GRID:10,7,1,1
    GroupBox 20,28,120,91,"Colours",.GroupBox1
    OptionGroup .Group1
      OptionButton 30,49,90,14,"Black",.OptionButton1
      OptionButton 30,70,90,14,"Red",.OptionButton2
      OptionButton 30,91,90,14,"Yellow",.OptionButton3
    OKButton 60,154,90,21
    CancelButton 230,154,90,21
    Picture 240,35,120,84,"C:\...Path..to..file\logo.bmp",0,.Picture1
  End Dialog
  Dim dlg As UserDialog
  If Dialog(dlg) = -1 Then
    Select Case dlg.Group1
      Case 0 'black
        MsgBox ("You selected Black")
      Case 1 'red
        MsgBox ("You selected Red")
      Case 2 'yellow
        MsgBox ("You selected Yellow")
    End Select
  Else
  End If
End Sub
```

Try it by saying:

"example group box and images" or in the **MyCommands Editor window**, click on the **"Start/Resume" icon (F5)**

Discuss

When creating GroupBoxes it is easier to create the GroupBox first and then create the intended enclosed items, otherwise, the items will appear to be hidden underneath. However, leaving the enclosed items hidden will not affect the look of the Dialog Form when the command is run.

 If the GroupBox is created after the intended items and they appear to be hidden, select the Groupbox item and click on the Move Behind icon until you achieve the required result.

 When exporting and distributing your scripts, it is important to bear in mind that any images will be referring to a directory path on your computer. A user importing your script may not have the same images in the same location and as a result no image will be displayed. Image files are not included in the export.

Allowing for Alt + Keys selection in Dialog Forms

When creating Dialog Forms, it is possible to allow users to use a shortcut key combination to move the cursor to a specific field or item. The shortcuts we can create use the *Alt* key in combination with another keyboard key.

The macro below shows how we can use shortcut keys to select or move to items on a Dialog Form. Figure 5-20 shows the Dialog Form that will be created.

Figure 5-20

The Dialog Form consists of Check boxes, Option buttons and a Text box.

Shortcut key combinations can be used to navigate to some of the items.

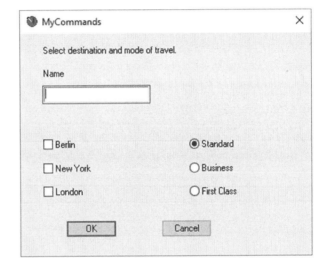

MyCommand Name: example short cut keys selection

Description: Shows an example of how we can add Shortcut keys for navigation within Dialog forms

Group: Dragon - A Step Further_Chapter_05

Availability: Global

Command Type: Advanced Scripting

Content:

```
Sub Main
Begin Dialog UserDialog 520,266 ' %GRID:10,7,1,1
    Text 40,14,300,14,"Select destination and mode of travel.",.formTitle
    Text 40,42,90,14,"Name",.Text2
    TextBox 40,63,190,21,.TextBox1
    CheckBox 40,126,90,14,"Berlin",.CheckBox1
    CheckBox 40,154,90,14,"New &York",.CheckBox2
    CheckBox 40,182,90,14,"London",.CheckBox3
    OptionGroup .travelClass
      OptionButton 300,126,100,14,"Standard",.OptionButton1
```

```
        OptionButton 300,154,100,14,"Business",.OptionButton2
        OptionButton 300,182,100,14,"&First Class",.OptionButton3
      OKButton 80,224,90,21
      CancelButton 250,224,90,21
    End Dialog
    Dim dlg As UserDialog
    Dialog dlg
End Sub
```

Try it by saying:

"example short cut keys selection" or in the **MyCommands Editor window**, click on the **"Start/Resume" icon (F5). Then press Alt+B to test it.**

In order that we can make *Alt+* key combinations available as a means of selection or navigation, we need to include ampersands (&) at specific positions within the script.

An ampersand (&) is placed before the character that is to be used as the accelerator key (the character to be used in conjunction with the *Alt* key).

As an example, to make a shortcut key for the CheckBox referred to as CheckBox1 with the Caption "Berlin" we would place an ampersand in front of any of the letters of the word "Berlin" (Caption field). Let's say that we want Alt+B to be our shortcut, we need to change the line:

```
CheckBox 40,126,90,14,"Berlin",.CheckBox1
```

To

```
CheckBox 40,126,90,14,"&Berlin",.CheckBox1
```

 The ampersand can be placed in front of any of the characters of the Caption text.

 If the same shortcut key is set up for multiple items, Dragon will ignore the shortcut key when attempted.

 When performing a shortcut on a CheckBox, you will notice that it also acts as a switch, checking then un-checking the CheckBox each time the shortcut is performed.

In order to create a keyboard shortcut (Alt+M) to the TextBox field (referred to as TextBox1) that does not have a Caption field, we need to create a shortcut to the Text Label preceding it (Text2). Therefore, in our script we would change the line:

```
Text 40,42,90,14,"Name",.Text2
```

To

```
Text 40,42,90,14,"Na&me",.Text2
```

Now when pressing Alt+M, the cursor will move to the TextBox field (TextBox1).

Set Focus

Sometimes when a command is run, and a Dialog Form is produced, you may want the cursor moved to a specific item/field within the Dialog Form.

The following steps outline how we can use the *DlgFocus* (set focus) command to place the cursor in a specific TextBox when a Dialog Form is presented:

Step 1. Create the Dialog Form using the following code between Sub Main and End Sub

```
Begin Dialog UserDialog 400,203,"Set the focus" ' %GRID:10,7,1,1
    Text 30,21,90,14,"Text Field 01",.Text1
    Text 240,21,90,14,"Text Field 02",.Text2
    Text 30,98,90,14,"Text Field 03",.Text3
    Text 240,98,90,14,"Text Field 04",.Text4
    TextBox 30,42,90,21,.TextBox1
    TextBox 250,42,90,21,.TextBox2
    TextBox 30,119,90,21,.TextBox3
    TextBox 250,119,90,21,.TextBox4
    OKButton 90,168,90,21
    CancelButton 220,168,90,21
End Dialog
Dim dlg As UserDialog
Dialog dlg
```

Step 2. Edit the UserDialog Properties.

- Highlight the code from Begin Dialog to End Dialog
- Click on the Edit UserDialog icon 📧 or press Ctrl+D to reveal the UserDialog Editor window (see Figure 5-21).

Figure 5-21

The UserDialog Editor consisting of four Text items and four TextBox items. Each TextBox item has a unique label/variable **Field** name (TextBox1 . . . 4)

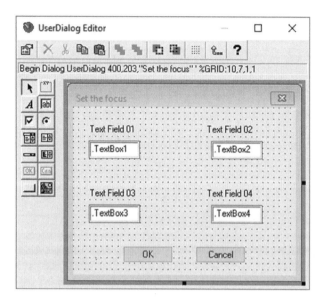

- Right-click on the grid area of the UserDialog Editor window to reveal the Edit UserDialog Properties window.
- Insert the text "dialogfunc" into the Dialog Function field, as shown in Figure 5-22 and press Enter.

Figure 5-22

Use the Edit UserDialog Properties window to change the properties of the Dialog Form. Insert the text "dialogfunc" into the **Dialog Function** field.

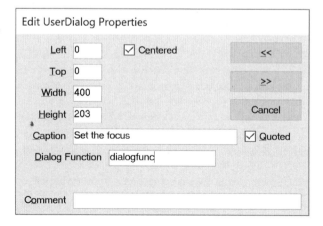

- Now, in the UserDialog Editor window, click on the Save and Exit icon 𝕃₀₀
- You will be presented with a pop-up window, as shown in Figure 5-23, click on the Yes button to create the skeleton dialog function. You will then be returned to the MyCommands Editor window.

Figure 5-23

The Dragon pop-up window will prompt the user to confirm the creation of the skeleton dialog function.

You should now notice that Dragon has made a small change to your Begin Dialog… line and if you scroll down within the MyCommands Editor window you will see that extra code has been inserted underneath the line End Sub.

Step 3. We now need to add a line of code to the bottom section of the script that will set the focus to TextBox4 when the command is run, rather than TextBox1 which would be the default.

Insert a blank line above the line Case 6 and insert the line DlgFocus("TextBox4"). Your section of code should look like this:

```
...
Case 5 ' Idle
   Rem Wait .1 : dialogfunc = True ' Continue getting idle actions
DlgFocus("TextBox4")
Case 6 ' Function key
   ...
```

 The positioning of this additional line of code is very important; it must be in the region of Case 5.

The line DlgFocus("TextBox4") instructs Dragon that when the Dialog Form is presented, the cursor/focus must move to the field "TextBox4".

The full script is below:

MyCommand Name: example set focus dialog form

Description: Shows how we can set focus to a specific TextBox

Group: Dragon - A Step Further_Chapter_05

Availability: Global

Command Type: Advanced Scripting

Content:

```
Sub Main
   Begin Dialog UserDialog 400,203,"Set the focus",.dialogfunc ' %GRID:10,7,1,1
```

```
      Text 30,21,90,14,"Text Field 01",.Text1
      Text 240,21,90,14,"Text Field 02",.Text2
      Text 30,98,90,14,"Text Field 03",.Text3
      Text 240,98,90,14,"Text Field 04",.Text4
      TextBox 30,42,90,21,.TextBox1
      TextBox 250,42,90,21,.TextBox2
      TextBox 30,119,90,21,.TextBox3
      TextBox 250,119,90,21,.TextBox4
      OKButton 90,168,90,21
      CancelButton 220,168,90,21
    End Dialog
Dim dlg As UserDialog
Dialog dlg
End Sub
Rem See DialogFunc help topic for more information.
Private Function dialogfunc(DlgItem$, Action%, SuppValue&) As Boolean
  Select Case Action%
  Case 1 ' Dialog box initialization
  Case 2 ' Value changing or button pressed
    Rem dialogfunc = True ' Prevent button press from closing the dialog box
  Case 3 ' TextBox or ComboBox text changed
  Case 4 ' Focus changed
  Case 5 ' Idle
    Rem Wait .1 : dialogfunc = True ' Continue getting idle actions
  DlgFocus("TextBox4")
  Case 6 ' Function key
  End Select
End Function
```

Try it by saying:

"example set focus dialog form" or in the **MyCommands Editor window**, click on the **"Start/Resume" icon (F5)**

Refer to:

Chapter 5: Advance Dialog Functions

Including Hidden Fields and how we can reveal them

When producing Dialog Forms there may be circumstances where you wish to include hidden fields (items) that will only be revealed to the user when a specific action is carried out.

To demonstrate this, the steps below will create a Dialog Form consisting of three CheckBoxes and a TextBox. The TextBox will be hidden at the point at which the command is run, and the form is presented. It is only when the CheckBox named "Other" is checked, that the form will reveal the hidden TextBox field. If the CheckBox is unchecked, the TextBox is again hidden.

Step 1. Create the Dialog Form.

```
Sub Main
  Begin Dialog UserDialog 400,203,"Hidden Fields"' %GRID:10,7,1,1
    Text 50,7,220,14,"Select the colours you like",.Text1
```

```
    CheckBox 30,35,70,14,"Black",.CheckBox1
    CheckBox 30,63,70,14,"Red",.CheckBox2
    CheckBox 30,91,70,14,"Other",.CheckBox3
    TextBox 110,91,280,21,.other_colour
    OKButton 60,154,90,21
    CancelButton 230,154,90,21
  End Dialog
  Dim dlg As UserDialog
  Dialog dlg
End Sub
```

Step 2. Edit the UserDialog Properties.

- Highlight the code from Begin Dialog to End Dialog
- Click on the Edit UserDialog icon [icon] or press Ctrl+D to reveal the UserDialog Editor window (see Figure 5-24).

Figure 5-24

The UserDialog Editor consisting of several items.

The TextBox item has its label/variable **Field** set to "other_colour".

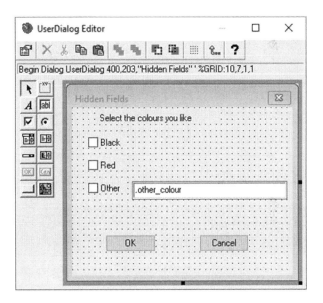

- Notice that the TextBox field contains the text other_colour. This is achieved by right-clicking on the TextBox and inserting the text "other_colour" into the field "Field". We will now be able to refer to this TextBox by the name "other_colour" when writing the rest of our script.
- Right-click on the grid area of the UserDialog Editor window to reveal the Edit UserDialog Properties window (see Figure 5-25).
- Insert the text "dialogfunc" into the Dialog Function field and press Enter

Figure 5-25

Use the Edit UserDialog Properties window to change the properties of the Dialog Form. Insert the text "dialogfunc" into the **Dialog Function** field.

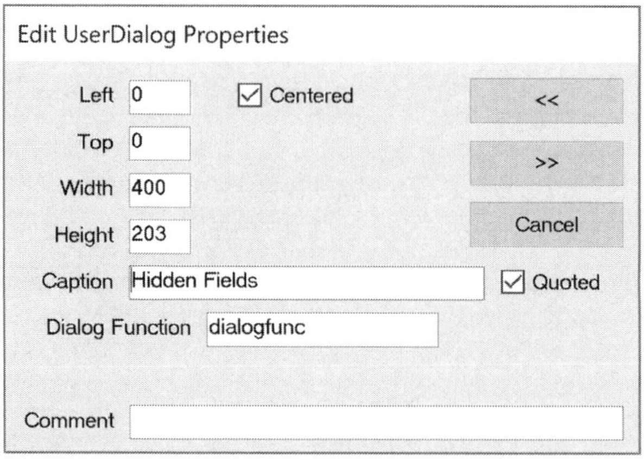

- Now in the UserDialog Editor window, click on the Save and Exit icon 🖺.. . You will be presented with a pop-up window, as shown in Figure 5-26.

Figure 5-26

The Dragon pop-up window will prompt the user to confirm the creation of the skeleton dialog function.

- Click on the Yes button to create the skeleton dialog function.

You will notice that Dragon has made a small change to your `Begin Dialog...` line and if you scroll down within the MyCommands Editor window you will see that extra code has been inserted underneath the line `End Sub`.

Step 3. We now need to add a line of code to the bottom section of the script that will make the TextBox hidden when the command is run.

Insert a blank line after the line `Case 1 ' Dialog box initialization` and type in the line `DlgVisible "other_colour", False`. Your section of code should look like this:

```
...
Case 1 ' Dialog box initialization
  DlgVisible "other_colour", False
Case 2 ' Value changing or button pressed
  ...
```

The positioning of this additional line of code is very important; it must be in the region of Case 1.

The line `DlgVisible "other_colour", False` instructs Dragon to make hidden/invisible the TextBox named "other_colour" when the Dialog Form is presented.

Step 4. We will now add extra code to the script that will check if the CheckBox named "CheckBox3" has been checked (ticked) or not. We do this by inserting an *If Then* statement within the `Case 2` area of the code.

Underneath the line `Rem dialogfunc = True ' Prevent button press from closing the dialog box`, make a blank line by pressing Enter and then Insert the following script:

```
If DlgItem = "CheckBox3" Then
   If SuppValue = 1 Then DlgVisible "other_colour", True
   If SuppValue = 0 Then DlgVisible "other_colour", False
End If
```

As you may well have noticed, I have inserted quite a few *If Then* statements, let me explain. Firstly, by placing this portion of script within the `Case 2` area means that while the Dialog Box is showing, Dragon will constantly be monitoring to see if the CheckBox named "CheckBox3" is checked or clicked on.

The line `If DlgItem = "CheckBox3" Then` means that, as soon as a user checks "CheckBox3" then Dragon will do something. That something is determined by the 2nd and 3rd lines of this portion of the script. It will either:

Follow the line `If SuppValue = 1 Then DlgVisible "other_colour", True` which means, is the SuppValue of CheckBox3 equal to 1? (basically, is CheckBox3 checked?), If it is checked, then make the TextBox named "other_colour" visible by carrying out the command `DlgVisible "other_colour", True`.

Or it will:

Follow the line `If SuppValue = 0 Then DlgVisible "other_colour", False` which means, is the SuppValue of CheckBox3 equal to 0? (basically, is it NOT checked?), If it is not checked, then make the TextBox named "other_colour" invisible/hidden by carrying out the command `DlgVisible "other_colour", False`.

`End If` closes our *If Then* statement.

The full script is below:

MyCommand Name: example hidden fields dialog form

Description: Shows how we can hide and reveal fields in Dialog forms

Group: Dragon - A Step Further_Chapter_05

Availability: Global

Command Type: Advanced Scripting

Content:

```
Sub Main
  Begin Dialog UserDialog 400,203,"Hidden Fields",.dialogfunc ' %GRID:10,7,1,1
    Text 50,7,220,14,"Select the colours you like",.Text1
    CheckBox 30,35,70,14,"Black",.CheckBox1
    CheckBox 30,63,70,14,"Red",.CheckBox2
    CheckBox 30,91,70,14,"Other",.CheckBox3
    TextBox 110,91,280,21,.other_colour
    OKButton 60,154,90,21
    CancelButton 230,154,90,21
  End Dialog
  Dim dlg As UserDialog
  Dialog dlg
End Sub
Rem See DialogFunc help topic for more information.
Private Function dialogfunc(DlgItem$, Action%, SuppValue&) As Boolean
  Select Case Action%
  Case 1 ' Dialog box initialization
    DlgVisible "other_colour", False
  Case 2 ' Value changing or button pressed
    Rem dialogfunc = True ' Prevent button press from closing the dialog box
  If DlgItem = "CheckBox3" Then
    If SuppValue = 1 Then DlgVisible "other_colour", True
    If SuppValue = 0 Then DlgVisible "other_colour", False
  End If
  Case 3 ' TextBox or ComboBox text changed
  Case 4 ' Focus changed
  Case 5 ' Idle
    Rem Wait .1 : dialogfunc = True ' Continue getting idle actions
  Case 6 ' Function key
  End Select
End Function
```

Try it by saying:

"example hidden fields dialog form" or in the **MyCommands Editor window**, click on the **"Start/Resume" icon (F5)**

Refer to:

Chapter 5: Advance Dialog Functions

Chapter 8: If Then Statement

Hidden Fields with Option/Radio buttons

The following command shows how we can include hidden elements within a Dialog Form. But this time we will reveal some text based upon a specific OptionButton that has been selected by the user.

The macro will produce a Dialog Form that contains six OptionButtons, two Text fields and the usual OK and Cancel buttons.

The user will be asked a question and can select any of the OptionButtons as the answer. When selecting the correct OptionButton, the Text field will become visible and display the text "WELL DONE". For all incorrect choices; the appropriate message will appear in a Message Box.

MyCommand Name: example hidden fields dialog form two

Description: Shows how we can hide and reveal fields in Dialog forms

Group: Dragon - A Step Further_Chapter_05

Availability: Global

Command Type: Advanced Scripting

Content:

```
Sub Main
  Begin Dialog UserDialog 400,203,"Quiz",.dialogfunc ' %GRID:10,7,1,1
    Text 10,7,170,21,"Which is most valuable?",.Text1
    OptionGroup .Group1
      OptionButton 20,35,100,14,"Bronze",.OptionButton1
      OptionButton 150,35,100,14,"Copper",.OptionButton2
      OptionButton 280,35,100,14,"Gold",.OptionButton3
      OptionButton 20,63,100,14,"Platinum",.OptionButton4
      OptionButton 150,63,100,14,"Silver",.OptionButton5
      OptionButton 280,63,100,14,"Tin",.OptionButton6
    Text 150,105,90,14,"WELL DONE",.Text2
    OKButton 50,154,90,21
    CancelButton 250,154,90,21
  End Dialog
  Dim dlg As UserDialog
  Dialog dlg
End Sub
Rem See DialogFunc help topic for more information.
Private Function dialogfunc(DlgItem$, Action%, SuppValue&) As Boolean
  Select Case Action%
  Case 1 ' Dialog box initialization
    DlgVisible "Text2", False
  Case 2 ' Value changing or button pressed
    Rem dialogfunc = True ' Prevent button press from closing the dialog box
If DlgItem = "Group1" Then
  If SuppValue = 0 Then MsgBox("Not Bronze")
  If SuppValue = 1 Then MsgBox("No, not Copper")
  If SuppValue = 2 Then MsgBox("Not Gold")
  If SuppValue = 3 Then DlgVisible "Text2", True
  If SuppValue = 4 Then MsgBox("No, not Silver")
  If SuppValue = 5 Then MsgBox("Not Tin")
End If
  Case 3 ' TextBox or ComboBox text changed
  Case 4 ' Focus changed
  Case 5 ' Idle
    Rem Wait .1 : dialogfunc = True ' Continue getting idle actions
  Case 6 ' Function key
  End Select
End Function
```

Try it by saying:

"example hidden fields dialog form two" or in the **MyCommands Editor window**, click on the **"Start/Resume" icon (F5)**

Discuss

This type of dynamic Dialog Form consists of the usual requirements:

- That the Dialog Form must have its Dialog Function field set to "dialogfunc" as represented by the line `Begin Dialog UserDialog 400,203,.dialogfunc`
- That it includes the lines `Dim dlg As UserDialog` and `Dialog dlg` in order to run the Dialog Form and make it ready for any actions that may take place, such as pressing a specific OptionButton.

The line `DlgVisible "Text2", False` is placed within the `Case 1` area of the script in order to make the Text field named `"Text2"` hidden at the point of running the command.

The main code to perform this command is placed within the `Case 2` area of the script. By placing it in the Case 2 area, the Dialog Form will constantly be monitoring for any change(s) and as a result, actions will be made in real time.

We use *If Then* statements to perform all of the checks.

The line `If DlgItem = "Group1" Then` means, as soon as a user selects any of the OptionButtons which are part of "Group1" then Dragon will do something. That something is determined by the six (`If SuppValue = ...`) lines.

Let's examine the first of these lines:

`If SuppValue = 0 Then MsgBox("Not Bronze")`, this line can be interpreted as meaning, if the first OptionButton of the group is selected then produce a Message Box that contains the text "Not Bronze".

The second `If SuppValue = 1 Then ...` performs virtually the same action, but only when the second OptionButton of the group has been selected and so on.

The line of code `If SuppValue = 3 Then DlgVisible "Text2", True` is the exception, whereby, when a user selects the fourth OptionBox, the portion of the code `DlgVisible "Text2", True` makes the Text field referred to as `"Text2"` become visible.

The values for the group name of a set of OptionButtons are expressed by:
"-1" represents that none of the OptionButtons have been selected.
"0" represents that the first OptionButton is selected.
"1" represents that the second OptionButton is selected.
"2" represents the third is selected – and so on.

Alternative

An alternative to this Dialog Form would be to have none of the OptionButtons selected at the point of running the command.

To do this, we need to add the line DlgValue "Group1", -1 into the Case 1 section of the script by placing it underneath the line DlgVisible "Text2", False and then save the script.

Dragon now knows that at the point of running the script, all OptionButtons within "Group1" are to be unselected. Run the command again to see the difference.

Refer to:

Chapter 5: Advance Dialog Functions

Chapter 8: If Then Statement, MsgBox Function

Creating List Boxes and Combo Boxes (menus) in Dialog Forms

Within Dialog Forms we can create List Box or Combo Box menus, which enable users to make a choice(s) from a list of items. List and Combo Boxes are useful when you want to limit the options available to a user and also to avoid any potential misspelt user input.

Whilst in the UserDialog Editor window, you will notice that Dragon allows us to create four different types, which are described below:

	ListBox: Allows a user to select only one of the items from the list of available items.
	DropListBox: Allows a user to select only one item from the list of available items. However, there is an option to allow the user to type in an alternative item.
	ComboBox: Allows a user to either select a single item from the list of items or insert an alternative into the TextBox field.
	MultiListBox: Allows a user to select one or more items from the list of available items.

At this point, and to avoid repetition, I will assume that you have an understanding of how a Dialog Form is created, so I will only focus on the sections of code that are pertinent to this topic.

Before we begin looking at the four available menu types, the first thing to consider when creating a menu is to decide which data/items will populate the menu.

Dragon requires that we create an Array that will hold the list of items to be placed in a menu. For example, if we create an Array called "fruits" and we want our list of items to be Apples, Pears and Oranges, then the following code would be required to set up the Array.

```
Dim fruits(2)
fruits (0) = "Apples"
fruits (1) = "Pears"
fruits (2) = "Oranges"
```

The code to create the Array should be placed in the script before/above the section of code that creates the Dialog Form.

Within the following four examples, the section of code that creates the Array can be found between the lines Sub Main **To** Begin Dialog UserDialog...

Refer to:

Chapter 8: Arrays

Using the ListBox item in Dialog Forms

Here we create a Dialog Form that contains a **ListBox** type of drop-down menu. The user will select their item of choice and then press OK. The result is a Message Box containing text that will confirm the choice made by the user. Figure 5-27 shows the ListBox that will be created.

Figure 5-27

An example ListBox, use a ListBox to control user input.

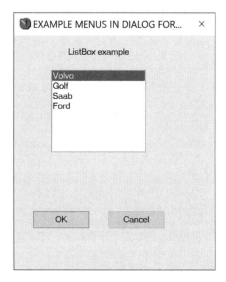

MyCommand Name: menu list box example

Description: Example of ListBox drop-down menu

Group: Dragon - A Step Further_Chapter_05

Availability: Global

Command Type: Advanced Scripting

Content:

```
Sub Main
  Dim cars$(3) 'Create Array of items for ListBox
    cars$(0) = "Volvo"
    cars$(1) = "Golf"
    cars$(2) = "Saab"
    cars$(3) = "Ford"
  Begin Dialog UserDialog 320,280,"EXAMPLE MENUS IN DIALOG FORMS" ' %GRID:10,7,1,1
    Text 60,14,150,14,"ListBox exmple",.Text3,2
    ListBox 60,42,150,98,cars(),.ListBox1
    OKButton 30,210,90,21
    CancelButton 150,210,90,21
  End Dialog
  Dim dlg As UserDialog
      If Dialog (dlg) = -1 Then 'Wait For "OK" then
    Select Case dlg.ListBox1
      Case 0 'Volvo
        MsgBox ("You selected Volvo")
      Case 1 'Golf
        MsgBox ("You selected Golf")
      Case 2 'Saab
        MsgBox ("You selected Saab")
      Case 3 'Ford
        MsgBox ("You selected Ford")
    End Select
  End If
End Sub
```

Try it by saying:

"menu list box example" or in the **MyCommands Editor window,** click on the **"Start/Resume" icon (F5)**

Discuss

When creating a ListBox and viewing its properties in the Edit ListBox Properties window (see Figure 5-28), we are presented with the usual options of being able to set the position and size dimensions.

Figure 5-28

Use the Edit ListBox Properties window to change the properties of the ListBox item.

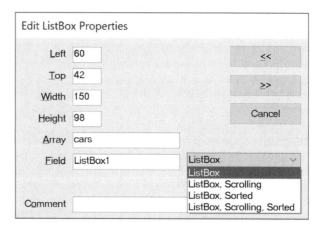

ListBox Properties explained:

The **Array** field contains the name of the Array (cars). The items within the Array cars will populate the ListBox when the command is run.

The **Field** field contains the name (ListBox1, also referred to as a label or variable) by which the ListBox item can be identified. We use this name to refer to the ListBox for further scripting and to access the value of the ListBox.

The **ListBox** drop-down menu gives us four choices which determine how the items will be displayed within the ListBox when the command is run:

- The default **ListBox** option will display the items in the order they have been inserted into the Array and produces the line ListBox 60,42,150,98,cars(),.ListBox1
- The **ListBox, Scrolling** option makes a slight adjustment to the size of the ListBox and produces the line ListBox 60,42,150,98,cars(),.ListBox1,1
- The **ListBox, Sorted** option will display the items in alphabetical order and produces the line ListBox 60,42,150,98,cars(),.ListBox1,2
- The **ListBox, Scrolling, Sorted** option makes an adjustment to the size of the ListBox, displays the items in alphabetical order and produces the line ListBox 60,42,150,98,cars(),.ListBox1,3

 If you have a large number of items in relation to the height of the ListBox, a scroll bar will automatically appear regardless of the option chosen.

In this script a *Select Case* function is used to determine which one of the items has been selected. As each of the items is within an Array, the value of the ListBox referred to as ListBox1 will be a number between 0 and 3.

The line `Select Case dlg.ListBox1` is the start of the *Select Case* function and the line `End Select` is where the function ends. All the *Case* lines in between check the value of `ListBox1` once the OK button has been pressed, and basically means; should it be the case that the value is 0 then produce a Message Box with the text "You selected Volvo" and so on.

The line `Dim cars$(3)` **is the statement used to create the Array called "cars". In this example the number** 3 **means that it can hold four values, as counting starts at zero.**

Alternative

The above method works well, but what if you have a large number of items? The code would soon become lengthy.

An alternative would be to replace the portion of the script from the line `Select Case...` **To** `End Select` with the following:

```
For counter = 0 To 4
  Select Case dlg.ListBox1
      Case counter
      MsgBox ("You selected " & (cars$(counter)))
  End Select
Next counter
```

Here we use a *For...Next Loop* as a counter to check which of the *Select Case* scenarios is equal to the value of `ListBox1`. Then we adjust the Message Box code to write out the contents of the `cars$` Array specific (counter) value, for example `cars$(1)` would type out the word "Golf".

Refer to:

Chapter 8: Arrays, For...Next Loop, Select Case Function, MsgBox Function

Using the DropListBox item in Dialog Forms

Here we create a Dialog Form that contains a **DropListBox** type of drop-down menu. The user will select their item of choice and then press OK. The result is a Message Box containing text that will confirm the choice made by the user. Figure 5-29 shows the DropListBox that will be created.

Figure 5-29

An example DropListBox, use a DropListBox to control user input.

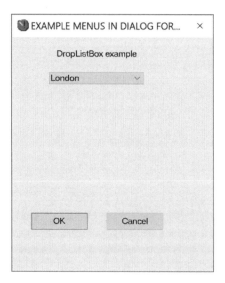

MyCommand Name: menu drop list box example

Description: Example of DropListBox drop-down menu

Group: Dragon - A Step Further_Chapter_05

Availability: Global

Command Type: Advanced Scripting

Content:

```
Sub Main
  Dim cities$(3) 'Create Array of items for DropListBox
    cities$(0) = "London"
    cities$(1) = "New York"
    cities$(2) = "Berlin"
    cities$(3) = "Bangkok"
  Begin Dialog*UserDialog 320,280,"EXAMPLE MENUS IN DIALOG FORMS" ' %GRID:10,7,1,1
    Text 60,14,150,14,"DropListBox example",.Text1,2
    DropListBox 60,42,150,98,cities(),.DropListBox1
    OKButton 30,210,90,21
    CancelButton 150,210,90,21
  End Dialog
  Dim dlg As UserDialog
  'Section 1. Use when DropListBox is set to NOT Editable
  'If Dialog (dlg) = -1 Then 'Wait For "OK" then
  ' MsgBox (cities$(dlg.DropListBox1))
  'End If
  'Section 2. Use when DropListBox is set to Editable
  'dlg.DropListBox1 = "xxx" ' list2 is a string field
  'If Dialog (dlg) = -1 Then 'Wait For "OK" then
```

```
   ' MsgBox (dlg.DropListBox1)
   'End If
   'Sections 1 & 2 CANNOT BE BOTH UNCOMMENTED
End Sub
```

Un-comment Section 1 and try it by saying:

"menu drop list box example" or in the **MyCommands Editor window**, click on the **"Start/Resume" icon (F5)**

Discuss

When creating a DropListBox and viewing its properties in the Edit DropListBox Properties window (see Figure 5-30), we are presented with the usual options of being able to set the position and size dimensions.

Figure 5-30

Use the Edit DropListBox Properties window to change the properties of the DropListBox item.

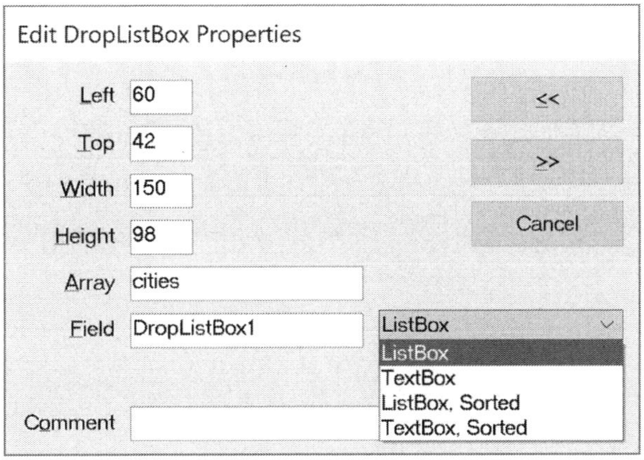

DropListBox Properties explained:

The **Array** field contains the name of the Array (cities). The items within the Array cities will populate the DropListBox when the command is run.

The **Field** field contains the name (DropListBox1, also referred to as a label or variable) by which the DropListBox item can be identified. We use this name to refer to the DropListBox for further scripting and to access the value of the DropListBox.

The **ListBox** drop-down menu gives us four choices; however, we need to be careful which one we choose, as the choice we make will affect how we will write the portion of the script needed to display the Message Box and its contents.

The default **ListBox** and **ListBox, Sorted** options both display what are called "**Non-Editable**" DropListBoxes and produce the following lines respectively:

- DropListBox 60,42,150,98,cities(),.DropListBox1
- DropListBox 60,42,150,98,cities(),.DropListBox1,2

The **TextBox** and **TextBox, Sorted** options both display what are called "**Editable**" DropListBoxes. These two options allow a user to insert an alternative item when the menu is presented and allows them to place a default item that has not been defined in the Array. They produce the following lines respectively:

- `DropListBox 60,42,150,98,cities(),.DropListBox1,1`
- `DropListBox 60,42,150,98,cities(),.DropListBox1,3`

In the above full script, I have decided to insert the two variations of code needed (commented Sections 1 & 2). To experiment with the command, only one of the two sections should be un-commented; which of them is dependent on the option you choose from the ListBox drop-down menu.

Section 1.

```
If Dialog (dlg) = -1 Then 'Wait For "OK" then
  MsgBox (cities$(dlg.DropListBox1))
End If
```

This section only works with the options **ListBox** (default) and **ListBox, Sorted**. In this instance we use the chosen items numerical value from the Array (cities) to display the correct choice in the Message Box.

Section 2.

```
dlg.DropListBox1 = "anywhere" ' list2 is a string field
If Dialog (dlg) = -1 Then 'Wait For "OK" then
  MsgBox (dlg.DropListBox1)
End If
```

This section only works with the options **TextBox** and **TextBox, Sorted**. Under these options `DropListBox1` is a string field and therefore our script within the Message Box is slightly different and simply displays the current string/text value (selected item) of the `DropListBox1`.

The line `dlg.DropListBox1 = "anywhere"` will populate the editable Text field with the text "anywhere". For a blank editable Text field use a set of double quotes (`""`).

Refer to:
Chapter 8: Arrays, If Then Statement, MsgBox Function

Using the ComboBox item in Dialog Forms

Here we create a Dialog Form that contains a **ComboBox** type of drop-down menu. The user will select their item of choice or enter a new one and then press OK. The result is a Message Box containing text that will confirm the choice made by the user. Figure 5-31 shows the ComboBox that will be created.

Figure 5-31

An example ComboBox, use a ComboBox to show options to a user. The user can also insert an alternative entry.

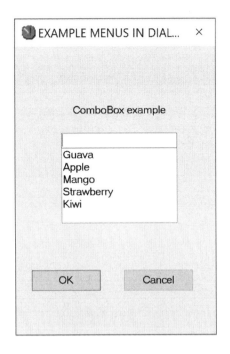

MyCommand Name: menu combo box example

Description: Example of ComboBox drop-down menu

Group: Dragon - A Step Further_Chapter_05

Availability: Global

Command Type: Advanced Scripting

Content:

```
Sub Main
  Dim fruits$(4) 'Create Array of items for ComboBox
    fruits$(0) = "Guava"
    fruits$(1) = "Apple"
    fruits$(2) = "Mango"
    fruits$(3) = "Strawberry"
    fruits$(4) = "Kiwi"
  Begin Dialog UserDialog 260,280,"EXAMPLE MENUS IN DIALOG FORMS" ' %GRID:10,7,1,1
    Text 60,56,150,14,"ComboBox example",.Text2,2
    ComboBox 60,84,150,98,fruits(),.ComboBox1
    OKButton 20,217,90,21
    CancelButton 140,217,90,21
  End Dialog
  Dim dlg As UserDialog
  'dlg.ComboBox1 = "other" 'Apply a default value of text within quotes if you wish
    If Dialog (dlg) = -1 Then 'Wait For "OK" then
```

```
        MsgBox (dlg.ComboBox1)
    End If
End Sub
```

Try it by saying:

"menu combo box example" or in the **MyCommands Editor window**, click on the **"Start/Resume" icon (F5)**

Discuss

When creating a ComboBox and viewing its properties in the Edit ComboBox Properties window (see Figure 5-32), we are presented with the usual options of being able to set the position and size dimensions.

Figure 5-32

Use the Edit ComboBox Properties window to change the properties of the ComboBox item.

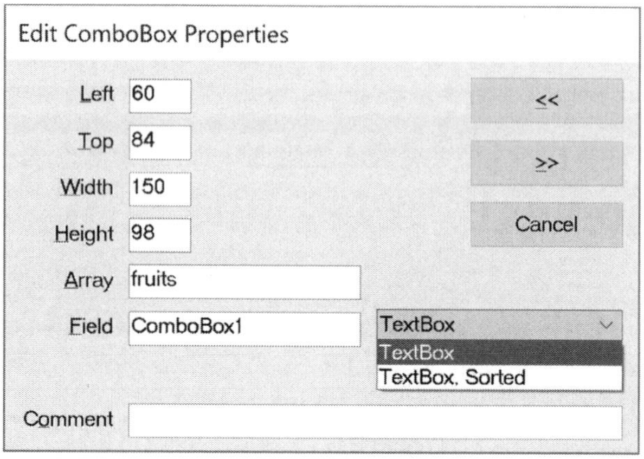

ComboBox Properties explained:

The **Array** field contains the name of the Array (fruits). The items within the Array `fruits` will populate the ComboBox when the command is run.

The **Field** field contains the name (`ComboBox1`, also referred to as a label or variable) by which the ComboBox item can be identified. We use this name to refer to the ComboBox for further scripting and to access the value of the ComboBox.

The **TextBox** drop-down menu gives us two choices which determine how the items will be displayed within the menu when the command is run:

- The default **TextBox** option will display the items in the order they have been inserted into the Array and creates the line `ComboBox 60,84,150,98,fruits(),.ComboBox1`
- The **TextBox, Sorted** option will display the items in alphabetical order and creates the line `ComboBox 60,84,150,98,fruits(),.ComboBox1,2`

If you have a large number of items in relation to the height of the ComboBox, scroll bars will automatically appear regardless of the option chosen.

Un-commenting the line `dlg.ComboBox1 = "other"` will insert the word "other" into the editable Text field (when the command is run), in other words, we set the value of the ComboBox1 to the string of text "other".

The line `MsgBox (dlg.ComboBox1)` is where we produce a Message Box to reveal the selected item (the current string value) of the ComboBox named "ComboBox1" which is within the Dialog Form referred to as `dlg`.

Refer to:

Chapter 8: Arrays, MsgBox Function

Using the MultiListBox item in Dialog Forms

Here we create a Dialog Form that contains a **MultiListBox** type of drop-down menu. The user will select their item or items of choice and then press OK. The result is a Message Box containing text that will confirm the choice(s) made by the user. Figure 5-33 shows an example of a MultiListBox.

Figure 5-33

An example MultiListBox, use a MultiListBox to control user input. The user can select one or more of the options.

MyCommand Name: menu multi list box example

Description: Example of MultiListBox drop-down menu

Group: Dragon - A Step Further_Chapter_05

Availability: Global

Command Type: Advanced Scripting

Content:

```
Sub Main
  Dim food$(3) 'Create Array of items for MultiListBox
    food$(0) = "Meat"
    food$(1) = "Fish"
    food$(2) = "Vegetables"
    food$(3) = "Fruit"
  Begin Dialog UserDialog 320,280,"EXAMPLE MENUS IN DIALOG FORMS" ' %GRID:10,7,1,1
    Text 60,14,150,14,"MultiListBox example",.Text1,2
    MultiListBox 60,42,150,98,food(),.MultiListBox1
    OKButton 30,210,90,21
    CancelButton 150,210,90,21
  End Dialog
  Dim dlg As UserDialog
  dlg.MultiListBox1 = Array
  If Dialog (dlg) = -1 Then
    For i = LBound(dlg.MultiListBox1) To UBound(dlg.MultiListBox1)
      MsgBox (food$(dlg.MultiListBox1(i)))
      Next i
  End If
End Sub
```

Try it by saying:

"menu multi list box example" or in the **MyCommands Editor window**, click on the **"Start/Resume" icon (F5)**

Discuss

When creating a MultiListBox and viewing its properties in the Edit MultiListBox Properties window (see Figure 5-34), we are presented with the usual options of being able to set the position and size dimensions.

Figure 5-34

Use the Edit MultiListBox Properties window to change the properties of the MultiListBox item.

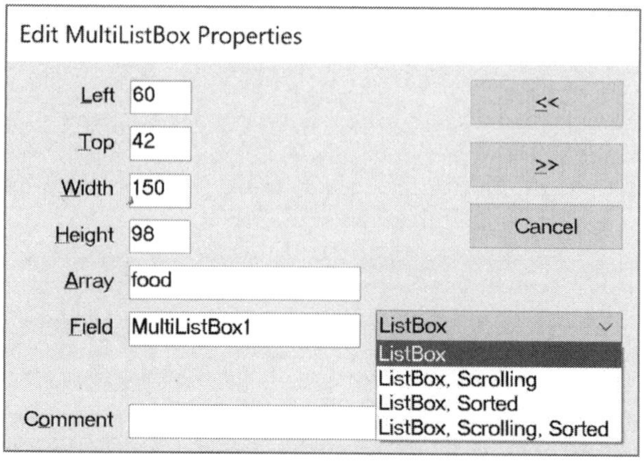

MultiListBox Properties explained:

The **Array** field contains the name of the Array (food). The items within the Array food will populate the MultiListBox when the command is run.

The **Field** field contains the name (MultiListBox1, also referred to as a label or variable) by which the MultiListBox item can be identified. We use this name to refer to the MultiListBox for further scripting and to access the value(s) of the MultiListBox.

The **ListBox** drop-down menu gives us four choices which determine how the items will be displayed within the MultiListBox when the command is run:

- The default **ListBox** option will display the items in the order they have been inserted into the Array and produces the line MultiListBox 60,42,150,98,food(),.MultiListBox1
- The **ListBox, Scrolling** option will display the items not sorted and shows a horizontal scroll bar when the width of the items exceeds the width of the MultiListBox. It produces the line MultiListBox 60,42,150,98,food(),.MultiListBox1,1
- The **ListBox, Sorted** option will display the items in alphabetical order and produces the line MultiListBox 60,42,150,98,food(),.MultiListBox1,2
- The **ListBox, Scrolling, Sorted** option will display the items in alphabetical order and shows a horizontal scroll bar when the width of the items exceeds the width of the MultiListBox. It produces the line MultiListBox 60,42,150,98,food(),.MultiListBox1,3

 The horizontal scroll bars will only show if the item string of characters is wider than the width of the MultiListBox.

 The vertical scroll bars will only show when the number of items exceeds the height of the MultiListBox.

In the case of MultiListBoxes we have to bear in mind that users are able to select one or more of the items from the list on display.

Therefore, we use a *For...Next Loop* to check which of the items have been selected once the OK button is pressed and if needed, produce a Message Box for each one.

In order to determine which of the items have been selected, we need an adjusted *For...Next Loop*. The following line of code achieves this:

```
For i = LBound(dlg.MultiListBox1) To UBound(dlg.MultiListBox1).
```

You will notice that there is the inclusion of two extra functions LBound(dlg.MultiListBox1) and UBound(dlg.MultiListBox1) where we would normally expect to see numbers.

By inserting these two functions we can get Dragon to produce the appropriate *For...Next Loop* dynamically at the point of running the command.

- LBound(dlg.MultiListBox1) returns the lowest index for the values of MultiListBox1
- UBound(dlg.MultiListBox1) returns the highest index for the values of MultiListBox1

The line MsgBox (food$(dlg.MultiListBox1(i))) will produce a Message Box for each of the selected items of the MultiListBox1.

Refer to:

Chapter 8: Arrays, For...Next Loop, LBound & UBound Functions, MsgBox Function

Setting an item to a specific value or state (DlgValue function)

When a Dialog Form is presented; items such as CheckBoxes, DropListBoxes and OptionButtons are displayed in their default state, for example a CheckBox will be displayed as unchecked.

The *DlgValue* function enables us to instruct Dragon to set the numerical value of an item. When used within the Case 1 area of a script, it will cause the items to be in the required state when a command is run, and the Dialog Form is presented to a user.

 The DlgValue should refer to the following items: CheckBox, ComboBox, DropListBox, ListBox, MultiListBox, or OptionGroup.

The macro below shows how we can use the *DlgValue* function within a script to produce a Dialog Form that consists of several items presented in a variety of states. Figure 5-35 shows the Dialog Form that will be created.

Figure 5-35

The Dialog Form consists of several items presented in a variety of states.

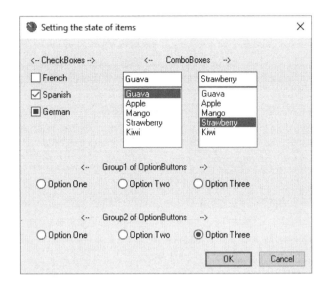

MyCommand Name: example set the state dialog form

Description: Shows the setting up of an item to a specific state

Group: Dragon - A Step Further_Chapter_05

Availability: Global

Command Type: Advanced Scripting

Content:

```
Sub Main
Dim fruits$(4) 'Create Array of items for ComboBox
fruits$(0) = "Guava"
fruits$(1) = "Apple"
fruits$(2) = "Mango"
fruits$(3) = "Strawberry"
fruits$(4) = "Kiwi"

    Begin Dialog UserDialog 540,294,"Setting the state of items",.dialogfunc '
%GRID:10,7,1,1
        CheckBox 20,42,130,14,"French",.CheckBox1
        CheckBox 20,63,130,14,"Spanish",.CheckBox2,1
        CheckBox 20,84,130,14,"German",.CheckBox3,2
        ComboBox 190,42,110,105,fruits(),.ComboBox1
        ComboBox 330,42,110,105,fruits(),.ComboBox2
        OptionGroup .Group1
            OptionButton 30,175,120,14,"Option One",.OptionButton1
            OptionButton 180,175,120,14,"Option Two",.OptionButton2
            OptionButton 320,175,120,14,"Option Three",.OptionButton3
        OptionGroup .Group2
            OptionButton 30,238,120,14,"Option One",.OptionButton4
```

```
                OptionButton 180,238,120,14,"Option Two",.OptionButton5
                OptionButton 320,238,120,14,"Option Three",.OptionButton6
        Text 30,154,400,14,"<--      Group1 of OptionButtons      -->",.Text1,2
        Text 30,217,400,14,"<--      Group2 of OptionButtons      -->",.Text4,2
        Text 190,21,240,14,"<--      ComboBoxes      -->",.Text2,2
        Text 10,21,140,14,"<-- CheckBoxes -->",.Text3,2
        OKButton 340,266,90,21
        CancelButton 440,266,90,21
    End Dialog

Dim dlg As UserDialog
Dialog dlg

End Sub

Rem See DialogFunc help topic for more information.
Private Function dialogfunc(DlgItem$, Action%, SuppValue&) As Boolean
    Select Case Action%
    Case 1 ' Dialog box initialization
        DlgValue "CheckBox1",0
        DlgValue "CheckBox2",1
        DlgValue "CheckBox3",2

        DlgValue "ComboBox1",0
        DlgValue "ComboBox2",3

        DlgValue "Group1",-1
        DlgValue "Group2",2

    Case 2 ' Value changing or button pressed
      Rem dialogfunc = True ' Prevent button press from closing the dialog box
    Case 3 ' TextBox or ComboBox text changed
    Case 4 ' Focus changed
    Case 5 ' Idle
      Rem Wait .1 : dialogfunc = True ' Continue getting idle actions
    Case 6 ' Function key
    End Select
End Function
```

Discuss

Using the DlgValue function with a CheckBox.

As I mentioned earlier, when a form is presented, all CheckBoxes by default will be set to the state of unchecked. The lines commencing with DlgValue "CheckBox… perform in the following ways:

- The line DlgValue "CheckBox1",0 instructs Dragon to present CheckBox1 in an unchecked (unticked) state (i.e. value = ,0).
- The line DlgValue "CheckBox2",1 instructs Dragon to present CheckBox2 in a checked (ticked) state (i.e. value = ,1).
- The line DlgValue "CheckBox3",2 instructs Dragon to present CheckBox3 in a greyed-out state (i.e. value = ,2).

A CheckBox can only be set to the greyed-out option (2) if the CheckBox has had its state changed to either "3 State" or "3 State, Auto" in the Edit CheckBox Properties window.

When working with the DlgValue function and CheckBoxes, the DlgValue must refer to the Field field value within the Edit CheckBox Properties window of the CheckBox and not the Caption value.

Using the DlgValue function with a ComboBox.

By default, when a ComboBox is presented, none of the options will be selected. The lines commencing with DlgValue "ComboBox... perform in the following ways:

- The line DlgValue "ComboBox1", 0 instructs Dragon to present ComboBox1 with the first option selected. (The value , 0 represents the first option of the ComboBox1 menu).
- The line DlgValue "ComboBox2", 3 instructs Dragon to present ComboBox2 with the fourth option selected. (The value , 3 represents the fourth option of the ComboBox2 menu).

Because ComboBoxes are populated by an Array, the value 0 refers to the first of the items within the Array, the value 1 is the second and so on. If the value inserted is beyond the number of items within the Array, the ComboBox will be presented in default (i.e. no items selected).

When working with the DlgValue function and ComboBoxes, the DlgValue must refer to the Field field value within the Edit ComboBox Properties window of the ComboBox and not the Array value.

Using the DlgValue function with a group of OptionButtons.

By default, when a group of OptionButtons are presented, the first OptionButton will be selected.

The lines commencing with DlgValue "Group... perform in the following ways:

- The line DlgValue "Group1", -1 instructs Dragon to present Group1 of the OptionButtons with none of the OptionButtons selected. (the value , -1 represents that no OptionButtons are selected).
- The line DlgValue "Group2", 2 instructs Dragon to present Group2 of the OptionButtons with the third OptionButton selected. (the value , 2 represents that the third OptionButton is selected).

When working with the DlgValue function and OptionButtons, the DlgValue must refer to the OptionGroup (name) value within the Edit OptionButton Properties window of the OptionButtons and not the Caption or Field values.

- **Group value = -1: No OptionButtons will be selected.**
- **Group value = 0: First OptionButton will be selected.**
- **Group value = 1: Second OptionButton will be selected.**
- **Group value = 2: Third OptionButton will be selected and so on.**

UserDialog Editor components

When we open the UserDialog Editor window we are presented with several components along the top (see Figure 5-36) and the most commonly used components along the left-hand side (see Figure 5-39).

Let's examine these components in more detail:

Top row icons

Figure 5-36

The top row of icons in the UserDialog Editor window.

Table 5-1 lists the function name of the top row icons of the UserDialog Editor.

Table 5-1

1. Edit Item Properties	7. Move Behind
2. Delete	8. Select in Front
3. Cut	9. Select Behind
4. Copy	10. Set Grid
5. Paste	11. Save and Exit
6. Move in Front	

Edit Item Properties

If you have selected an item in the UserDialog Editor, clicking this icon will reveal the Edit Item Properties window for the selected item.

The contents of the Edit Properties window will vary depending on the item selected; however, more often than not they will include options to name, alter, resize and position various aspects of the selected item. The result of any change(s) you make will be reflected in a line of code produced in the MyCommand Editor.

To quickly navigate between the Edit Properties windows of the various items you may have in your Dialog form, you can use the arrow keys (see Figure 5-37) to go to the next or previous items.

Figure 5-37

Use the arrow keys in the Edit Properties window of an item to navigate to the next or previous items.

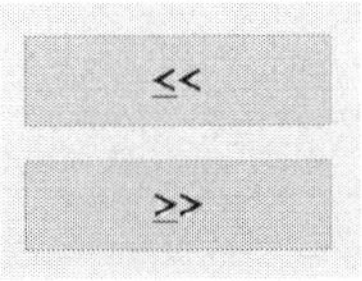

Delete

Delete works as one would expect; which is to delete the selected item. This deletion will also be reflected in the MyCommand Editor by removing the appropriate line of code.

Cut / Copy / Paste

These buttons work as expected by performing Cut, Copy, or Paste operations respectively on whatever is selected, however, there are a few further points to bear in mind.

As you start to build a Dialog Form by adding items, an order develops. This order can be seen when the Tab key is pressed whilst in the UserDialog Editor window. Dragon selects the next item based on the order in which they were created in the form.

 In the UserDialog Editor window there is an information line just below the top row of icons. As you select various items, information relating to the item, including the item number (order) is displayed.

When an item is Cut it will most often change the order of the other items within the Dialog Form by moving their position up or down.

If an item has been Cut and additional items added, when the Cut item is pasted its order will be the same as it was originally, and the new and existing items will be re-ordered accordingly.

When an item is copied and then pasted, the pasted version of the item will be positioned after the original selected item's position (within the order of the items). All of the other items will adjust accordingly. For example, a TextBox currently in position 5, when copied, the pasted version of the TextBox will be at position 6. If there was already an item at position 6 then that item will move to position 7 and so on.

Move in Front / Move Behind

Use the Move in Front icon when you wish to change the order of the items. For example, let's take a Dialog Form that consist of three items, whereby the first item is a Text label (item number one), the second is a CheckBox (item number two) and the third is a TextBox (item number three). By selecting the Text label and then clicking on the Move in Front icon, this will result in the Text label becoming item number two and the other items will move consecutively.

Clicking on the Move Behind icon, carries out the reverse by moving an item to a lower position in the order.

 Once the UserDialog Editor has been saved, I often find it useful to re-order, by cutting and pasting the produced lines of code situated between `Begin Dialog...` To `End Dialog.`

Select in Front / Select Behind

The Select in Front and Select Behind icons can be used to navigate through the various items of the Dialog Form. If you click on the UserDialog Editor window and then click the Select in Front icon, the first item will be selected, click on it again and it will select the next item and so on.

Clicking on the Select Behind icon, carries out the reverse by selecting the previous item.

Set Grid

Figure 5-38

Use the Grid Settings window to change the properties of the grid and how the items align in the UserDialog Editor window.

Clicking on the Set Grid icon reveals the Grid Settings window (see Figure 5-38) with the following options:

- Adjust the size of the gaps between the grid dots/lines.
- Choose whether to display the grid.
- Choose whether to have items snap to the grid lines when placed.

Save and Exit

Clicking the Save and Exit icon will save the changes made in the UserDialog Editor window and return you to the MyCommands Editor window.

Left-Hand side options

Figure 5-39

The left-hand side options in the UserDialog Editor window.

Table 5-2 lists the function name of the left side icons of the UserDialog Editor.

Table 5-2

1. Select	8. Add ListBox
2. Add GroupBox	9. Add DropListBox
3. Add Text	10. Add MultiListBox
4. Add TextBox	11. Add OKButton
5. Add CheckBox	12. Add Cancel Button
6. Add OptionButton	13. Add PushButton
7. Add ComboBox	14. Add Picture

 If you position your mouse over any of the icons, a short description of the control will appear.

The icons on the left are predominantly used to add items to your Dialog Form. Let's have a look at some of the options in more detail.

Select:
This is the pointer, selection tool and default tool.

Add GroupBox:
This allows us to create a rectangular box, with or without a caption title, at a defined position and defined size in a Dialog Form.

Refer to:
Chapter 5: Placing GroupBoxes and Images in Dialog Forms

Add Text:
This enables text to be added to a Dialog Form. More often than not this is used to add some fixed text, such as a headline or caption to Dialog Forms. It is possible to change this text dynamically within a dialog script.

Refer to:
Chapter 5: Create a Simple Dialog Form

Add TextBox:

Adding a TextBox allows a user to enter text into a Dialog Form. A TextBox can range in size from a single character to a large block of text consisting of multiple lines. There is also the option to make the entered text appear as asterisk, which would be handy for a password protected form.

Refer to:

Chapter 5: Create a Simple Dialog Form

Add CheckBox:

Adds a conventional Yes/No or On/Off type of CheckBox to the Dialog Form.

Dragon does allow for CheckBoxes to have three states. Changing the setting in the Edit CheckBox Properties window to the "3 State" value, will result in a CheckBox being allowed to be either, checked, not checked or greyed out.

Refer to:

Chapter 5: Using CheckBoxes in Dialog Forms, An Advanced Dialog Form

Add OptionButton:

Click to place OptionButtons which are also referred to as Radio buttons onto the Dialog Form. Each OptionButton belongs to a group which is set by the OptionGroup value in the properties of each OptionButton.

- When the Dialog Form is run, only one of the OptionButtons within a group can be selected.
- You can have more than one group of OptionButtons on a Dialog Form.

For scripting purposes, the values of a group in a functioning Dialog Form will result in the following:

- The value **-1** is returned if no OptionButtons are selected.
- The value **0** is returned if the first OptionButton is selected.
- The value **1** is returned if the second OptionButton is selected.
- The value **2** is returned if the third is selected and so on.

Refer to:

Chapter 5: Using OptionButtons (Radio buttons) in Dialog Forms, An Advanced Dialog Form

Add ComboBox:

Adds a drop-down list to the Dialog Form that allows a user to either select a single item from a list or alternatively enter/insert a different item into a small TextBox.

Refer to:

Chapter 5: Using the ComboBox item in Dialog Forms

Add ListBox:

Adds a drop-down list to the Dialog Form that allows a user to select only one item from the list of available items.

Refer to:

Chapter 5: Using the ListBox item in Dialog Forms

Add DropListBox:

Adds a drop-down list that allows a user to select one of the items from the list of available items. There is also an option to allow a user to enter/insert a different item into a small TextBox.

Refer to:

Chapter 5: Using the DropListBox item in Dialog Forms

Add MultiListBox:

Adds a drop-down list to the Dialog Form that allows a user to select one or more items from the list of available items.

Refer to:

Chapter 5: Using the MultiListBox item in Dialog Forms

Add OKButton, Add CancelButton:

Adds either an OKButton or CancelButton to the Dialog Form. It is a requirement to have either an OK button or Cancel button included on your form, unless you have added a PushButton.

- Only one OKButton is allowed on a Dialog Form.
- Only one CancelButton is allowed on a Dialog Form.

For scripting purposes, the values of these buttons in a functioning Dialog Form will result in the following:

- A value of **-1** is returned when the OK button is pressed.
- A value of **0** is returned when the Cancel button is pressed.

Refer to:

Chapter 5: Create a Simple Dialog Form

Add PushButton:

Adding a PushButton enables us to add buttons with our own titles to the Dialog Form. By default, each PushButton created on a form is named (as set in the Caption field) in sequence; "PushButton1", "PushButton2", and so on. You can of course change the Caption field to suit your requirements.

A PushButton can be used as a replacement for an OK or Cancel button; however, they are commonly used to provide extra options to a user.

For scripting purposes, the values returned when PushButtons are pressed in a functioning Dialog Form, will return the following:

- A value of **1** is returned for the first placed PushButton.
- A value of **2** is returned for the second placed PushButton.
- A value of **3** for a third PushButton and so on.

Refer to:

Chapter 5: Using Push Buttons (user defined buttons) in Dialog Forms, An Advanced Dialog Form

Add Picture:

Enables a bitmap image (.bmp) to be included in a Dialog Form.

Refer to:

Chapter 5: Placing GroupBoxes and Images in Dialog Forms

Advanced Dialog Functions

You may have noticed in some of the previous Dialog Form commands that when we created the forms, we also added the term "dialogfunc" to the Dialog function field within the Edit UserDialog Properties window. As a result, Dragon adds extra code to our scripts and also gives us the means by which we can increase control and functionality of our forms by using what is referred to as "Dialog functions".

Examples of Dialog functions include the ability to: hide items (DlgVisible), set focus to items (DlgFocus) and change the state of items (DlgValue).

The generated code produced as a result of adding the term "dialogfunc" includes a *Select Case* Action statement which consists of six *Case* options. Let's look at how we can use them to enhance our Dialog Form macros.

Case 1:

Code placed within this section is executed immediately once the Dialog Form is presented.

Example actions might be:

- To hide an item, such as a TextBox.
- To set a CheckBox to its checked state.
- To set all OptionButtons within a group to be unselected.

Case 2:

Code within this section is executed/run when a button is pressed, a CheckBox is checked (or unchecked), when OptionButtons are selected or when a value in a box is changed.

Because we are able to inspect the values, we can use the values returned, to determine if some other action should be carried out while the Dialog Form is still active.

Case 3:

Code within this section is run after a TextBox or the text within a ComboBox changes.

Case 4:

When focus changes from one item to another in the Dialog Form, scripts within this section are then run.

Case 5:

Is referred to as the "idle function", an example action might be:

- To set the initial focus to a specific TextBox.

Case 6:

Scripts within this section are used to process function keys that have been defined for the Dialog Form.

 When creating a script that includes Dialog functions, you can remove the Case areas that are not used, if you wish.

Creating a Dialog Form in the style of a simple Input Box

By creating a Dialog Form in the style of an Input Box (see Figure 5-40) ensures that we achieve a pop-up window that appears above any running applications.

The following script when run; will produce a styled Dialog Form and once the form has been addressed a Message Box is revealed to confirm the input.

Figure 5-40

A Dialog Form in the style of an Input Box.

MyCommand Name: dialog form as an input box

Description: Creating a Dialog Form to act as an input box

Group: Dragon - A Step Further_Chapter_05

Availability: Global

Command Type: Advanced Scripting

Content:

```
Sub Main
myVariableIn = 11
    Begin Dialog UserDialog 460,98,"Dialog Form - Input Box",.dialogfunc '
%GRID:10,7,1,1
        Text 10,7,310,35,"Enter a value between 1 and ",.Text1
        Text 200,7,100,21,myVariableIn,.Text2
        TextBox 10,56,320,21,.TextBox1
        OKButton 350,7,90,21
        CancelButton 350,35,90,21
    End Dialog

  Dim dlg As UserDialog
  value_form_one=Dialog (dlg)
  valueOfTextBoxEntry = dlg.TextBox1

  Select Case value_form_one
    Case 0 'Cancel button pressed
      Exit All 'Exit script
  End Select

  MsgBox ("You entered " & valueOfTextBoxEntry, 4096)
End Sub

Rem See DialogFunc help topic for more information.
Private Function dialogfunc(DlgItem$, Action%, SuppValue&) As Boolean
    Select Case Action%
    Case 1 ' Dialog box initialization
    Case 2 ' Value changing or button pressed
      Rem dialogfunc = True ' Prevent button press from closing the dialog box
    Case 3 ' TextBox or ComboBox text changed
    Case 4 ' Focus changed
    Case 5 ' Idle
      Rem Wait .1 : dialogfunc = True ' Continue getting idle actions
DlgFocus("TextBox1")
    Case 6 ' Function key
    End Select
End Function
```

Try it by saying:

"dialog form as an input box" or in the **MyCommands Editor window**, click on the **"Start/Resume" icon (F5)**

Discuss

The above script shows how we can create and design a Dialog Form which visually looks and works in a similar way to a conventional pop-up window produced by using the *InputBox* function.

Now that we have created the Dialog Form, we need to know how to parse values into and out of the Dialog Form.

Let's break down the script:

The line `myVariableIn = 11` sets up the variable `myVariableIn` and assigns a value of `11` to it. We will use this variable's value in the text to be written in our box. This could just as easily be a string of text.

The lines `Begin Dialog UserDialog...` to `End Dialog` defines the form size and its contents. Also, while creating the form within the UserDialog Editor window, there are a few points to bear in mind.

- The message "Enter a value between 1 and 11" is produced by using two Text fields (`Text1` & `Text2`) positioned next to each other.
- The Caption field of `Text1` contains the text "Enter a value between 1 and ".
- The Caption field of `Text2` contains the text "myVariableIn". However, because the CheckBox for the Quoted option is unchecked, Dragon knows that we are in fact referring to the value of the variable `myVariableIn`.
- Within the written-out text, the number "11" is revealed, in other words we parse the value of the variable `myVariableIn` into the Dialog Form. You can of course change the value of the variable (`myVariableIn`) to see how it changes the line of text when run.

Next is the inclusion of a TextBox; which has been left with its default name of `TextBox1`. This holds the value of whatever a user inserts into the Text field when the Dialog Form is presented.

Within the Edit UserDialog Properties window, the title of the form is determined by the text "Dialog Form – Input Box" in the Caption field. The text "dialogfunc" in the Dialog Function field makes the form ready for Dialog functions to be included.

The line `value_form_one=Dialog (dlg)` makes the variable `value_form_one` equal to a value of either -1 or 0 depending on whether the user clicks the OK button (-1) or the Cancel button (0).

The line `valueOfTextBoxEntry = dlg.TextBox1` makes the variable `valueOfTextBoxEntry` equal to whatever the user has inserted.

The *Case* statement is used to carry out the action of exiting the script if the user has clicked the Cancel button, i.e. where the variable `value_form_one` has a value of zero.

If the value of the variable `value_form_one` is not zero then the script moves on to the line `MsgBox ("You entered " & valueOfTextBoxEntry, 4096)` where we use the *MsgBox* function to type out a sentence with whatever the user has inputted into the Text field, therefore achieving the parsing out of data from the Dialog Form.

The line `DlgFocus("TextBox1")` in the `Case 5` area, is used to instruct Dragon to apply focus to the Text field `TextBox1` when the command is run. This will force our styled Dialog Form to pop up above any running applications.

This may seem like a long way to produce an Input Box, but trust me, there is nothing worse than running a command with an *InputBox* function, where your end-users are sitting there waiting for a pop-up window that seemingly does not appear to work.

An Advanced Dialog Form

The following example shows a more complex Dialog Form. Here we create a car sales purchase system, whereby the user is able to select a car with several options and the system will produce a summary with the price based on the choices made.

The Dialog Form demonstrates a range of functions, for example:

- How we can define two Dialog Forms within a Dragon script.
- Hiding and revealing fields based upon choices.
- Enabling and disabling options based upon choices.
- How we carry out calculations based on choices made.
- How we update captions dynamically.

MyCommand Name: example advanced dialog form

Description: Shows a multitude of options available in Dialog Forms

Group: Dragon - A Step Further_Chapter_05

Availability: Global

Command Type: Advanced Scripting

Content:

```
Sub Main
'Set up Variables and Arrays
theStart:
Dim colours$(5)
colours$(0) = "Black"
colours$(1) = "Blue"
colours$(2) = "Green"
colours$(3) = "Red"
colours$(4) = "Silver"
colours$(5) = "White"
Dim CaptionHeaderTextDlg02 As String 'Text Header for 2nd Dialog form
Dim CaptionTitleTextDlg02 As String 'Text Title for 2nd Dialog form
Dim CaptionPushBtnVal As String 'Text label for a PushButton
Dim car_choice As String 'holds choice of car
Dim car_type As String 'holds type of car
```

```
Dim col_choice As String 'holds colour choice
Dim audio_choice As String 'holds choice of audio system
Dim interior_choice As String 'holds choice of interior
Dim interior_h_seats As String 'holds heated seats Yes/No
Dim interior_sat_nav As String 'holds sat nav Yes/No
  'Default values
  CaptionHeaderTextDlg02 = "Price Plan"
  CaptionTitleTextDlg02 = "Summary & Price"
  CaptionPushBtnVal = "Click for Ford Price Plan"
  car_choice = "Ford"
  car_type = "4 door"
  col_choice = "Black"
  audio_choice = "Standard Audio system"
  interior_choice = "Material"
  interior_h_seats = "No"
  interior_sat_nav = "No"
  'Create Dialog Form 1
  Begin Dialog UserDialog01 450,301,"DRAGON CAR SALES",.dialogfunc ' %GRID:10,7,1,1
     Text 10,14,220,14,"MODEL:",.Text1
     ListBox 140,84,120,56,colours(),.coloursList
     OptionGroup .cars_radio_buttons_group
       OptionButton 80,14,90,14,"FORD",.ford
       OptionButton 180,14,90,14,"VOLVO",.volvo
     Text 10,63,90,14,"TYPE:",.typeOfCarLabel
     CheckBox 10,84,100,14,"4 DOOR",.doors4
     CheckBox 10,112,100,14,"CABRIOLET",.cabriolet
     Text 150,63,90,14,"COLOUR",.colourOfCarLabel
     Text 10,35,230,14,"Select specifications for Volvo cars",.volvoSpecLabel
     Text 10,35,230,14,"Select specifications for Ford cars:",.fordSpecLabel
     Text 10,140,90,14,"INTERIOR:",.interior_label
     CheckBox 10,161,120,14,"Leather seats",.interior1
     CheckBox 10,182,120,14,"Material seats",.interior2
     CheckBox 140,161,140,14,"Heated seats",.interior3
     CheckBox 140,182,140,14,"Sat Nav",.interior4
     Text 290,63,90,14,"AUDIO:",.typeOfAudioLabel
     OptionGroup .audio_group_options
       OptionButton 290,84,90,14,"Standard",.standard_audio
       OptionButton 290,105,90,14,"Dolby B",.dolby_b_audio
       OptionButton 290,126,130,14,"Surround sound",.s_s_audio
     CancelButton 60,252,90,28
     PushButton 210,252,180,28,CaptionPushBtnVal,.specButton
  End Dialog
  Dim dlg01 As UserDialog01
  value_form_one=Dialog (dlg01) 'Capture value into the variable value_form_one
  If value_form_one = 0 Then Exit All 'If Cancel btn on Dialog form 1 is pressed, exit
  'Create Dialog Form 2
  Begin Dialog UserDialog02 450,301,CaptionTitleTextDlg02,.dialogfunc ' %GRID:10,7,1,1
     Text 30,21,220,14,CaptionHeaderTextDlg02,.model_specs_label
     OKButton 40,231,90,21
     CancelButton 290,231,90,21
     PushButton 130,119,160,35,"Summary & Price",.PushButton1
  End Dialog
  Dim dlg02 As UserDialog02
  value_form_two=Dialog (dlg02) 'Capture value into the variable value_form_two
```

```
If value_form_two = 0 Then 'If Cancel btn on Dialog form 2 is pressed, start again
    GoTo theStart
End If
If value_form_two = 1 Then 'If Push button on Dialog form 2 is pressed
'Perform Calculations for choices made
total_price = 0 'Set total price to zero
If dlg01.doors4 = 1 Then car_type = "4 Door"
If dlg01.cabriolet = 1 Then car_type = "Cabriolet"
If dlg01.interior1 = 1 Then interior_choice = "Leather"
If dlg01.interior1 = 1 Then total_price = total_price + 111
If dlg01.interior2 = 1 Then interior_choice = "Material"
If dlg01.interior3 = 1 Then interior_h_seats = "Yes"
If dlg01.interior4 = 1 Then interior_sat_nav = "Yes"
'Use a For Next Loop to discover which colour has been selected from
'the ListBox referred to as colourList
For counter = 0 To 5 'Get the chosen colour
    Select Case dlg01.coloursList
      Case counter
      col_choice = colours$(counter) 'variable col_choice equals colour chosen
    End Select
Next counter
Select Case dlg01.cars_radio_buttons_group
    Case 0 'Specific Ford choice calculations
      car_choice = "Ford"
      total_price = total_price + 10000
    'Increment total price based on choice of type of Ford
      If dlg01.doors4 = 1 Then total_price = total_price + 499
      If dlg01.cabriolet = 1 Then total_price = total_price + 695
    'Increment total price based on choice of audio for Ford
      Select Case dlg01.audio_group_options
        Case 0 'standard_audio
            total_price = total_price + 39
            audio_choice = "Standard Audio system"
        Case 1 'dolby_b_audio
            total_price = total_price + 49
            audio_choice = "Dolby B Audio system"
        Case 2 's_s_audio
            total_price = total_price + 79
            audio_choice = "Surround Sound Audio system"
      End Select
    Case 1 'Specific Volvo choice calculations
      car_choice = "Volvo"
      total_price = total_price + 20000
    'Increment total price based on choice of type of Volvo
      If dlg01.cabriolet = 1 Then total_price = total_price + 999
End Select
MsgBox ("Summary:" & Chr$(13) & "" & Chr$(13) & _
"You selected a " & car_choice & " " & car_type & " in " & col_choice _
& Chr$(13) & Chr$(13) & _
"With:" & Chr$(13) & _
interior_choice & " Interior" & Chr$(13) & _
"Heated Seats: " & interior_h_seats & Chr$(13) & _
"Sat Nav: " & interior_sat_nav & Chr$(13) & _
"Audio: " & audio_choice & Chr$(13) & Chr$(13) & _
```

```
    "Price: £" & total_price,,"Summary & Price")
  Else
  End If
End Sub
Rem See DialogFunc help topic for more information.
Private Function dialogfunc(DlgItem$, Action%, SuppValue&) As Boolean
  Select Case Action%
  Case 1 ' Dialog box initialization
  Case 2 ' Value changing or button pressed
     Rem dialogfunc = True ' Prevent button press from closing the dialog box
  If DlgItem = "cars_radio_buttons_group" Then
     'If Option button Ford is selected do:
     If SuppValue = 0 Then DlgValue "doors4",0 'checkbox doors4 is un-checked
     If SuppValue = 0 Then DlgValue "cabriolet",0 'checkbox cabriolet is un-checked
     If SuppValue = 0 Then DlgEnable "doors4",True 'checkbox doors4 is ENABLED
     If SuppValue = 0 Then DlgVisible "fordSpecLabel",True 'Show fordSpecLabel
     If SuppValue = 0 Then DlgVisible "volvoSpecLabel",False 'Hide fordSpecLabel
     If SuppValue = 0 Then CaptionPushBtnVal = "Click for Ford Price Plan"
     If SuppValue = 0 Then DlgText (22, CaptionPushBtnVal) 'PushButton is item 22
     If SuppValue = 0 Then DlgEnable "s_s_audio",True 'option button s_s_audio is
ENABLED
     'If Option button Volvo is selected do:
     If SuppValue = 1 Then DlgValue "doors4",0 'checkbox doors4 is un-checked
     If SuppValue = 1 Then DlgValue "cabriolet",1 'checkbox cabriolet is checked
     If SuppValue = 1 Then DlgEnable "doors4",False 'checkbox doors4 is DISABLED
     If SuppValue = 1 Then DlgVisible "volvoSpecLabel",True 'Show fordSpecLabel
     If SuppValue = 1 Then DlgVisible "fordSpecLabel",False 'Hide fordSpecLabel
     If SuppValue = 1 Then CaptionPushBtnVal = "Click for Volvo Price Plan"
     If SuppValue = 1 Then DlgText (22, CaptionPushBtnVal) 'PushButton is item 22
     If SuppValue = 1 Then DlgEnable "s_s_audio",False 'option button s_s_audio is
DISABLED
  End If
  'Switch for Material or Leather interior checkboxes
  If DlgItem = "interior1" Then
     If SuppValue = 1 Then DlgValue "interior2",0 'Check box interior2 becomes empty
  End If
  If DlgItem = "interior2" Then
     If SuppValue = 1 Then DlgValue "interior1",0 'Check box interior1 becomes empty
  End If
  Case 3 ' TextBox or ComboBox text changed
  Case 4 ' Focus changed
  Case 5 ' Idle
     Rem Wait .1 : dialogfunc = True ' Continue getting idle actions
  Case 6 ' Function key
  End Select
End Function
```

Try it by saying:

"example advanced dialog form" or in the **MyCommands Editor window**, click on the **"Start/Resume" icon (F5)**

Discuss

Although you will find a number of comment statements (') included in the code. Let's examine some portions of this script in more detail.

Dynamically altering the Caption text in a PushButton, DlgText function:

The Caption text within the PushButton of the first Dialog Form is dependent (changes dynamically) on the choice of car selected by the user. To achieve this, when creating the PushButton, we make sure the Quoted option is not checked in the Edit PushButton Properties window (see Figure 5-41). Dragon will then treat the Caption field value as a variable.

Figure 5-41

Use the Edit PushButton Properties window to change the properties of the PushButton.

Insert a variable name into the **Caption** field and uncheck the **Quoted** option.

Dragon will now treat the **Caption** text as a variable which can now be changed dynamically by code.

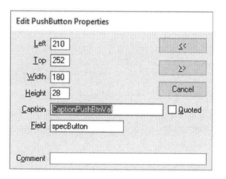

Notice that this variable is created and given a value in the early stages of the script before the actual Dialog Form is created, by the lines:

- `Dim CaptionPushBtnVal As String 'Text label for a PushButton`
- `CaptionPushBtnVal = "Click for Ford Price Plan"`

Within the `Case 2` section of the script, two lines are needed to perform our objective:

- The line `If SuppValue = 1 Then CaptionPushBtnVal = "Click for Volvo Price Plan"` will change the value of the variable `CaptionPushBtnVal` if the user selects the OptionButton "Volvo".
- The line `If SuppValue = 1 Then DlgText (22, CaptionPushBtnVal) 'PushButton is item 22` uses the ***DlgText*** function to populate item number 22 (the PushButton) with the value of the `CaptionPushBtnVal` variable and as such changes the Caption text within the PushButton. There are two similar lines that perform the action of changing the Caption when "Ford" is selected, see if you can spot them.

Using the DlgEnable function:

When the command is run you will notice that if the user selects "Volvo", the CheckBox 4 Door becomes disabled, greyed out and cannot be checked.

This is achieved by placing the line `If SuppValue = 1 Then DlgEnable "doors4",False` in the `Case 2` section of the script. We use the ***DlgEnable*** function to disable the CheckBox labelled `doors4`.

Dynamically changing the Dialog Form title:

The 2nd Dialog Form title is created by using the value of the variable `CaptionTitleTextDlg02`. This variable name must also be the name in the Caption field of the Edit UserDialog Properties window of the 2nd Dialog Form and the Quoted option must be un-checked. The variable is defined, assigned a value and placed within the script before the portion of code that creates the Dialog Form.

 To change the Caption title of a Dialog Form dynamically (i.e. Not just at the point that the Dialog Form appears) you can use a line such as `DlgText (-1, "New Caption Title")` and place it in the `Case 2` area along with an If Then statement. The -1 is the item number for a Dialog Form's title.

Refer to:

Chapter 5: Advanced Dialog Functions

Chapter 8: Arrays, If Then Statement, MsgBox Function, Select Case Function

Section 4: Distributing and Encrypting Dragon Macros

Chapter 6: Importing, Exporting and Distributing Dragon Commands

Exporting your Dragon Commands

There will undoubtedly be times when you will want to backup or share your custom Dragon commands with others.

It might be a case of distributing your macros with fellow work or student colleagues, or, you may have been hired to create full-on in-depth scripts for a company or organisation.

Dragon enables us to export our macros individually or as a group resulting in either an *.xml* or *.dat* file being produced.

Criteria for Exporting your Dragon Macros

Before we look at the number of ways, we can export our Dragon commands, it is important that you understand the environments/criteria where exporting is available.

In previous versions of Dragon NaturallySpeaking (version 13 and below), Nuance placed certain restrictions based upon the product version. If a user had the "Premium version", they would not be able to create Advanced Scripting commands and consequently would be unable to import or export any Advanced Scripting type commands.

The "Home" version went a step further by restricting users from creating both "Advanced Scripts" and "Text and Graphics" macros. Therefore, you needed to have the "Professional version" to take full advantage of importing, exporting and creating all types of macros.

This all changed with the arrival of Dragon Professional version 14. Thankfully the guys at Nuance decided to move away from these variations in products and reduced it to two versions, Dragon Professional Individual (DPI) and Dragon Professional Group (DPG) both of which allow for full scripting.

Exporting a Macro as an XML file

Open the Command Browser via the DragonBar >> Tools menu, select the macro you wish to export (see Figure 6-1).

Figure 6-1

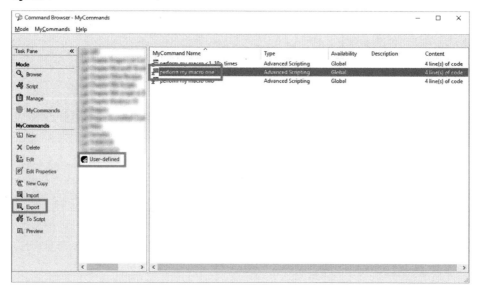

In this example our command is called "perform my macro one" and is located in the "User-defined" folder. Your command may be in a different folder, dependent on where you save your commands.

Click the Export button on the left-hand side of the Command Browser in order to reveal the Export Commands window (see Figure 6-2).

Figure 6-2

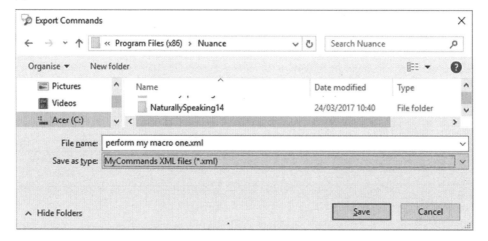

Insert a file name for the file to be saved.

Click the down arrow on the Save as type: drop-down menu and select MyCommands files (*.xml).

Click the Save button.

Saving your command as an .xml file creates a file that is in a readable format, it can be easily emailed and is less likely to be quarantined by virus protection programs on an end-user's machine.

Exporting a Macro as a DAT file

Open the Command Browser via the DragonBar >> Tools menu, select the macro you wish to export (see Figure 6-3).

Figure 6-3

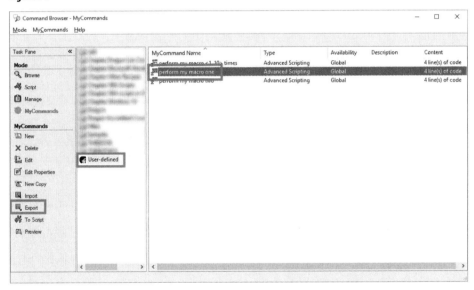

In this example our command is called "perform my macro one" and is located in the "User-defined" folder, your command may be in a different folder, dependent on where you save your commands.

Click the Export button on the left-hand side of the Command Browser in order to reveal the Export Commands window.

Insert a file name for the file to be saved.

Click the down arrow on the Save as type: drop-down menu and select MyCommands files (*.dat).

Click the Save button.

Saving your command as a .dat file creates a non-readable format file. If you have any problems sending the file by email, I would suggest that you zip the file and then send the zip file out to your end-users.

Only .dat files can be encrypted.

Refer to:

Chapter 7: How to create an Encrypted Macro

Exporting several Macros at once

It is possible to export a group or several of your Dragon commands at once.

Carry out the procedure of opening the Command browser and select the commands that you wish to export (see Figure 6-4).

Figure 6-4

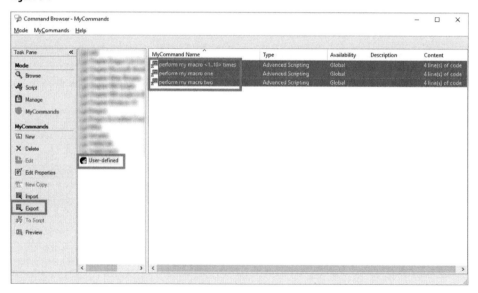

In this example we have selected three macros and they are located in the "User-defined" folder, your commands may be in a different folder, dependent on where you save your commands.

Click the Export button on the left-hand side of the Command Browser in order to reveal the Export Commands window.

Insert a file name for the file to be saved.

Click the down arrow on the Save as type: drop-down menu and select either to save as "MyCommands files (*.dat)" or "MyCommands files (*.xml)".

Click the Save button.

You will notice that, even though we have selected more than one command, Dragon creates only one *.dat* or *.xml* file.

Exporting as a .xml file:
- Creates a file that is in a readable format.
- File can be emailed easily and is less likely to be quarantined by virus protection.

Exporting as a .dat file:
- Creates a non-readable format file.
- You may have to zip the file, in order to send by email to end-users.
- File can be encrypted.

Refer to:

Chapter 7: Locking, Protecting, Encrypting your created Dragon Commands

The difference between Overwriting and Merging when exporting your Macros

When exporting macros, if you decide to name and place the resultant *.dat* file in the same location as an existing *.dat* file with the same name, you will be presented with the option of either overwriting or merging with the existing *.dat* file, as shown in Figure 6-5.

Figure 6-5

Choose whether you want to overwrite or merge with an existing exported file.

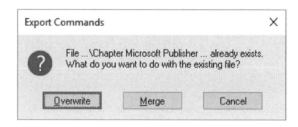

The **Overwrite** option will replace the macros in the existing *.dat* file with the ones selected.

Here is an example, if you have previously created a *.dat* file that contained five macros; then in the Command Browser delete three of the macros and create a new one; then select and export the remaining three as the same *.dat* filename. The result would be three macros in the *.dat* file. Figure 6-6 illustrates this.

Figure 6-6

The **Merge** option adds the macros you have selected in the Command Browser to the ones in the existing *.dat* file.

Again, if you have previously created a *.dat* file that contained five macros; then in the Command Browser delete three of the macros and create a new one; then select and export the remaining three as the same *.dat* filename. The result would be six macros in the *.dat* file. Figure 6-7 illustrates this.

Figure 6-7

Importing Macros

To import macros into Dragon, open the Command Browser (see Figure 6-8) via the DragonBar >> Tools menu.

Figure 6-8

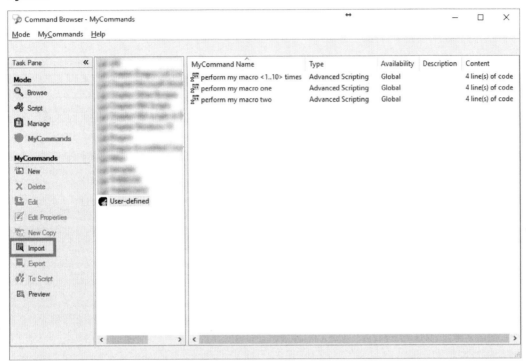

Click the Import button on the left-hand side of the Command Browser to reveal the File Explorer Import Commands window.

Navigate to the location of the *.xml* or *.dat* file that you wish to import and click the Open button.

 If you do not see your intended file, make sure the file type next to the filename field ("MyCommands files (*.dat)" etc.) is the same as the type of file you wish to import or select "All files (*.*)" from the list in the menu. You will then be presented with the Import Commands window:

Figure 6-9

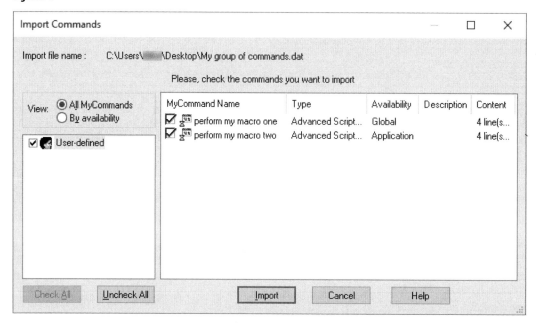

In this scenario, we have selected the "My group of commands.dat" file to be imported. The Import Commands window (see Figure 6-9) displays all the commands that are contained within the *.dat* file.

On the left-hand side of the window, "User-defined" is the name of the folder into which these commands will be placed.

There are two view options, as shown in Figure 6-10.

Figure 6-10

Selecting one of the two View options when importing Dragon commands.

All MyCommands, will display the list of macros contained within the *.dat* file (as can be seen in Figure 6-9)

By Availability, displays a more detailed breakdown of the commands contained within the *.dat* file. This view breaks up the commands into their availability state (whether they are Global, Application-specific or Window-specific types of commands). By clicking on Global, the section on the right will show the commands that are Global in the *.dat* file and the same applies for Application-specific and Window-specific (see Figure 6-11).

You can now either import all the ticked macros or select only the macros you require. Click the Import button to import the commands.

Figure 6-11

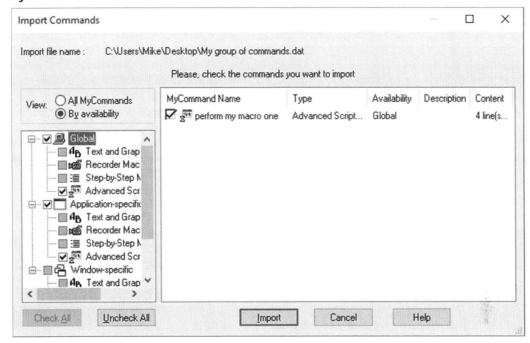

 When commands are imported they will be placed in the same named folder they were exported from.

 In a scenario where a user imports an Application-specific command but does not have the application on their PC. Dragon will still allow you to import the command, however, Dragon will not respond to the voice command until the application has been installed on the target PC.

Importing Macros that contain Dragon Lists

When importing a command that contains a Dragon List, Dragon automatically imports the List and its items.

However, if there is already a Dragon List with the same name on the end-user's PC then Dragon will display a warning, as shown in Figure 6-12.

Figure 6-12

When a user attempts to import a Dragon command containing a Dragon List, Dragon will check to see if the List name conflicts with an existing List name. If it does, Dragon will prompt the user for confirmation.

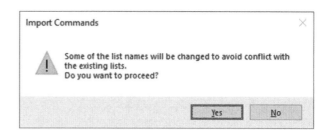

Once you give the go ahead, Dragon will create a newly named version of the List and edit the imported command's name to include the new List name.

Refer to:

Chapter 4: What are Dragon List Commands?

Importing Macros that contain References to Application Object Libraries

When writing and distributing commands that contain a reference to an application Object Library (see Chapter 2: "Object Library References"), we are not only writing a macro that requires a specific application in order to work; the specific version of that application is important as well.

An application Object Library will often be updated and renamed by software companies for different versions of an application, for example.

The Object Library for Microsoft Word:

- Version 2010 - Microsoft Word 14.0 Object Library (8.5)
- Version 2016 - Microsoft Word 16.0 Object Library (8.7)

The Object Library for Mindjet's MindManager:

- MindManager version 16 - MindManager 16 Type Library (10.0)
- MindManager version 18 - MindManager 18 Type Library (12.0)

Therefore, don't be surprised that if you import such a macro, it may not work, and of course you should consider this possibility when distributing your macros to others. Should this be the case, in order to get these macros to work again, you will need to edit the script and re-reference to the appropriate Object Library, as shown below:

- Open the Command Browser and locate the imported command.
- Double click the command in order to edit it.
- Place your cursor over the code between the lines Sub Main and End Sub

- Right-click your mouse and select "References" from the drop-down menu. The References - mycommand window will appear.
- Look out for any "Bad reference: …" and make sure you un-check them.
- Look for the application's Object Library for the version that is on your PC.
- Check the box next to your application version Object Library and click Save.

Figure 6-13 shows an example of a Bad reference.

Figure 6-13

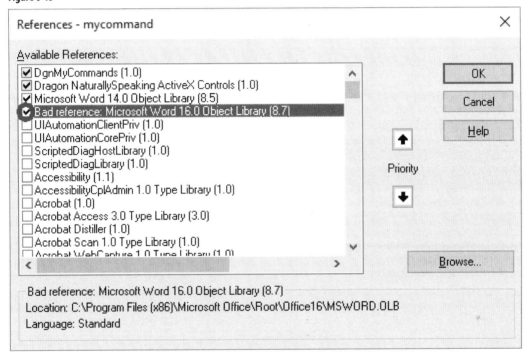

The command should now work.

Refer to:

Chapter 2: Using VBA Macros in Dragon Advanced Scripting Commands

Updating Application-specific Macros

From time to time you may find yourself in a situation where you have created several macros for a specific version of an application. Only to find that after a period of time a new version of the application has been installed onto the system and now your macros no longer work.

You'd be forgiven for thinking "OK, I will change each macro to the new version". Well yes, that will work, but what if there are 20 plus commands? This would be quite tedious.

The best approach would be to change them all at once and this can be done by:

Opening the Command Browser via the DragonBar >> Tools menu, locate and select the macros you wish to change, as shown in Figure 6-14 (Use the Ctrl or Shift keys to select the intended macros).

Figure 6-14

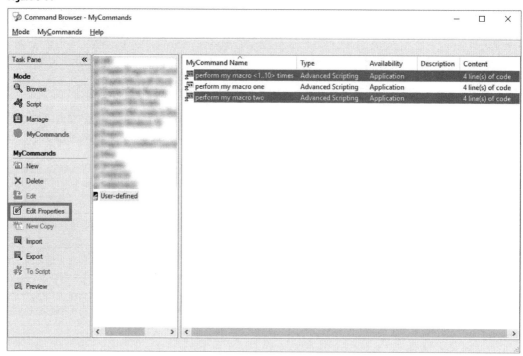

Click on the Edit Properties button in order to reveal the MyCommands Properties window (see Figure 6-15).

Figure 6-15

You can use the MyCommands Properties window to view and change the command properties of the selected commands.

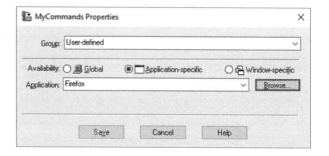

You can now select the Application-specific radio button and then click the Browse button to locate the new application executable file. Once done, click the Save button.

All selected macros will now be updated to the new application version.

Chapter 7: Locking, Protecting, Encrypting your created Dragon Commands

There may be times when you will want to distribute protected/locked versions of your macros. Whether it's to prevent end users editing and corrupting your scripts resulting in your macros not working or for privacy, to conceal the hard work you have put into your code to stop/prevent others from copying it.

Thankfully, Dragon comes with a handy utility called the "MyCommands Protection Utility", which enables you to lock and encrypt your created macros. Once an encrypted macro has been imported into Dragon, the command will work as normal; however, it cannot be edited, viewed or exported.

 Where an encrypted command includes a Dragon List, the actual Dragon List is not encrypted as part of this process and can be modified on an end-user's system.

 You cannot change the Object Reference of an imported encrypted command.

Refer to:

Chapter 2: Object Library References
Chapter 4: What are Dragon List Commands?

How to create an Encrypted Macro

To create an encrypted version of one of your Dragon commands, follow the steps below:

Step 1. Export your macro

Open the Command Browser via the DragonBar >> Tools menu, locate and select the macro you wish to encrypt (see Figure 7-1).

Figure 7-1

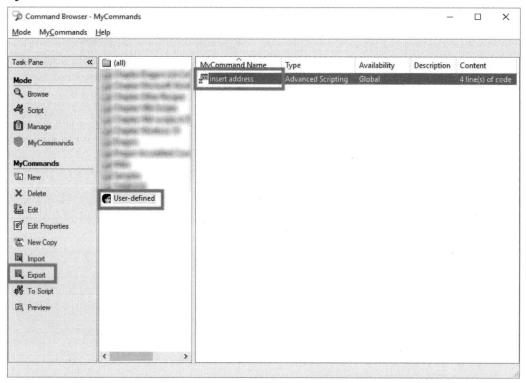

In this example our command is called "insert address" and is located in the "User-defined" folder, your command may be in a different folder.

Click the Export button on the left-hand side of the Command Browser to reveal the Export Commands window (see Figure 7-2).

Insert the name of the file to be saved, notice that I have inserted an underscore in between the words and named our file "insert_address".

Make sure that the Save as type: is set to "MyCommands files (*.dat)". This is important, as it is only *.dat* files that can be encrypted.

 When saving, choose a simple location such as a folder on your desktop as this will make it easier to type the path location in the MyCommands Protection Utility tool.

Figure 7-2

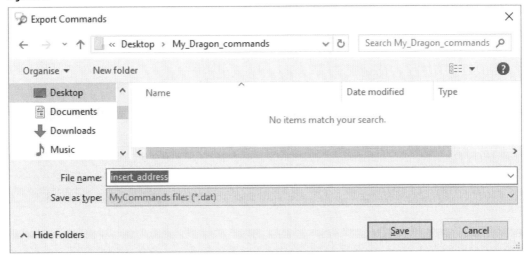

Step 2. Encrypt your exported macro

 Before creating the encrypted command (.dat file), be sure to back up the exported macro (.dat file), as once the encrypted version is imported into the Command Browser, it will overwrite the original macro and you will not be able to edit or export the macro again.

In the Windows Start Menu, select Dragon >> MyCommands Protection Utility, as shown in Figure 7-3.

Figure 7-3

Click on the Windows Start button to reveal the Windows Start menu. Look for the Dragon folder and click it to reveal its sub menu. Select the MyCommands Protection Utility.

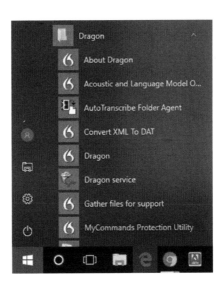

This will reveal the MyCommands Protection Utility window (see Figure 7-4), with a prompt ready for you to insert the command to carry out the encryption.

Figure 7-4

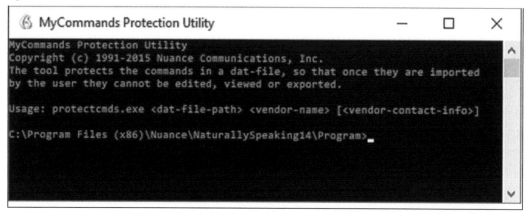

This is the command line utility that we use to lock and encrypt our macro. The important thing to note is how we write our command to perform the encryption.

In fact, the MyCommands Protection Utility shows us the general format for running the encryption process in the line:

`Usage: protectcmds.exe <dat-file-path> <vendor-name> [<vendor-contact-info>]`

Let's break this down:

`protectcmds.exe` is the executable file that will run the process, however it needs a few parameters in order to work:

- `<dat-file-path>`, refers to the full path to the *.dat* file.
- `<vendor-name>`, gives you the opportunity to name yourself as the author of the macro.
- `[<vendor-contact-info>]`, gives you the opportunity to insert your company name.

In our scenario, our macro file name is "insert_address.dat".

The location of our file is in the folder "My_Dragon_commands" situated on the Windows desktop.

I will have an author name of "Mike" and a company name of "MyCompany".

Therefore, we will type the following into the MyCommands Protection Utility and press the Enter key:

`protectcmds.exe C:\Path...\Desktop\My_Dragon_commands\insert_address.dat Mike MyCompany`

If there are any spaces in the path/file name, vendor-name, or vendor-contact-info details, then you will need to use double quotes in the command line. Therefore, in a scenario where the folder name is "My macros", the filename is "open report.dat", the vendor name is "Mike Lloyd" and vendor-contact-info is "Temple Tech Ltd" the following command will work:

`protectcmds.exe "C:\Path...to..file\My macros\open report.dat" "Mike Lloyd" "Temple Tech Ltd"`

I would advise typing the full command in an application such as Notepad and then copying and pasting it into the MyCommands Protection Utility.

Provided you have inserted the correct details and spacings (considering any adjustments on your part) you will see the following confirmation message within the MyCommands Protection Utility:

```
Protected 1 commands in "C:\Path...\Desktop\My_Dragon_commands\insert_address.dat"
```

That's it! your command is now encrypted. Next, let's import this macro back into Dragon to see the difference.

Remember, once you import the encrypted command, it will overwrite your original unencrypted command.

Step 3. Importing the Encrypted Command

Once you have imported your macro, you will notice a difference in the Command Browser next to the macro name.

Figure 7-5 shows how the macro looks in the Command Browser before encryption.

Figure 7-5

MyCommand Name	Type	Availability	Description	Content
insert address	Advanced Scripting	Global		4 line(s) of code

Figure 7-6 shows how the macro looks in the Command Browser after encryption.

Figure 7-6

MyCommand Name	Type	Availability	Description	Content
insert address	Advanced Scripting	Global		Protected by Mike

The macro can be used as freely as before, however, now try double clicking on the macro as if to edit it and you will be presented with the Protected Command window (see Figure 7-7).

Figure 7-7

The Protected Command window will appear when you double click (attempt to edit) on a protected command.

Details of the person who protected the command are also shown.

"The command was protected by [vendor-name]. Please contact [vendor-contact-info] for more information."

Encrypting a bunch of Commands

To encrypt several commands at the same time, you will need to first export them as a bunch. The encryption process can then be performed on the *.dat* file created.

Open the MyCommand Protection Utility and write the instructions for encryption in exactly the same way as if you were encrypting a single command.

For example, `protectcmds.exe C:\Path...\Desktop\My_Dragon_commands\myBunchMacros.dat Mike MyCompany`

You will notice that the confirmation message will differ according to the number of commands in the bunch. For example, if your *.dat* file contains three commands then the resulting confirmation message within the MyCommands Protection Utility will be similar to:

`Protected 3 commands in "C:\Path...\Desktop\My_Dragon_commands\myBunchMacros.dat"`

Importing the encrypted *.dat* file into Dragon will import all the commands (now encrypted).

Refer to:

Chapter 6: Importing, Exporting and Distributing Dragon Commands

MyCommands Protection Utility Command Line examples

Example command lines that are required under various naming alternatives are listed below:

Scenario 1 - Where there are no spaces in the directory folder, macro name, author or company name.

Macro name: `print_twice.dat`

Folder name: `my_commands` (situated on the windows desktop)

Author: `Michael`

Company name: Office

Command to run encryption: protectcmds.exe C:\Path...\Desktop\my_commands\print_twice.dat Michael Office

 Spaces are important for the command to work.

Scenario 2 - Where there are spaces in the directory folder and macro name.

Macro name: open report.dat

Folder name: my macros (situated on the windows desktop)

Author: Yvette

Company name: Newtons

Command to run encryption: protectcmds.exe "C:\Path...\Desktop\my macros\open_report.dat" Yvette Newtons

 When there are spaces in the folder name or macro name, we need to use quotes ("") to surround the file path for the command to work.

Scenario 3 - Where there are spaces in the author (vendor) and company name.

Macro name: open_report.dat

Folder name: my macros (situated on the windows desktop)

Author: Billy Paul

Company name: Temple Ltd

Command to run encryption: protectcmds.exe "C:\Path...\Desktop\my_commands\open_report.dat" "Mike Lloyd" "Temple Ltd"

 When there are spaces in the vendor or company name, we need to use quotes ("") to surround the vendor name and company name for the command to work.

If you do not require a vendor or company name, the encryption command will take the form of:

protectcmds.exe "C:\Path...\Desktop\my_commands\open_report.dat" "" ""

If you require only the vendor name, the encryption command will take the form of:

```
protectcmds.exe "C:\Path...\Desktop\my_commands\open_report.dat" "Mike"
```

Once a macro has been successfully encrypted, the following confirmation message will appear within the Mycommands Protection Utility:

```
Protected 1 commands in "C:\...Path..to..file\my_macro_name.dat"
```

Section 5: Dragon Scripting Commands and Extensions

Chapter 8: Overview of Dragon Script Functions and Statements

AppBringUp

Within Advanced Scripts the *AppBringUp* command can be used to open/start or reactivate an application if it is already running. It can also be used to start up a specific file such has a *.doc* document and as a result MS Word would start.

Below are examples of how the *AppBringUp* command can be used:

Opening an application:

```
AppBringUp "Application"
```

```
Sub Main
AppBringUp "winword.exe"
End Sub
```

Here we use the command to start the application MS Word.

For applications that Dragon knows about, you do not need the `.exe` portion of the script. `AppBringUp "winword"` would work just as well.

Where Dragon does not know the application, you can adjust the command by including the path to the executable file of the application. For example, `AppBringUp "C:\...Path..to..file\application.exe"`.

Opening a specific file:

```
AppBringUp "Path\fileName.ext"
```

```
Sub Main
AppBringUp "C:\...Path..to..file\myDocument.docx"
End Sub
```

This example shows how *AppBringUp* is used to open a specific document. Dragon recognises the document type and will then open the associated application to reveal it.

 The application opened for a specific file type is determined by a user's system settings.

Opening a specific file with a specific application:

```
AppBringUp "Label", "Application Path\fileName.ext"
```

```
Sub Main
AppBringUp "myLabel","WordPad C:\...Path..to..file\myDoc.txt"
End Sub
```

The above example shows how we can force Dragon to open the text file myDoc.txt with the application WordPad instead of Notepad, which is the usual default application for opening text files on most people's PCs.

The parameter myLabel can be used later in a script to reactivate the application and file by using the line AppBringUp "myLabel".

A second parameter (WordPad) is inserted before the path to the file which instructs Dragon to open the file with the application WordPad. An alternative could be where we want the myDoc.txt to be opened with the application MS Word in which case the line would become AppBringUp "myLabel","Winword C:\...Path..to..file\myDoc.txt".

When including the application parameter and where Dragon knows the application, inserting application names such as WordPad, Notepad or Winword will work.

However, with some applications you may need to insert the directory path to the executable file of that application. For example, AppBringUp "myLabel","C:\Program Files\Sublime Text 2\sublime_text.exe C:\...Path..to..file\myDoc.txt" would be needed to have a document opened by the application Sublime Text 2.

 AppBringUp does not work with long filenames or folder names containing spaces (the directory path to the file must not contain spaces).

Opening an application in a specific state:

```
AppBringUp "Label", "Application Path\fileName.ext", State
```

```
Sub Main
AppBringUp "myLabel","WordPad C:\...Path..to..file\myDoc.txt",3
End Sub
```

The *AppBringUp* function allows us to open an application in either a minimised, maximised or default window state. To set this, we include a parameter at the end of the line with a value of 1, 2 or 3.

Some developers prefer to use the VB Defined names rather than a numerical value for determining the window state. Table 8-1 lists the VB Defined names and their numerical values.

Table 8-1

VB Defined name	Value	Window state
vbNormalFocus	1	Window has focus and is restored to its original size and position.
vbMinimizedFocus	2	Window is displayed as an icon with focus.
vbMaximizedFocus	3	Window is maximised with focus.

Therefore, changing the line to `AppBringUp "myLabel","WordPad C:\...Path..to..file\myDoc.txt",vbMaximizedFocus` would be allowed.

 For some developers, when writing a simple script that opens an application, the preferred way is to use a Step-by-Step command script.

Arrays

An *Array* is a list of values/items which are stored in a single variable.

The format for creating an *Array* is to:

- Define the variable (name of the Array) that will hold the values (the name of a string variable may be followed by the "$" sign).
- Define the number of items (in brackets) it will contain.
- Define (on the proceeding lines) each of the items for the *Array*.

The values are assigned to the Array by attaching an Array Index number against each item specified.

```
Sub Main
Dim variableName$(4) 'Create String Array
  variableName$(0) = "Sun"
  variableName$(1) = "Moon"
  variableName$(2) = "Stars"
  variableName$(3) = "Galaxy"
  variableName$(4) = "Universe"
MsgBox (variableName$(4))
End Sub
```

It is important to note that when working with *Arrays* the first item is referred to as position "0". Therefore, in the above example, even though the line `Dim variableName$(4)` appears to indicate space for four items, it is in fact five items that can be placed.

Arrays can store any type of variable including integers and strings.

An array and its items can also be created in the following format; `VariableName =`
`Array(0,2,5,8)`

Beep

By including the *Beep* command Dragon will generate the Windows default beep sound. The actual sound heard will depend on the hardware and operating system configuration.

I personally use the *Beep* command in situations where I would like an indication that a command has completed its task.

The script below is an example of how we can turn off the microphone, play the beep sound, wait for two seconds to ensure that the sound finishes playing, and then turn the microphone back on.

```
Sub Main
SetMicrophone 0
Beep
Wait 2
SetMicrophone 1
End Sub
```

On some systems (especially where you notice that a sound cannot be heard) it is a requirement to turn off the microphone before executing the Beep command and then turning the microphone back on afterwards.

ButtonClick Command

There are times when writing scripts that we need to emulate/generate the pressing of a mouse button.

For example, if you are writing a macro for an application that involves moving the cursor to a specific position on the screen and then clicking the left mouse button in order to carry out the required function.

The *ButtonClick* command requires two parameters.

```
ButtonClick [button[,count]]
```

The **button** parameter determines which of the mouse buttons to press. This is determined by the values:

Value	Button
1	Left button
2	Right button
4	Third (middle) button

The **count** parameter determines how many times the button should be pressed:

Value	Count
1	Single click
2	Double click

Below is a simple example of how the *ButtonClick* command can be used. Try it out on the Windows desktop.

```
Sub Main
ButtonClick 2,1
End Sub
```

This command will press the right mouse button, once, in order to reveal a drop-down menu.

 It is a good idea to include a Wait statement before and after the ButtonClick command within your scripts.

Refer to:

Chapter 8: MouseGrid Function

Chr and Asc Functions

Chr function

The *Chr* function is used to insert special characters into our scripts. An example would be when working with Message Boxes, you may need to place characters such as quotations, brackets or include line breaks in a Message Box prompt text. In such cases the *Chr* function is used and is sometimes necessary to prevent your script from failing.

The *Chr* function works by interpreting the ASCII code value used in the statement and reveals the character or an action associated with that value.

Please refer to the Appendix for a comprehensive list of ASCII codes and their associated characters and actions.

Below is an example of how we need to use the *Chr* function in order to insert double quotes and perform a Carriage Return (line break) in a Message Box prompt message.

```
Sub Main
  MsgBox ("He said " & Chr(34) & "No" & Chr(34) & Chr(13) & "Yesterday")
End Sub
```

Discuss

The ASCII character code value for quotes (") is 34 and the ASCII character code value for a Carriage Return (line break) is (13). This is why we use the Chr(34) and Chr(13) statements in our script.

The Ampersand (&) symbol is used to connect the *Chr* statement to the text in order that Dragon treats this as one line of code.

Placing the *Chr* function is similar to how we place a variable, in that it is not enclosed within quotes.

In the above example, if we were to remove the *Chr* functions and change the script to the following: MsgBox ("He said "No"")- It would not work!

The following script uses a *For...Next Loop* and an *Array* to type out some of the popular ASCII code values and their associated characters or actions.

MyCommand Name: produce ascii code list

Description: Example of a script using the Chr function

Group: Dragon - A Step Further_Chapter_08

Availability: Global

Command Type: Advanced Scripting

Content:

```
Sub Main
SetMicrophone 0
Dim popularAsciis$(4) 'Create String Array
    popularAsciis$(0) = "9 | horizontal tab"
    popularAsciis$(1) = "10 | new line"
    popularAsciis$(2) = "13 | carriage return"
    popularAsciis$(3) = "31 | unit separator"
    popularAsciis$(4) = "32 | Space"
  SendDragonKeys ("ASCII CHARACTER CODES" & Chr(13)) 'carriage return
  For count = 0 To 4
    SendDragonKeys (Chr(13))
    SendDragonKeys ("ASCII Code No. " & popularAsciis(count) & Chr(32)) 'space
  Next count
  For count = 33 To 47
    SendDragonKeys (Chr(13))
    SendDragonKeys ("ASCII Code No. " & count & Chr(32))
    SendDragonKeys (Chr(124) & Chr(32)) '124 - pipe character
    SendDragonKeys (Chr(count))
  Next count
  For count = 58 To 64
    SendDragonKeys (Chr(13))
    SendDragonKeys ("ASCII Code No. " & count & Chr(32))
    SendDragonKeys (Chr(124) & Chr(32))
    SendDragonKeys (Chr(count))
```

```
  Next count
  For count = 91 To 96
    SendDragonKeys (Chr(13))
    SendDragonKeys ("ASCII Code No. " & count & Chr(32))
    SendDragonKeys (Chr(124) & Chr(32))
    SendDragonKeys (Chr(count))
  Next count
  For count = 123 To 126
    SendDragonKeys (Chr(13))
    SendDragonKeys ("ASCII Code No. " & count & Chr(32))
    SendDragonKeys (Chr(124) & Chr(32))
    SendDragonKeys (Chr(count))
  Next count
SetMicrophone 1
End Sub
```

Open a word processing application and try it by saying:

"produce ascii code list"

When working with Chr functions and sending out text, it is always best to use the **SendDragonKeys** function.

Asc function

The *Asc* function works in reverse to the *Chr* function by revealing the ASCII character code that is associated with a character. How this function can be used is shown below.

```
Sub Main
  MsgBox ("" & Asc("M")) 'Will reveal the ASCII code value of 77
End Sub
```

Refer to:

Chapter 8: Arrays, For…Next Loop, MsgBox Function, SendDragonKeys, SendKeys & SendSystemKeys

Appendix: Popular Ascii Character Codes

ClearDesktop

The *ClearDesktop* function can be used within a script to clear the Windows desktop and minimise all currently running applications.

It's a good idea to use this function when your script includes the opening of an application.

```
Sub Main
ClearDesktop
End Sub
```

Clipboard Function

The *Clipboard* function enables us to send and access data from the Clipboard within our scripts. This is extremely useful where you might want a string variable to become equal to text that has been copied to the Clipboard with the intention of using or manipulating that variable elsewhere in your script. Equally, you may have altered some text or performed some form of calculation in a script and now you want the results to be sent to the Clipboard in order that it can be pasted later to the appropriate place within a document or application.

In a basic form we can send a string of text to the Clipboard by using the following lines of code:

```
Sub Main
  Clipboard "Happy Birthday"
End Sub
```

This will send the text "Happy Birthday" to the Clipboard (the same as performing the Ctrl+C keystroke). Take note that the string of text is within quotes.

The Clipboard function also works with variables, in that we can either:

- Send the value/contents of a variable to the Clipboard.
- Make the value of a variable become equal to the contents of the Clipboard.

The following script demonstrates how we can send and receive data from the Clipboard using the *Clipboard* function with variables.

MyCommand Name: example clipboard script

Description: Example of a script using the Clipboard function

Group: Dragon - A Step Further_Chapter_08

Availability: Global

Command Type: Advanced Scripting

Content:

```
Sub Main
  Dim sendToClipboard As String
  Dim getFromClipboard As String
  Dim sendToClipboardTwo As Long
  Dim getFromClipboardTwo As Long

  sendToClipboard = "The quick brown fox"
  getFromClipboard = ""
  sendToClipboardTwo = 20
  getFromClipboardTwo = 0
'Send the value of the String variable to the Clipboard
  Clipboard sendToClipboard
  getFromClipboard = Clipboard
```

```
  MsgBox (getFromClipboard & " jumped over the lazy dog", 4096)
'Send the value of the Long variable to the Clipboard
  Clipboard CStr(sendToClipboardTwo)
  getFromClipboardTwo = Clipboard
  getFromClipboardTwo = getFromClipboardTwo * 2
  MsgBox ("The new doubled value is " & CStr(getFromClipboardTwo))
End Sub
```

Try it by saying:
"example clipboard script" or in the **MyCommands Editor window**, click on the **"Start/Resume" icon (F5)**

Discuss
The first part of this script is where we create and set up the String and Numerical variables (Dim...). Both the variables sendToClipboard and sendToClipboardTwo have values assigned to them.

The line Clipboard sendToClipboard sends the value of the variable sendToClipboard to the Clipboard.

The line getFromClipboard = Clipboard makes the value of the variable getFromClipboard equal to whatever data is in the Clipboard.

We then use the line MsgBox (getFromClipboard & " jumped over the lazy dog") to create a Message Box that contains the text of the variable getFromClipboard which has become populated with data from the Clipboard, with some extra text thrown in to complete the well-known phrase.

The second part of this script is where we work with the Long variables.

Pay close attention to the line Clipboard CStr(sendToClipboardTwo) as it includes the extra function *CStr*. This is needed as the *Clipboard* function cannot work directly with Long or Integer variables and as a result we need to perform the *CStr* function on the variable sendToClipboardTwo to convert its value to a string and therefore enable the *Clipboard* statement to work.

The line getFromClipboardTwo = Clipboard makes the value of the variable getFromClipboardTwo equal to whatever data is in the Clipboard.

The line getFromClipboardTwo = getFromClipboardTwo * 2 makes the value of the variable getFromClipboardTwo equal to its new value retrieved from the Clipboard times two. In other words, the value of the variable getFromClipboardTwo is doubled.

We then use the line MsgBox ("The new doubled value is " & CStr(getFromClipboardTwo)) to create a Message Box that contains the text of the variable getFromClipboardTwo which has become populated with data from the Clipboard that has been multiplied by 2. In this instance I have included the *CStr* function for consistency rather than necessity.

The Clipboard function only works with strings of text, therefore when using Long or Integer variables within your script, you will need to convert its value to a string by using the CStr function.

Refer to:

Chapter 8: CStr Function, MsgBox Function

CLng Function

In situations where you want to perform mathematical calculations on the values of your variables, Dragon may or may not make this possible; as depending on the variable type (Integer, Long, String etc.) you are working with, errors may occur.

The *CLng* function (CLng(variable)) is used to convert the value of a variable to a type **Integer** which then enables us to perform calculations on the variable.

The macro below includes various lines of code that demonstrate where the use of the *Clng* function may be necessary to enable calculations with different variable types. Notice the variable types that have been set up and experiment by un-commenting the lines. A Message Box is used to reveal the results.

MyCommand Name: example convert variables one

Description: Example of using the CLng function

Group: Dragon - A Step Further_Chapter_08

Availability: Global

Command Type: Advanced Scripting

Content:

```
Sub Main
Dim no_of_red_apples As Long
Dim no_of_green_apples As String
no_of_red_apples = 20
no_of_green_apples = "55"
'Adding the number of Red & Green apples

total_apples = no_of_red_apples + CLng(no_of_green_apples) 'WORKS
'total_apples = CLng(no_of_green_apples) + CLng(no_of_green_apples) 'WORKS

'total_apples = no_of_red_apples + no_of_red_apples 'WORKS

'total_apples = no_of_red_apples + no_of_green_apples 'NOT ALLOWED
'total_apples = no_of_green_apples + no_of_green_apples 'DOES NOT WORK

MsgBox ("The total number of apples = " & total_apples)
End Sub
```

Try it by saying:

"example convert variables one" or in the **MyCommands Editor window**, click on the **"Start/Resume" icon (F5)**

CStr Function

In situations where you want the values of your variables to be typed out in a word processing application, Dragon may or may not make this possible; as depending on the variable type (Integer, Long, String etc.) you are working with, errors may occur.

The *CStr* function (`CStr(variable)`) is used to convert the value of a variable to a type **String** which then enables us to use the *SendKeys, SendDragonKeys and SendSystemKeys* commands to type out results.

The macro below includes various lines of code that demonstrate where the use of the *CStr* function may be necessary to enable the *SendKeys* command to work with different variable types. Notice the variable types that have been set up and experiment by un-commenting the *Sendkeys* lines.

MyCommand Name: example convert variables two

Description: Example of using the CStr function

Group: Dragon - A Step Further_Chapter_08

Availability: Global

Command Type: Advanced Scripting

Content:

```
Sub Main
Dim no_of_red_apples As Integer
Dim no_of_green_apples As String
Dim total_apples As Long
no_of_red_apples = 20
no_of_green_apples = "55"

'Adding the number of Red & Green apples
total_apples = no_of_red_apples + CLng(no_of_green_apples)

SendKeys (CStr(total_apples)) 'WORKS
'SendKeys total_apples 'NOT ALLOWED

'SendKeys (CStr(no_of_red_apples)) 'WORKS
'SendKeys no_of_red_apples 'NOT ALLOWED

'SendKeys no_of_green_apples 'WORKS

'SendDragonKeys no_of_green_apples 'WORKS
'SendDragonKeys no_of_red_apples 'NOT ALLOWED

End Sub
```

Open a word processing application and try it by saying:

"example convert variables two" or in the **MyCommands Editor window**, click on the **"Start/Resume" icon (F5)**

Refer to:

Chapter 8: MsgBox Function, SendDragonKeys, SendKeys & SendSystemKeys

Do While Loop

The *Do While Loop* is used in situations where we want to repeat a group of statements/instructions as long as a specific condition is true. The condition may be checked at the beginning of the loop or at the end of the loop.

The script below demonstrates how we can use a *Do While Loop* to produce a set number of Message Boxes:

```
Sub Main
Dim counter As Integer
counter = 0
   Do While counter < 5
      counter = counter + 1
      MsgBox ("This is Message Box number: " & counter, 4096)
   Loop
  MsgBox("Finished, out of loop")
End Sub
```

In the first part of the script we create a variable called counter and assign to it a value of 0

The line Do While counter < 5 is the start of the loop and is the line that controls whether the loop will repeatedly loop all the statements between the line Do While counter < 5 and the line Loop.

Basically, the loop will check the value of the variable counter and if its value is less than 5, then it will carry out the statements within the loop.

To stop this loop from repeating forever, the line counter = counter + 1 increments the value of the variable counter each time the loop is repeated. Therefore, at some point the value of the variable counter will reach 5 and it is at this point that the loop ends, and Dragon will move out of the loop and on to the next line in the script, which is: MsgBox("Finished, out of loop").

 If we set the initial value of the variable counter **to 6 or above, then the statements within the loop would not run at all.**

Exit Sub

By including the *Exit Sub* function within a script, the script will stop and end at that point regardless of any further lines of code. When debugging your scripts, it can serve as a valuable tool to highlight where your script might be going wrong.

Notice that in the Dragon script below, the Message Box containing the words "All Done" will not show as the script is forced to end before it reaches that line of code.

```
Sub Main
  MsgBox("Message Box 1", 64, "Warning")
  MsgBox("Message Box 2", 64, "Warning")
  Exit Sub
  MsgBox("All Done", 64, "Warning")
End Sub
```

For...Next Loop

The *For...Next Loop* can be used within a script to repeat a group of statements a specific number of times.

A *For...Next Loop* will loop (*x*) times the statements that are placed between the line beginning with For and the line Next.

Below is an example of how we can use the *For...Next Loop* to produce six Message Box pop-up windows.

```
Sub Main
  For counter = 1 To 6
    MsgBox ("This is Message Box number " & counter, 4096)
  Next
  MsgBox("Finished, out of loop")
End Sub
```

The line For counter = 1 to 6 is the starting line of the loop. It creates a variable called counter with an initial value of 1.

The line MsgBox ("This is Message Box number " & counter, 4096) is the statement within the *For...Next Loop.*

Each time the script reaches the line Next it will loop back, and the value of the variable counter will be incremented by 1 up to a maximum value of 6.

This when run causes Dragon to produce each of the six pop-up messages in turn, with each containing the number of the pop-up window.

The line For counter = 1 to 6 can be set up in alternative ways to cater to a developer's requirements, below are some examples:

Example 1.
```
Sub Main
  For counter = 2 To 7
    MsgBox ("Value of counter = " & counter, 4096)
  Next
  MsgBox("Finished, out of loop")
End Sub
```

For counter = 2 to 7: This would give the variable counter an initial value of 2 and will increment as expected by 1 each time until its value becomes equal to 7. Therefore, statements within the loop will be carried out 6 times.

Example 2.
```
Sub Main
  For counter = 2 To 10 Step 2
    MsgBox ("Value of counter = " & counter, 4096)
  Next
  MsgBox("Finished, out of loop")
End Sub
```

For counter = 2 to 10 Step 2: This again gives the variable counter an initial value of 2. However, the portion of the script Step 2 means that the variable counter will increment by plus 2 each time, until its value becomes equal to 10. Therefore, in this situation, statements within the loop will be carried out 5 times.

Example 3.

The *For…Next Loop* also allows us to count down.

```
Sub Main
  For myCounter = 75 To 15 Step -15
    MsgBox ("Value of myCounter = " & myCounter, 4096)
  Next
  MsgBox("Finished, out of loop")
End Sub
```

For myCounter = 75 to 15 Step -15: In this case the initial value of the variable myCounter is set to 75 and with each loop the value is reduced by 15 until the variable myCounter becomes equal to 15 and ultimately exits the loop.

 It is not necessary to create the variable that is going to be used in the For…Next Loop beforehand.

HeardWord

The *HeardWord* command makes Dragon behave as though the specified words (which are comma separated and within quotes) have been dictated. Its primary use is to run an existing command from within your script, which can be very useful and a real time-saver for script writers.

You will need to be specific when using the *HeardWord* command, especially when it comes to upper and lower case of the words being used. As a rule, you will generally use lowercase for the words of existing built-in commands. When it comes to custom commands that you have created, make sure your capitalisation matches the name of your custom command and ensure you separate the words.

In instances where the *HeardWord* command is not being recognized, you can check for the exact spelling and capitalisation by dictating the intended command directly and then checking the recognition history.

To view the recognition history, click on the DragonBar >> Tools >> Recognition History...

Below are examples of using the *HeardWord* command in a Dragon script in order to send the microphone to sleep; and where it will, or will not work:

```
Sub Main
  HeardWord "go", "to", "sleep" 'lowercase works
  HeardWord "Go", "To", "Sleep" 'caps do not work
End Sub
```

The command below demonstrates that for the *HeardWord* command to execute, the microphone must be in the ON state. This is why we do not see the word "after" typed out.

MyCommand Name: example heard word script

Description: Example of a script using the HeardWord command

Group: Dragon - A Step Further_Chapter_08

Availability: Global

Command Type: Advanced Scripting

Content:

```
Sub Main
  'Try this in your word processing software
  HeardWord "before" 'works and types out the word "before"
  HeardWord "go", "to", "sleep"
  HeardWord "after" 'will not work, nothing is typed out
End Sub
```

Open a word processing application and try it by saying:
"example heard word script"

The microphone must be in the ON state for the HeardWord command to work.

The HeardWord command cannot be used to write out a sentence. For example, HeardWord "Hello how are you" will not work. The SendKeys command should be used instead.

The commands below demonstrate various examples of the *HeardWord* command in use. Open a word processing application and give them a try.

Remember the microphone must be in the ON state and I would also suggest using the "New Copy" option by right-clicking on an existing command in the Command Browser - MyCommands window to quickly create a new command (Ctrl+Shift+C).

Example 1.

```
Sub Main
   'Try this in your word processing software
   HeardWord "Here is some dummy text"
   HeardWord "select", "all"
   HeardWord "set", "font", "bold"
End Sub
```

Example 2.

```
Sub Main
   'Try this in your word processing software
   HeardWord "London"
   HeardWord "new", "line"
   HeardWord "after"
End Sub
```

Refer to:

Chapter 8: SendDragonKeys, SendKeys & SendSystemKeys

If Then Statement

The *If Then* statement is a decision-making statement that we can use when we want to control the execution flow of a script. It is made up of a Boolean expression followed by one or more statements and basically works by testing if the condition between the lines If Then and End If is true or false and will do one of two things:

- If the condition is True, then the statements within the *If* condition(s) are executed (the statements between the lines If Then and End If).
- If the condition is False, then the statements after the End If statement are executed.

In the example script below, we use the *If Then* statement to check which of the two variables (a or b) are largest in value.

```
Sub Main
   Dim a As Integer
   Dim b As Integer
   a = 234
   b = 32
   If a > b Then
      MsgBox ("a is Greater than b")
   End If
End Sub
```

An alternative to using the *If Then* statement is to use the *If Then Else* statement. We can expand on the previous script by incorporating an *Else* statement, the following script demonstrates this:

```
Sub Main
   Dim a As Integer
   Dim b As Integer
   a = 234
   b = 32
   If a > b Then
      MsgBox ("a is Greater than b")
  Else
    MsgBox ("a is Lower than b")
   End If
End Sub
```

Further use of the *If Then* statement can also include using the *ElseIf* statement. We could have written the previous script in the following way:

```
Sub Main
   Dim a As Integer
   Dim b As Integer
   a = 234
   b = 32
   If a > b Then
      MsgBox ("a is Greater than b")
   ElseIf a < b Then
      MsgBox ("a is Lower than b")
   End If
End Sub
```

 You can have an If or ElseIf statement inside another If or ElseIf statement(s). The inner If statements are executed based on the outermost If statements. These are referred to as Nested If statements.

InputBox Function

The *InputBox* function is used to make simple Input Boxes that offers a means of allowing a user to input a value or string of text. Figure 8-1 shows an example of a generated Input Box.

Once the user has pressed the OK button the value becomes assigned to a variable and we can take that value/variable and work with it in a script.

An *InputBox* function can be broken up into the following parameters:

```
InputBox(prompt[,title][,default][,Xpos,Ypos])
```

Figure 8-1

An example Input Box.

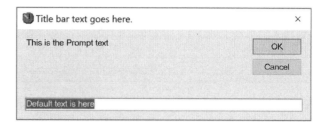

The **prompt** contains a string expression which is displayed as the message in the Input Box. The string is surrounded by quotes (") and is the only required parameter when creating Input Boxes.

The **title** parameter is optional and can contain a string expression surrounded by quotes ("). The string will be displayed in the title bar of the Input Box.

The **default** parameter is optional and can contain a string expression surrounded by quotes ("). This parameter can be used to insert a default value within the Input Box. If left blank, then no message will be displayed.

The **Xpos, Ypos** parameters are optional and can be used to place the Input Box in a specific position on the screen. The values inserted will be the position of the left edge of the Input Box. If left blank, the Input Box will be positioned in the center of the screen.

Below is a simple example of where we ask a user their name and then the name will become part of a welcome message within a Message Box:

```
Sub Main
returnedValue = InputBox("Enter your name:")
MsgBox ("Hello " & returnedValue)
End Sub
```

Let's take the *InputBox* function a step further by including calculations and using more than one Input Box within a command.

In the following script, you will see how it's possible to have one Input Box appear after the other; it records the values entered by the user into variables; and then performs a calculation on those variables. A Message Box which contains the result of the calculation will then be displayed:

MyCommand Name: example input box one

Description: Example of using the InputBox command

Group: Dragon - A Step Further_Chapter_08

Availability: Global

Command Type: Advanced Scripting

Content:

```
Sub Main
Dim number_of_red_apples As Long
Dim number_of_green_apples As Long
Dim total_apples As Long

number_of_red_apples = InputBox("Enter number of red apples:")
number_of_green_apples = InputBox("Enter number of green apples:")

total_apples = number_of_red_apples + _
number_of_green_apples

MsgBox ("The total number of apples = " & total_apples)
End Sub
```

Try it by saying:

"example input box one" or in the **MyCommands Editor window**, click on the **"Start/Resume" icon (F5)**

Discuss

In this script, the variables created are of the type Long. Therefore, if a user does not input a numerical value an error will occur. To avoid such errors; you should include the *On Error* instruction within your scripts.

The script below shows how variables can be used to populate, position and define the look of Input Boxes:

MyCommand Name: example input box two

Description: Example of using the InputBox command

Group: Dragon - A Step Further_Chapter_08

Availability: Global

Command Type: Advanced Scripting

Content:

```
Sub Main
Dim promptText as String
Dim titleBarTitle as String
Dim defaultText as String
Dim xCoord as Long
Dim yCoord as long
PromptText = "How many moons orbit Earth?"
titleBarTitle =  "Your title bar text goes here."
defaultText = "Insert a number"
xCoord = 0
yCoord = 0
returnedValue = InputBox(promptText, titleBarTitle, _
DefaultText, xCoord,yCoord)
'Check if returned value is equal to the correct answer
If returnedValue = "1" Then MsgBox ("WELL DONE")
'Check if returned value does not equal (<>) the correct answer
If returnedValue <> "1" Then MsgBox ("WRONG ANSWER")
End Sub
```

Try it by saying:

"example input box two" or in the **MyCommands Editor window**, click on the **"Start/Resume" icon (F5)**

 When incorporating the InputBox function into your Advanced scripts, you may find that when run, the Input Box does not appear on top of other applications. As an alternative, a Dialog Form can be created and styled in the form of an Input Box. It would contain a TextBox field and you will have the ability to set the focus on the TextBox when the macro is run. I have found this works fine.

Refer to:

Chapter 5: Creating a Dialog Form in the style of a simple Input Box

Chapter 8: On Error Instruction

InStr Function

The *InStr* function is used to return (tell us) the position of the first occurrence of a specific character in a string of text.

The *InStr* function can be broken up into the following parameters:

InStr (string1,string2)

The **string1** parameter is required and is the string that is to be searched. If text is placed here, you will need to surround it in quotes (") - No quotes are placed if it is a variable.

The **string2** parameter is required and is the character/string that we are searching for. If text is placed here, you will need to surround it in quotes (") - No quotes are placed if it is a variable.

The script below shows several examples of how we can use the *InStr* command in a Dragon Script. Uncomment them (remove the apostrophes) one by one to see the results:

MyCommand Name: example in string function

Description: Example of using the InStr command

Group: Dragon - A Step Further_Chapter_08

Availability: Global

Command Type: Advanced Scripting

Content:

```
Sub Main
    Dim text_variable As String
    Dim start_pos As Long
    Dim char_to_find As String
    text_variable = "Have a nice\fun day"
    char_to_find = "\"
```

```
    'result = InStr ("text to check @*/£","@") 'Example 1
    'result = InStr ("text to check @*/£","#") 'Example 2
    'Using variables with InStr
    result = InStr (text_variable,char_to_find) 'Example 3
    MsgBox (result)
End Sub
```

Try it by saying:

"example in string function" or in the **MyCommands Editor window**, click on the **"Start/Resume" icon (F5)**

Example 1.

The variable result becomes equal to **15** as the character @ is the 15th character in the string of text.

Example 2.

The variable result becomes equal to **0** as the character # is not within the string of text we are searching.

Example 3.

Here we use created variables to populate the *InStr* parameters. The variable result becomes equal to **12** as the character \ (value of char_to_find variable) is the 12th character in the string of text (value of text_variable variable).

 Spaces are included when counting character positions.

 If the character we are searching for does not exist in the text then the value zero (0) is returned.

 When working with Dragon Written\Spoken words Lists, the InStr command plays an important role in analysing the contents of Written\Spoken words Lists and ultimately enables us to reveal and work with the written portions of the Lists.

Refer to:

Chapter 4: Dragon Written\Spoken words List

LBound and UBound Functions

The *LBound* function is used to return the lowest index for an Array variable.

The *UBound* function does the opposite in that it will return the highest index for an Array variable.

The following script shows examples of how we can use the *LBound* & *UBound* functions in a Dragon Script:

```
Sub Main
Dim myArray01$(4)
myArray02 = Array(9,2,5,8,5,67,2)
lowest01 = LBound(myArray01)
highest01 = UBound(myArray01)
lowest02 = LBound(myArray02)
highest02 = UBound(myArray02)
MsgBox ("myArray01:" & _
Chr$(13) & "Lowest index = " & lowest01 & _
Chr$(13) & "Highest index = " & highest01 & _
Chr$(13) & Chr$(13) & _
Chr$(13) & "myArray02:" & _
Chr$(13) & "Lowest index = " & lowest02 & _
Chr$(13) & "Highest index = " & highest02)
End Sub
```

In order to make the *MsgBox* command more readable, a continuation character "_" is used at the end of each line apart from the last.

Refer to:

Chapter 8: Arrays, MsgBox Function

LCase and UCase Functions

The *LCase* function is used to return a lowercase version of the string held in a variable or string of text.

The *UCase* function does the opposite in that it will return an uppercase version of the string held in a variable or string of text.

The script below shows several examples of how we can use the *UCase* & *LCase* functions in a Dragon Script. Un-comment them (remove the apostrophes) one by one to see the results:

MyCommand Name: example upper and lower case functions

Description: Examples of using the UCase and LCase functions

Group: Dragon - A Step Further_Chapter_08

Availability: Global

Command Type: Advanced Scripting

Content:

```
Sub Main
  Dim text_string As String
  text_string = "HELLO how are YOU?"

  result = UCase ("CAPITAL letters")          'CAPITAL LETTERS
  'result = UCase ("Item-ID: 212")            'ITEM-ID: 212
  'result = LCase ("CAPITAL letters")         'capital letters
  'result = LCase ("Item-ID: 212")            'item-id: 212
```

```
'Using variables with the LCase & UCase functions

  'result = LCase (text_string) 'hello how are you?
  'result = UCase (text_string) 'HELLO HOW ARE YOU?

MsgBox (result)
End Sub
```

Try it by saying:

"example upper and lower case functions" or in the **MyCommands Editor window**, click on the **"Start/Resume" icon (F5)**

Mid Function

The *Mid* function is used to return (tell us) the string of characters from the start to end position in a string of text. The end position is determined by the number of characters from the start position.

The *Mid* function can be broken up into the following parameters:

```
MID( string, start_position, number_of_characters )
```

The **string** parameter is required and is the string that is to be searched. If text is placed here, you will need to surround it in quotes (") - No quotes are placed if it is a variable.

The **start_position** parameter refers to the starting position of the search to be carried out on the variable **string**. By default, the search will begin at character position 1.

The **number_of_characters** parameter is an optional numerical value. It determines the number of characters from the **start_position** that will be returned. If this parameter is omitted, then the characters returned will be from the **start_position** to the end of the text within the variable **string**.

The script below shows several examples of how we can use the *Mid* command in a Dragon Script. Un-comment them (remove the apostrophes) one by one to see the results:

MyCommand Name: example mid string function

Description: Example of using the Mid command

Group: Dragon - A Step Further_Chapter_08

Availability: Global

Command Type: Advanced Scripting

Content:

```
Sub Main
  Dim text_variable As String
  Dim start_pos As Long
  Dim no_of_characters As Long
```

```
    text_variable = "Welcome to my home"
    start_pos = 2
    no_of_characters = 2
    'result = Mid ("How are you today",5) 'Example 1
    'result = Mid ("How are you today",12) 'Example 2
    'result = Mid ("How are you today",9,3) 'Example 3
    'Using variables with Mid
'result = Mid (text_variable,start_pos,no_of_characters) 'Example 4
MsgBox (result)
End Sub
```

Try it by saying:

"example Mid String function" or in the **MyCommands Editor window**, click on the **"Start/Resume" icon (F5)**

Example 1.

The variable result becomes equal to the string of text "**are you today**" as the *Mid* command returns all characters from the 5th position in the string of text examined.

Example 2.

The variable result becomes equal to "**today**" as the *Mid* command returns all characters from the 12th position in the string of text examined.

Example 3.

The variable result becomes equal to "**you**" as the *Mid* command returns the next three (3) characters from the 9th position in the string of text examined.

Example 4.

Here we use created variables to populate the *Mid* parameters. The variable result becomes equal to "**to my**" as the *Mid* command returns the next 2 characters (value of no_of_characters variable) from the 2nd position (value of start_pos variable) in the string of text examined.

 Spaces are included when counting character positions.

MouseGrid Function

The *MouseGrid* function can be used within your scripts to emulate the built-in dictated MouseGrid command. This can be useful where you want to write a macro that positions the mouse pointer at a specific point on the screen or within an active window, as shown in Figure 8-2.

Figure 8-2

The MouseGrid as shown within an active window.

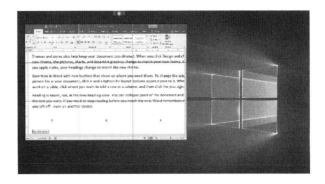

The *MouseGrid* function requires two parameters.

```
MouseGrid [state[,gridbox]]
```

The **state** parameter determines whether the *MouseGrid*, when revealed, will either be sized to fill the whole screen, the active window or be used to turn off the *MouseGrid*. This is determined by the values:

Value	Description
1	Opens the MouseGrid relative to the screen size
2	Opens the MouseGrid relative to the active window
0	Turns the MouseGrid off

The **gridbox** parameter determines the numbered (1-9) area of the screen, window or open MouseGrid to which the MouseGrid will be sized.

 The gridbox parameter can be set to the value 0, this will undo the last MouseGrid action.

The command below is an example of how variables can also be used with the *MouseGrid* function within a script:

MyCommand Name: example mouse grid function

Description: Example of using the MouseGrid function

Group: Dragon - A Step Further_Chapter_08

Availability: Global

Command Type: Advanced Scripting

Content:

```
Sub Main
Dim stateValue As Integer
'StateValue = 1: Opens MouseGrid relative to the screen
```

```
'StateValue = 2: Opens MouseGrid relative to the active window

stateValue = 1 'Change the value to 1 or 2

    MouseGrid stateValue,1
    Wait 2
    MouseGrid stateValue,5
    Wait 2
    MouseGrid stateValue,0 'Undoes the last MouseGrid action
    Wait 2
    MouseGrid 0 'Closes the MouseGrid

End Sub
```

Set the variable stateValue to either 1 or 2 and try it by saying:

"example mouse grid function"

 When using the MouseGrid function in your scripts, make sure the intended window is maximised before executing the function.

Refer to:

Chapter 8: ButtonClick Command, Wait

On Error Instruction

There will probably be times where you have created a specific type of variable in anticipation that the user will input data of the same type. In such an instance, if the user makes a mistake, for example, inputting words where a numerical value is expected, Dragon will produce an error.

The *On Error* instruction enables us to do something whenever an error occurs while our code is being run. This will in turn prevent users of your scripts from having the pleasure of looking at a scary error code as can be seen in Figure 8-3.

Figure 8-3

Dragon produces a pop-up window with an error message when something is wrong with your script.

Use the message to help you identify the potential line of code causing the problem.

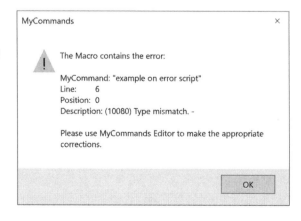

The following script uses an Input Box to show how, even though we think we have accounted for all possibilities, we haven't! As the script stands, it checks to see whether the variable ans is equal to the numerical value 3 or not and displays a Message Box accordingly. However, if the user types in the word "three", Dragon will produce an error code pop-up window. This occurs because we defined the variable ans as the type "Long"; so therefore, Dragon is expecting and will only allow a numerical value to be inserted. Hence the error code!

MyCommand Name: example on error script

Description: Shows On Error command in action

Group: Dragon - A Step Further_Chapter_08

Availability: Global

Command Type: Advanced Scripting

Content:

```
Sub Main
Dim Name As String
Dim ans As Long
'On Error GoTo X
ans = InputBox("How many sides are there in a triangle?")
'Check if the variable "ans" is equal to 3
If ans = 3 Then MsgBox ("WELL DONE")
'Check if the variable "ans" does not equal (<>) 3
If ans  <> 3 Then MsgBox ("WRONG ANSWER")
'X: MsgBox ("Only numerals please", 4096)
End Sub
```

Open a word processing application and try it by saying:
"example on error script"

Test the script by entering a numerical value, and then try it by entering a value in words.

Discuss

This is an easy oversight that programmers can make with their code. Thankfully, the *On Error* instruction comes in handy and prevents users encountering such errors. The *On Error* instruction can also be used within a script to check that your code is working as you want it to.

To prevent the unsightly error message from appearing, un-comment (remove the apostrophe) the lines 'On Error GoTo X and 'X: MsgBox ("Only numerals please"). Now run the same script again and type in the word "three". Voila! No unsightly error code pop-up window.

The line On Error GoTo X must be placed before the line ans = InputBox("How many sides are there in a triangle?") (displays the Input Box), which tells Dragon that if at any time there is an error, go to the line X: MsgBox ("Only numerals please") and produce a Message Box with the message "Only numerals please". This line is deliberately placed at the end of the script so that no other actions within the script will run if an error occurs.

PlaySound

The *PlaySound* command enables us to play an internal or external audio/sound file while our script is running.

When I refer to internal audio, I mean the audio files that come with your Windows operating system. The most common can be found in the directory "C:\Windows\Media\" and includes such files as Windows Logon.wav and Chimes.wav. An example of using an internal file would be the following:

```
Sub Main
  PlaySound "C:\Windows\Media\Windows Notify.wav"
End Sub
```

When referring to external audio files, I mean the audio that you may have made yourself, imported or been given. When working with such audio, it is important that you record the directory path and folder where the file is stored. It is this path and the filename that will be used to make the *PlaySound* command work. Below is an example:

```
Sub Main
  PlaySound "C:\...Path..to..file\myAudio.wav"
End Sub
```

According to documentation I have read, the *PlaySound* command should pause the script while it plays the audio file and continue to the next line of the script once the audio file has finished playing. This appears to work under some conditions and not under others, the following two examples demonstrate the inconsistencies.

```
Sub Main
  PlaySound "C:\...Path..to..file\audio1.wav"
  PlaySound "C:\...Path..to..file\audio2.wav"
  SendKeys ("Hello, how are you today?")
End Sub
```

In the script above, the audio1.wav will be played and once finished, audio2.wav will start playing and the *SendKeys* message will be revealed before audio2.wav has finished playing.

```
Sub Main
  PlaySound "C:\...Path..to..file\audio1.wav"
  SendKeys ("Hello, how are you today?")
  PlaySound "C:\...Path..to..file\audio2.wav"
End Sub
```

In the script above, the audio1.wav will start playing and the *SendKeys* message will be revealed before the audio1.wav has finished playing. Once audio1.wav has finished playing, audio2.wav will then start playing.

Overall, when you write any scripts that include the *PlaySound* command, make sure you check and double check that the flow of your script is working in the way you require.

While the audio is playing the PlaySound command turns the microphone off and then returns the microphone back to its previous state once the audio has finished playing.

 PlaySound only plays audio files of .wav format.

Refer to:

Chapter 8: SendDragonKeys, SendKeys & SendSystemKeys

PromptValue Function

The *PromptValue* function is an alternative method for gathering a user's choice. When run, it will display a Prompt Box containing a list of values from which the user can select one of the options either by voice or with the mouse.

The parameters are as follows:

```
EngineControl.PromptValue( Values, Description, Xpos, Ypos )
```

The **Values** is the Array of values that will be displayed to the user.

The **Description** parameter contains a string expression surrounded by quotes which is what will be displayed in the title bar of the Prompt Box.

The **Xpos, Ypos** parameters are optional and can be used to place the Prompt Box in a specific position on the screen. The values inserted will be the position of the left edge of the Prompt Box. If left blank, Dragon will self-determine the most appropriate positioning of the Prompt Box.

Below is an example of how the Prompt Box is created and how we use a variable to record the user's choice:

MyCommand Name: produce my prompt box

Description: Produces a Prompt Box

Group: Dragon - A Step Further_Chapter_08

Availability: Global

Command Type: Advanced Scripting

Content:

```
Sub Main
'We create an array that will hold all the values/options
Dim Values(7) As String
 Values (0) = "Spanish"
 Values (1) = "French"
```

```
 Values (2) = "English"
 Values (3) = "German"
SetState "" 'We set the state to null before displaying the prompt box
Dim x As Long
Dim y As Long
x = 500 'used to position the prompt box
y = 200 'used to position the prompt box
Dim userChoice As String 'The string variable that will hold the user choice
userChoice  = EngineControl.PromptValue (Values(), "Select your preferred language", x,
y) 'Produces the prompt box popup, ready for the user response
MsgBox("The item selected = " & userChoice,4096)
End Sub
```

Try it by saying:

"produce my prompt box" or in the **MyCommands Editor window**, click on the **"Start/Resume" icon (F5)**

 PromptValue returns a string and populates the variable userChoice **with the value chosen by the user. If the Prompt Box is closed or dismissed without making a choice, the variable** userChoice **will be empty.**

Refer to:

Chapter 8: Arrays, MsgBox Function

Select Case Statement

The *Select Case* statement is used to test the contents/value of a variable and perform an action accordingly. It is often used when you know there are only a limited number of values that a variable could be equal to. In addition, it is sometimes used as a substitute for the *If Then* statement.

Below is an example of using the *Select Case* statement within a script:

MyCommand Name: example select case statement

Description: Example of using the Select Case Statement

Group: Dragon - A Step Further_Chapter_08

Availability: Global

Command Type: Advanced Scripting

Content:

```
Sub Main
userInput = InputBox("Enter in caps Mercury, Jupiter or Saturn:")
  Select Case (userInput)
    Case "MERCURY"
    MsgBox ("Mercury is the closest planet to the sun.")
    Case "Jupiter"
    MsgBox ("Jupiter, the largest of the planets")
    Case "SATURN"
    MsgBox ("Saturn is famous for its rings.")
```

```
      Case Else
      MsgBox ("Pardon?")
   End Select
End Sub
```

Try it by saying:

"example select case statement" or in the **MyCommands Editor window**, click on the **"Start/Resume" icon (F5)**

In the first part of the script we use an Input Box to gather an entry from a user and populate the variable `userInput` with the inputted text.

The line `Select Case userInput` is the start of the *Select Case* statement and tells Dragon that we wish to set up a *Select Case* statement to test what is inside the variable called `userInput`.

The line `Case "MERCURY"` is where we check if the variable `userInput` is equal to the word "MERCURY" (case sensitive). In other words, is it the case that ...?

If it is the case that the variable `userInput` is equal to the word "MERCURY", then Dragon will move to the next line of code `MsgBox ("Mercury is the closest planet to the sun.")` and performs the action of creating a Message Box with the appropriate message.

If the variable `userInput` is **not** equal to the word "MERCURY", then Dragon will skip the line or lines of code below and jump to the next *Case* (`Case "JUPITER"`).

The script continues to check whether all the words after each *Case* are equal to the variable `userInput`. If it finds one, it will carry out the code below the *Case* word; if it doesn't find any matches, it will do nothing!

The line `Case Else` is used as our safety net, in that, if any of the *Case* statements are not matched, it will then execute the code below the line `Case Else`, in which case the statement `MsgBox ("Pardon?")` will be carried out.

The line `End Select` ends the *Select Case* statement.

 When using Case "string...", bear in mind that it will only look for an exact match ("Mercury" is not the same as "MERCURY"). Therefore, if you are working with user inputs, I would suggest using the UCase or LCase functions on the inputted text. Changing the line `Select Case userInput` **to** `Select Case UCase(userInput)` **would cater for lower or uppercase user entries.**

SetMicrophone

The *SetMicrophone* function can be used within your script to turn the microphone On or Off while the command is running. In situations where you have created a script that takes a significant amount of time to execute or is running in the background of a word processing application, you might want to turn off the microphone so that it does not pick up on any unintentional heard words.

The following script demonstrates how we can use the *SetMicrophone* function:

```
Sub Main
  SetMicrophone 0
  Wait 5 ' wait for 5 seconds
  SetMicrophone 1
  Wait 5 ' wait for 5 seconds
  SetMicrophone
End Sub
```

The *SetMicrophone* function can be used in three ways as described by the script lines below:

SetMicrophone 0: Turns off the microphone.

SetMicrophone 1: Turns on the microphone.

SetMicrophone: The microphone is switched from its current state to the opposite state (no value is specified).

SetRecognitionMode

The *SetRecognitionMode* command is used to change Dragon into one of its five dictation modes. To use the command within an Advanced script, it is written in the following format:

```
ExecuteScript "SetRecognitionMode mode",0
```

The parameter mode can have a value of between 0 to 4, where:

0 = Normal Mode (can speak commands and dictation)

1 = Dictation Mode (dictation only, with a few available commands)

2 = Command Mode (dictate commands only)

3 = Numbers Mode (dictate numbers only, only numerals will be typed out)

4 = Spell Mode (dictate characters only, only characters will be typed out)

The *SetRecognitionMode* command can be handy in situations where you might want a user to interact with your script in a specific way. For example, you might want a script that produces an *InputBox* and you want the user to only dictate characters (e.g. a student membership number).

In this type of scenario, turning Dragon into Spell mode would prevent Dragon from interpreting what the user dictates as words.

The following example script shows how we can use the *SetRecognitionMode* command:

```
Sub Main
ExecuteScript "SetRecognitionMode 4", 0
returnedValue = InputBox("Enter your student number:")
ExecuteScript "SetRecognitionMode 0", 0
MsgBox ("Your student number " & returnedValue)
End Sub
```

The line ExecuteScript "SetRecognitionMode 4", 0 is where we turn Dragon into Spell Mode.

We then use the InputBox statement to prompt a user for a response.

The line ExecuteScript "SetRecognitionMode 0", 0 is where we revert back to Normal mode.

The *MsgBox* function is then used to reveal the dictated characters.

 When changing the dictation mode, it is advisable to turn the mode back to Normal after your set of statements has been carried out.

ShellExecute

The *ShellExecute* statement enables us to run another application from within an Advanced script. If the application is already running, it will open a new instance of the application. It can also be used to open a specific file/document.

Below are examples of how the *ShellExecute* command can be used:

Open the Chrome browser to a specific website page.

```
ShellExecute "commandLine", windowStyle
```

```
Sub Main
ShellExecute "chrome www.dragonspeechtips.com/",3
End Sub
```

In this example chrome www.dragonspeechtips.com/ is the commandLine portion of the script. Dragon knows the application Chrome and by including the URL knows to open it at that specific web page. We could replace chrome with firefox if the Firefox application is installed on the PC.

The ",3" is the parameter to set the windowStyle and determines whether Chrome will either be opened in a minimised, maximised or default window state dependent on the value used.

Some developers prefer to use the VB defined names rather than a numerical value for determining the window state. Table 8-2 lists the VB Defined names and their numerical values.

Table 8-2

VB Defined name	Value	Window state
vbNormalFocus	1	Window has focus and is restored to its original size and position.
vbMinimizedFocus	2	Window is displayed as an icon with focus.
vbMaximizedFocus	3	Window is maximised with focus.

Therefore, changing the line to ShellExecute "chrome www.dragonspeechtips.com/", vbMaximizedFocus would be allowed.

When including the application parameter and where Dragon knows the application, inserting application names such as Chrome will work.

However, with some applications you may need to insert the directory path to the executable file of that application. For example, ShellExecute "C:\Program Files\Mozilla Firefox\firefox.exe http://www.bbc.co.uk/news", 3 could be used to have the browser Firefox open at a specific webpage.

Opening a specific file:

```
ShellExecute "Path\fileName.ext"
```

```
Sub Main
ShellExecute "C:\...Path..to..file\myDoc.docx"
End Sub
```

This example shows how *ShellExecute* is used to open a specific document. Dragon recognises the document type and will then open the default application as determined by a user's system settings.

 The directory path to the file should not contain spaces.

Opening a specific file with a specific application:

```
ShellExecute "application Path\fileName.ext"
```

```
Sub Main
ShellExecute "WordPad C:\...Path..to..file\myDoc.txt"
End Sub
```

By inserting the additional parameter WordPad before the directory path, the document will open in the application WordPad.

Where Dragon does not know the application, we could replace WordPad with a directory path to the executable file of the required application, for example, an alternative would be:

```
ShellExecute "C:\Program Files\Sublime Text 2\sublime_text.exe
C:\...Path..to..file\myDoc.txt"
```

TTSPlayString

The *TTSPlayString* command is what we use to send an instruction to the text-to-speech utility within Dragon.

Imagine a scenario where you want your script, at the end of processing, to get the computer to speak the words "Processing has finished". By using the *TTSPlayString* command we can achieve this and more...

The *TTSPlayString* command consists of one parameter and two optional switches that can be included.

```
TTSPlayString ["text to be read out load" [, "switches"]]
```

A simple version of this command would be the following:

```
TTSPlayString "Processing has finished", "/s80 /l255"
```

The first parameter is the string of text "Processing has finished" which will be the actual text to be read out.

There are two optional types of switches that can also be used within the structure of the command:

The switch /s80 refers to the playback speed at which the text will be read out and can have a numerical value between 0 - 255, where the default value is 127.

The switch /l255 refers to the playback volume relative to the current volume control settings and can have a numerical value between 0 - 255. The default value is 255, which when reading out, will be at the volume equal to the computer's volume setting.

Reading out the contents of the Clipboard.

By inserting two quotes without any text in between ("") instructs the *TTSPlayString* command to read out text that has been copied to the Clipboard. The command would look like this:

```
TTSPlayString "", "/s80 /l255" or TTSPlayString ""
```

String variables can also be used within *TTSPlayString* commands.

 You can stop the output by pressing the Esc key or turning on the microphone.

In the following example, we use an Input Box to ask a user "how many times they took their driving test?". The objective is to get the computer to read out a phrase depending on the answer given.

MyCommand Name: example read string script

Description: Example of a script using the TTSPlayString command

Group: Dragon - A Step Further_Chapter_08

Availability: Global

Command Type: Advanced Scripting

Content:

```
Sub Main
On Error GoTo X
Dim dtest$(4) 'Create Array of phrases
    dtest$(0) = "Don't you think you should get it done?"
    dtest$(1) = "Fantastic, well done!"
    dtest$(2) = "Very good, that is average!"
    dtest$(3) = "Not bad!"
    dtest$(4) = "wow, that is a lot!"
choice = InputBox("How many times did you take your driving test? (0-4 times)")
TTSPlayString dtest$(choice)
Exit Sub
X: TTSPlayString "Sorry, only numbers between zero and four are allowed"
End Sub
```

Try it by saying:

"example read string script" or in the **MyCommands Editor window**, click on the **"Start/Resume" icon (F5)**

Discuss

In the first part of the script we set up and use an *Array* to hold the strings of text that could possibly be read out.

The variable choice becomes equal to the value that the user inserts when prompted by the *Input Box*.

The line TTSPlayString dtest$(choice) uses the value inserted by the user to form part of the *Array* element. In other words, we have already set up that dtest$(0), dtest$(1)... all have their own individual string values. As long as the value of the variable choice is between zero and four, Dragon will be aware of it. We then use the *Array* element as part of the *TTSPlayString* command in order that it reads out the correct text.

The line On Error GoTo X is our way of telling Dragon that if the user inserts a character or an invalid number then go to the line X: TTSPlayString "Sorry, only numbers between zero and four are allowed" in the script. It will then read out the sorry message.

The line Exit Sub is used to stop the script running when a correct value has been chosen and read out. It is specifically placed in the script at this position to stop the flow of the script moving onto the next line of X: TTSPlayString "Sorry,...

When Dragon reaches a line in your script using the TTSPlayString command, it will continue to the next line of the script regardless of it still reading out the text or contents of the Clipboard. Basically, the script does not pause while text or Clipboard content is read out.

If your script has started reading out a TTSPlayString command and it comes across another TTSPlayString command, the first command will stop reading out (even in mid flow) and immediately switch to reading out the second. Dragon cannot read out two TTSPlayString commands at the same time.

Refer to:

Chapter 8: Arrays, Exit Sub, InputBox Function, On Error Instruction

Wait

There are times, especially when working with Advanced Scripts that the speed at which Dragon processes a macro is way too fast for a computer to keep up. An example could be a script that opens an application and sends specific keystrokes to access menus within that application. Now, because of the speed of your computer, the process of opening the application can take a set amount of time and you don't want Dragon to start any keystrokes until the application has fully opened otherwise the script will fail.

This is where the *Wait* function comes in handy, in that it will make a script pause for a set amount of time.

A typical line of code containing the *Wait* command would look like the following:

```
Sub Main
  Wait 5 ' wait for 5 seconds
End Sub
```

The value of 5 is the number of seconds that the script will pause before moving on to the next line of code.

Variables can also be used within a *Wait* instruction. Below, the script demonstrates how we can set the wait time in a variable and then have a Message Box appear after the set amount of time has elapsed:

```
Sub Main
  Dim delayTimeInSeconds as Long
  delayTimeInSeconds = 5
  Wait delayTimeInSeconds
  MsgBox ("You have waited " & delayTimeInSeconds & " seconds.")
End Sub
```

Refer to:

Chapter 8: MsgBox Function

Date and Time Functions

Dragon has many built-in functions which enables us to work with Date and Time within our scripts. These built-in variables allow us to convert Dates and Times from one format into another and display Dates and Times in a specific format to suit our needs.

Let's look at these functions/variables and how we can use them.

The Now, Date & Time Functions

Now – Returns the current system Date and Time (the moment the function is run).

Date – Returns the current system date (the moment the function is run).

Time – Returns the current system time (the moment the function is run).

The script below shows examples of how we can use the *Now, Date & Time* functions on their own as variables, how we can create our own variables (my…) and make them become equal to the values of these functions:

MyCommand Name: example dates and times functions one

Description: Example of using the date and time functions

Group: Dragon - A Step Further_Chapter_08

Availability: Global

Command Type: Advanced Scripting

Content:

```
Sub Main
Dim myNow As Variant
Dim myDate As Variant
Dim myTime As Variant
myNow = Now
myDate = Date
myTime = Time
MsgBox ("Now function produces: " & Now)
MsgBox ("Date function produces: " & Date)
MsgBox ("Time function produces: " & Time)
MsgBox ("The Date and Time is: " & myNow)
MsgBox ("The Date is: " & myDate)
MsgBox ("The Time is: " & myTime)
End Sub
```

More Date and Time Functions

More often than not you will want your displayed Date and Time results to be defined. Table 8-3 lists several *Date* and *Time* functions we can use to achieve this.

Table 8-3

Function	What it returns
Day function	Returns an integer number of between 1 and 31, which represents the day of the specified date.
WeekDay function	Returns an integer number of between 1 and 7, which represents the day of the week for the specified day. 1-Sunday, 2-Monday, 3-Tuesday etc.
Month function	Returns an integer number of between 1 and 12, which represents the month of the specified date.
Year function	Returns an integer number that represents the year of the specified date.
Hour function	Returns an integer between 0 and 23 that represents the hour part of the given time.
Minute function	Returns an integer between 0 and 59 that represents the minutes part of the given time.
Second function	Returns an integer between 0 and 59 that represents the seconds part of the given time.

On their own, these functions do not work, for example, trying to produce a Message Box by the line MsgBox ("The day is: " & Day) will produce an error. In fact, Dragon will not allow you to save the script.

Strings and variables can also be used. The script below shows how these additional functions are used with either a *Date*, *Time* or *Now* function. Experiment with the commented code to view the results:

MyCommand Name: example dates and times functions two

Description: Example of using the date and time functions

Group: Dragon - A Step Further_Chapter_08

Availability: Global

Command Type: Advanced Scripting

Content:

```
Sub Main
Dim myVarString As String
myVarString = "2018-04-25"
MsgBox("Day number: " & Day("2018-05-31"))
'MsgBox("Day number: " & Day(myVarString))
```

```
'MsgBox("Todays day number is: " & Day(Now))
'MsgBox("Todays day of the week number is: " & Weekday(Now))
'MsgBox("Todays month number is: " & Month(Date))
'MsgBox("Todays year number is: " & Year(Date))

'MsgBox ("The current hour is " & Hour(Now))
'MsgBox ("The current minute is " & Minute(Time))
'MsgBox ("The current second is " & Second(Time))
End Sub
```

 If you are using your own created variables with these date functions, create them as String variables, otherwise you may get some odd and undesired results.

Making Date Results More Readable

So far, our results have all been integers/numbers, which is all well and good. But telling someone "Your appointment is on day 4" would be better written as "Your appointment is on Wednesday". We can achieve this by using further functions, as listed in Table 8-4.

Table 8-4

Function	What it returns
WeekDayName function	Returns the weekday name for the specified day.
MonthName function	Returns the name of the month for the specified date.

The script below shows how we can use the *WeekDayName* and *MonthName* functions:

MyCommand Name: example dates and times functions three

Description: Example of using the date and time functions

Group: Dragon - A Step Further_Chapter_08

Availability: Global

Command Type: Advanced Scripting

Content:

```
Sub Main
Dim myVarInteger As Integer
myVarInteger = 5
MsgBox("Day 1 is a: " & WeekDayName (1))
MsgBox("Day 5 is a: " & WeekDayName (myVarInteger))
MsgBox("Today is a: " & WeekdayName(Weekday(Now)))
MsgBox("Month 1 is: " & MonthName (1))
MsgBox("Month 5 is: " & MonthName (myVarInteger))
MsgBox("This is the month of: " & MonthName(Month(Now)))
End Sub
```

When using variables with the WeekDayName and MonthName functions, use Integer variables.

The WeekDayName and MonthName functions will not work directly with the Now function, you will need to include the WeekDay and Month functions as part of the line of code.

Performing Calculations on Dates

There may be times when you will want to perform calculations on your Dates. For example, writing a letter or report where you are required to insert the correct date(s) in the future.

The script below demonstrates how we can carry out calculations on Dates. Un-comment the lines of code (remove the apostrophes) one at a time to see the results:

MyCommand Name: example dates and times functions four

Description: Examples of performing calculation with date and time functions

Group: Dragon - A Step Further_Chapter_08

Availability: Global

Command Type: Advanced Scripting

Content:

```
Sub Main
Dim yesterday As Date
Dim futureDate As Date
Dim toDay As Date
Dim numberOfDays As Integer
toDay = Now
numberOfDays = 5
numberOfDays02 = 60
futureDate = Now +(numberOfDays)
yesterday = Now - 1
MsgBox ("The date and time 5 days in the future is: " & futureDate)
'MsgBox ("The date 5 days in the future is: " & Date + numberOfDays)
'MsgBox ("The week day in 5 days is: " & WeekdayName(Weekday(futureDate)))
'MsgBox ("It was " & WeekdayName(Weekday(Now - 1)) & " yesterday.")
'MsgBox ("It was " & WeekdayName(Weekday(yesterday)) & " yesterday.")
'MsgBox ("It will be " & MonthName(Month(Now + numberOfDays02)) & " in " &
numberOfDays02 & " days time.")
End Sub
```

In situations where calculations with your variables does not work, check if your code needs either the CStr or CLng functions in order to convert the variables to the correct type.

Changing the Display Format of Date & Time

It is the *Format* function which enables us to change the format or style of our Date and Time results. For some it may be necessary to have the dates typed out in UK or US formats, short dates or long date versions dependent on the end user's requirements.

The *Format* function consists of two parameters which are enclosed within parentheses. The first parameter is the Date and Time, usually obtained using the *Now* Function. The second parameter is the desired format constant.

The *Format* function can be used with the *MsgBox* function or *Send...Keys* functions (in order that results can be typed out in a word processing application).

The following script shows examples of how we can determine how the dates and times will be displayed. Uncomment them (remove the apostrophes) one at a time to see the results:

MyCommand Name: example dates and times functions five

Description: Examples of styling dates and times

Group: Dragon - A Step Further_Chapter_08

Availability: Global

Command Type: Advanced Scripting

Content:

```
Sub Main
myDateTime = "2018-05-02 20:25" 'US format for date
'MsgBox (Format(myDateTime, "dddd, mmmm d yyyy"))
'MsgBox (Format(myDateTime, "dd-mm-yyyy")) 'UK version
'MsgBox (Format(myDateTime, "hh:mm:ss AM/PM"))
'MsgBox (Format(Now, "mmm, d/yyyy"))
'MsgBox ("Todays date is " & (Format(Now, "dddd, mmmm d yyyy ""and the time is""
h:mmAM/PM")))
'SendKeys "Your appointment is set for " & (Format(myDateTime, "dddd, mmmm d yyyy"))
'SendDragonKeys "Your appointment is set for " & (Format(myDateTime, "dddd mmmm d, yyyy
""at the time of"" h:mmAM/PM " ))
'SendKeys (Format(myDateTime, "hh:mm:ss am/pm"))
'SendKeys "the time is now " & (Format(Now, "hh:mm:ss AM/PM"))
'SendKeys "the time is " & (Format(Now, "hh:mm")) & " you are late."
End Sub
```

The most useful Format constants are listed in Table 8-5.

Overview of formatting dates

- By default, Dragon works with dates in the US format. Therefore, it is important that when working with or manipulating dates you are aware of this and act accordingly to your requirements. For example, there is a distinct difference between having a parcel delivered on "2018-05-02" and "2018-02-05".
- Sometimes you will need to use double quotes to surround additional text within a line of code if you require your output to be in a more readable style.
- Characters such as hyphens, underscores, colons and slashes will be displayed when used in the Format function.
- The strings produced are dependent upon the regional settings of the end user's Windows operating system. A French user would see "Mai" instead of "May" as the 5th month of the year.

Table of Date and Time Formatting Styles

Table 8-5

Formatting Styles available		
Format Constants	**Description**	**Example, Date and Time: 2018-09-17 15:06:23 Outcome**
d	day of month with no leading 0	17
dd	two-digit day of month	17
ddd	abbreviated day of week (e.g. "Fri" for Friday)	Tue
dddd	day of week (e.g. "Saturday")	Tuesday
ddddd	date expressed "m/d/yyyy"	17/09/2018
dddddd	date expressed "dd mmmm yyyy"	17 September 2018
m	The number of the month with no leading zeros (e.g. "5" for May)	9
mm	two-digit number of month (e.g. "05" for May)	09
mmm	three-character abbreviated name of month	Sep
mmmm	name of month	September
yy	two-digit year	18

Formatting Styles available (cont'd)		
Format Constants	**Description**	**Example, Date and Time: 2018-09-17 15:06:23 Outcome**
yyyy	four-digit year	2018
h	hour of day, no leading 0	15
hh	two-digit hour of day	15
ham/pm	am or pm, changes the format for hour to 12-hour clock	3pm
hham/pm	am or pm, changes the format for hour to 12-hour clock	03pm
hAM/PM	AM or PM changes the format for hour to 12-hour clock	3PM
hhAM/PM	AM or PM changes the format for hour to 12-hour clock	03PM
h:m	minutes, no leading 0, must follow a format for hour	15:6
hh:mm	two-digit minutes must follow a format for hour	15:06
s	seconds, no leading 0	23
ss	two-digit seconds	23
q	Date is in the 1, 2, 3 or 4th quarter of the year	3
c	complete date/time in format "dd/mm/yyyy hh:mm:ss"	18/09/2018 19:30:23
dddd, mmmm dd yyyy		Tuesday, September 17 2018
dddd, dd mmmm yyyy		Tuesday, 17 September 2018
dd-mm-yyyy		17-09-2018
Dd_mm.yyyy		17_09.2018
mmmm (yy)		September (18)

Refer to:

Chapter 8: CLng Function, CStr Functions, MsgBox Function

MsgBox Function - Message Boxes

Message Boxes are an ideal way to interact with users of your scripts. They also serve as a valuable tool for debugging and checking your command actions as they are being carried out.

When a Message Box is revealed, Dragon will pause the flow of the script until the Message Box has been responded to. Once the Message Box has been addressed the flow of the script will continue from that point onwards.

I have created Dragon scripts in the past that have taken the best part of 5 – 10 minutes to perform the process of actions. In these circumstances I always use a Message Box which simply states "All done" at the end of the process. Basically, it means I can go away, have a cup of tea and not have to watch the screen.

The *MsgBox* function is used to create Message Boxes, and it is the various parameters we include that determine the look and make-up of the Message Box when it is displayed.

Let's have a look at the various Message Box types we can create and how we go about creating them.

Message Box Types

A MsgBox function can be broken up into the following parameters:

```
MsgBox (prompt[,buttons][,title])
```

The **prompt** contains a string expression which is displayed as the message in the Message Box. The string is surrounded by quotes (") and is the only required parameter when creating Message Boxes.

The optional **buttons** parameter can contain either a numeric value or a defined symbol which will determine the type of Message Box to be displayed. It has a default value of "0".

The **title** parameter is optional and can contain a string expression surrounded by quotes. The string will be displayed in the title bar of the Message Box.

As we do not need to include all the parameters or their values in order to produce a Message Box, the most basic form of a Message Box (see Figure 8-4) can be created with the following code:

MyCommand Name: example message box one

Description: Produce a message box

Group: Dragon - A Step Further_Chapter_08

Availability: Global

Command Type: Advanced Scripting

Content:

```
Sub Main
  MsgBox ("Hello, how are you today?")
End Sub
```

Try it by saying:

"example message box one" or in the **MyCommands Editor window**, click on the **"Start/Resume" icon (F5)**

Figure 8-4

The MsgBox function is used to display information and obtain a basic response from the user.

As you can see, this produces a simple Message Box with our text on one line and the inclusion of an OK button that is placed there by default.

The same Message Box could have been created by replacing the line MsgBox ("hello, how are you today?") with either of the following lines of code:

- MsgBox ("hello, how are you today?",0)
- MsgBox ("hello, how are you today?",vbOkOnly)

The lines above include the use of the **buttons** parameter; either the value 0 or the defined symbol vbOkOnly can be used to instruct Dragon to produce the OK button for this Message Box and ultimately defines the type of Message Box created.

 Some developers prefer to use the defined symbol instead of numerical values when writing their code, this makes it easier for others to debug or decipher.

Table 8-6 shows a list of *MsgBox* defined symbols, actions and their numerical values.

Table 8-6

Defined Symbol	Value	Description
vbOKOnly	0	Displays OK button only
vbOKCancel	1	Displays OK and Cancel buttons
vbAbortRetryIgnore	2	Displays Abort, Retry, and Ignore buttons
vbYesNoCancel	3	Displays Yes, No, and Cancel buttons
vbYesNo	4	Displays Yes and No buttons
vbRetryCancel	5	Displays Retry and Cancel buttons
vbCritical	16	Displays Critical Message icon
vbQuestion	32	Displays Warning Query icon
vbExclamation	48	Displays Warning Message icon
vbInformation	64	Displays Information Message icon
vbDefaultButton1	0	First button is default
vbDefaultButton2	256	Second button is default (if two buttons are on show, for example, where there is an "OK" and a "Cancel" button, the "Cancel" button becomes the default.)
vbDefaultButton3	512	Third button is default
vbSystemModal	4096	Makes the Message Box pop up in front of all other running applications

Below is a command consisting of several Message Box examples. Un-comment the examples individually by removing the apostrophe (') at the beginning of each line of code or alternatively un-comment them all and run the command, each Message Box will then appear one after the other:

MyCommand Name: example message box two

Description: Produce message box examples

Group: Dragon - A Step Further_Chapter_08

Availability: Global

Command Type: Advanced Scripting

Content:

```
Sub Main
   MsgBox ("Displaying Ok and Cancel buttons",vbOKCancel)
   'MsgBox ("The script is still processing",2)
   'MsgBox ("Are you over 18?",vbYesNo)
   'MsgBox ("Displays critical icon",16)
   'MsgBox ("Displays information icon",vbInformation)
End Sub
```

Try it by saying:

"example message box two" or in the **MyCommands Editor window**, click on the **"Start/Resume" icon (F5)**

Including a Message Box Title

The **title** parameter is used to place text in the title bar of the Message Boxes we create. You will notice that Dragon will truncate the text in the title bar if the text to be displayed in the prompt area is long in length.

If it is important for you to see the title bar text in full, add blank spaces to the end of the string of text in the **prompt** parameter. See the example below of how we achieve this:

```
Sub Main
  MsgBox ("Hello",0,"Long Text Title")
End Sub
```

Figure 8-5 shows an example of a Message Box with truncated text in the title bar.

Figure 8-5

An example of a Message Box which shows truncated text in the title bar of the window.

```
Sub Main
  MsgBox ("hello                    ",0,"Long Text Title")
End Sub
```

Figure 8-6 shows an example of a Message Box with the full length of text in the title bar.

Figure 8-6

An example of a Message Box which shows the full length of text in the title bar of the window.

If you wish to create Message Boxes with your own labelled buttons refer to Chapter 5: Using Push Buttons (user defined buttons) in Dialog Forms.

Refer to:

Chapter 5: Using Push Buttons (user defined buttons) in Dialog Forms

Combining Defined Symbols and their Values to produce Alternative Message Boxes

Alternative Message Boxes can be created by combining Defined Symbols or adding their values together.

As an example, if we want to create a Message Box that contains Yes & No buttons with a question mark icon. We need to perform the following calculation first:

To produce the Yes & No buttons the value of the Defined Symbols = "4".

To produce a question mark icon the value of the Defined Symbol = "32".

Therefore, to create the Message Box the buttons parameter must be equal to 4+32 = "36". To produce our desired result, the code would be similar to the following:

```
MsgBox ("My text is here", 36)
```

An alternative way of producing the same Message Box would be:

```
MsgBox ("My text is here", vbYesNo + vbQuestion)
```

Not all combinations are valid when combining the Defined Symbols or adding their values. You could end up with unexpected results.

When using the Defined Symbols in your code, you must use the plus sign (+). The Ampersand (&) does not work when combining Defined Symbols and will produce some unexpected results.

The command below consists of a few Message Box examples. Un-comment the examples by removing the apostrophe (') at the beginning of each line of code or un-comment them all and each Message Box will appear one after the other:

MyCommand Name: example message box three

Description: Produce alternative message box examples

Group: Dragon - A Step Further_Chapter_08

Availability: Global

Command Type: Advanced Scripting

Content:

```
Sub Main
    MsgBox ("My text is here", vbAbortRetryIgnore + vbCritical )
    'MsgBox ("My text is here", 69)
    'MsgBox ("My text is here", vbYesNoCancel + vbExclamation)
End Sub
```

Try it by saying:

"example message box three" or in the **MyCommands Editor window**, click on the **"Start/Resume" icon (F5)**

Refer to:

Chapter 5: Using Push Buttons (user defined buttons) in Dialog Forms

Multiple Lines of Text in Message Boxes

There may be times where you require your prompt message to be spread over multiple lines (include line breaks). To do this, we need to include the character code that represents a Carriage Return.

Figure 8-7

An example of a Message Box that consists of multiple lines of text.

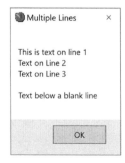

Figure 8-7 is an example of a Message Box consisting of multiple lines of text. To produce the Message Box the command script would be as follows:

```
Sub Main
  MsgBox ("This is text on line 1" & _
  Chr$(13) & "Text on Line 2" & _
  Chr$(13) & "Text on Line 3" & _
  Chr$(13) & Chr$(13) & _
  "Text below a blank line",4096,"Multiple Lines")
End Sub
```

In this example the first thing to note, is that this is in fact, one single line of code. Each portion of actual text to be displayed is enclosed within speech marks (").

The ampersand sign (&) joins the desired text to the Chr$(13) statement in order to maintain this as one single line of code.

The Chr$(13) uses the *Chr* function to return a string containing the character associated with the specified character code (13), in this case a Carriage Return is returned.

When it is required to write a single long line of code, use the underscore character (_) followed by pressing enter to make your code more readable. The underscore has no effect on the workings of the actual script.

Refer to:

Chapter 8: Chr and Asc Functions

Appendix: Popular Ascii Character Codes

Displaying Special Characters in the Prompt Message of Message Boxes

There may be times when you need to insert special characters such as speech marks in your prompt message. As an example, you want the message "*Need help? Click "Yes" or "No"*", whereby we actually want to display the speech marks surrounding the words Yes and No. The following script will achieve this:

```
Sub Main
  MsgBox ("Need help? Click " & Chr$(34) & "Yes" & _
  Chr$(34) & " or " & Chr$(34) & "No" & Chr$(34),vbYesNo)
End Sub
```

To display the text, we have used a single line of code.

Each portion of the text to be displayed is enclosed within speech marks ("). Notice how before and after certain words we insert an extra space; these spaces are inserted to make the outcome a more readable sentence.

The Ampersand sign (&) is what joins the desired text to the Chr$(34) in order to keep this as one single line of code.

The Chr$(34) uses the *Chr* function to return a String containing the character associated with the specified character code (34), in this case, a speech mark is returned.

Refer to:

Chapter 8: Chr and Asc Functions

Appendix: Popular Ascii Character Codes

Using Variables in Message Boxes

We can use both user-defined and built-in variables such as the *Now* variable (used to insert dates and times) in our Message Boxes.

Here are some examples:

Example 1 String variables.

```
Sub Main
Dim name As String
name = "Here is some text"
MsgBox (Name)
End Sub
```

- In the example above, the line Dim Name As String tells Dragon to create a variable called name and that this variable is of the type String, which also means that any values we decide to assign to it, will be a string of characters (predominately text).
- The line name = "Here is some text" makes the variable called name equal to the value of "here is some text". Notice that this value **is** within quotes (").
- Finally, the line MsgBox (name) produces a Message Box where the prompt text displayed will be the value of the variable name, which in this case is the text "Here is some text".

A point to note is that up until now, we have used quotes (") to surround our Message Box prompt text, however when working with variables we do not place quotes around a variable name.

Example 2 (Long/Integer variables (numbers)).

```
Sub Main
Dim age As Long
age = 32
MsgBox (CStr(age))
End Sub
```

- In the above example, we are working with variables containing numbers and at times these variables may be used to perform calculations within your scripts.
- The line Dim age As Integer tells Dragon to create a variable called age and that this variable is of the type Long, therefore we must assign a numerical value (a number) to it.
- The line age = 32 makes the variable called age equal to the value of 32. Notice that this value is **not** within quotes (")

You would be forgiven for thinking that the last line should read as "MsgBox (age)". But no, that is not the case! Dragon does not allow us to simply display the value of Integer or Long variable types. We have to convert these types of variables into String type variables first, before they can be displayed. The *CStr* function is used to do this.

Refer to Chapter 8: CStr Function for more information on the *CStr* function.

- As a result, the final line `MsgBox (CStr(age))` produces a Message Box where the prompt text displayed will be the value of the (Long) variable `age`, which has been converted into a String type variable by the command `CStr` which in this case displays the number/string "32".

Example 3 Message Boxes with the built-in variable *Now*

```
Sub Main
    MsgBox ("" & Now)
End Sub
```

The above example shows how we use the built-in variable *Now* within a Message Box. The important thing to note is that the `""` & are required as part of the line of code, as *Now* on its own will not work. You could also write `MsgBox (Now & "" )` or use these quotes to place some text, for example `MsgBox ("Today's date and time is " & Now)`.

Example 4 Message Boxes with *Date* type variables.

```
Sub Main
Dim inTwoWeeksFromToday As Date
inTwoWeeksFromToday = Now + 14
MsgBox ("Your appointment is on " & WeekdayName(Weekday(inTwoWeeksFromToday)) & _
" " & Day(inTwoWeeksFromToday))
End Sub
```

- In the above example, the line `Dim inTwoWeeksFromToday As Date` tells Dragon to create a variable called `inTwoWeeksFromToday` and that this variable is of the type `Date`, which means its values will only be dates or times or both.
- The line `inTwoWeeksFromToday = Now + 14` makes the variable called `inTwoWeeksFromToday` equal to the value of the date and time of `Now` (the point at which the command is run) plus 14 days into the future. Notice that this value is **not** within quotes (").
- Finally, the line `MsgBox ("Your appointment is on " & WeekdayName(Weekday(inTwoWeeksFromToday)) & _ " " & Day(inTwoWeeksFromToday))` produces a Message Box where the prompt text displayed will be the date 14 days from now, where only the day of the week and the day number will be written out. Notice the deliberate extra spaces to make the written-out text more readable.

Refer to:

Chapter 8: The Now, Date & Time Functions

Chapter 8: CStr Function

An Advanced Message Box Example using Variables

With thought and careful planning, you can produce informative Message Boxes, where the information presented is made up of user-defined and built-in variables.

The following script shows such an example, more than likely, we would use a Dialog Form to populate the variables, but in this case, we will do that within the code.

Have a read through the script to see if you understand how we arrive at the final outcome and hopefully you will become familiar with the type of Message Boxes you can create for yourself.

MyCommand Name: example message box four

Description: advanced example using variables

Group: Dragon - A Step Further_Chapter_08

Availability: Global

Command Type: Advanced Scripting

Content:

```
Sub Main
' Client requirements
Dim clientName As String
Dim daysInTheFuture As Long
Dim hours_booked As Long
Dim bookingDate As Date
Dim bookedOn As Date
'Populate the variables
clientName = "Victoria"
daysInTheFuture = 2
hours_booked = 3
bookedOn = Now
bookingDate = Now + daysInTheFuture
' Look of the message box
Dim boxType As Long
Dim boxIcon As Long
Dim boxTitle As String
'Populate the variables
boxType = 3
boxIcon = 64
boxTitle = "Room booking confirmation"
MsgBox ("Student name: " & clientName & Chr$(13) & Chr$(13) & _
"The library room is booked for " & _
CStr(hours_booked) & " hours " & Chr$(13) & _
"on " & _
WeekdayName(Weekday(bookingDate )) & _
" " & Day(bookingDate ) & " " & _
MonthName(Month(bookingDate )) & Chr$(13)& "Which is in " & _
CStr(daysInTheFuture) & " days time." & Chr$(13) & Chr$(13) & _
"Please confirm.", boxType + boxIcon, boxTitle  )
End Sub
```

Try it by saying:
"example message box four" or in the **MyCommands Editor window**, click on the **"Start/Resume" icon (F5)**

Discuss
Dragon allows us to add the variables Now and DaysInTheFuture even though they are of different types.

There is no requirement to perform the *CStr* function on the variable DaysInTheFuture in the calculation bookingDate = Now + DaysInTheFuture.

Refer to:
Chapter 5: Dialog Form
Chapter 8: Chr and Asc Functions, CStr Function, The Now and Date & Time Functions

Recording User Response from Message Boxes
There will be times when you need to know what a user's response to a Message Box has been. For example, you may want your script to perform a specific action when they click the OK button and an alternative action when they click on the Cancel button.

The following example shows how we can achieve this:

MyCommand Name: example message box five

Description: User response to message box

Group: Dragon - A Step Further_Chapter_08

Availability: Global

Command Type: Advanced Scripting

Content:

```
Sub Main
  responseValue = MsgBox ("Click a button",1)
  If responseValue = 1 Then MsgBox("You pressed the OK button.")
  If responseValue = 2 Then MsgBox("You pressed the Cancel button.")
End Sub
```

Try it by saying:
"example message box five" or in the **MyCommands Editor window**, click on the **"Start/Resume" icon (F5)**

The line responseValue = MsgBox ("Click a button") will store a value in the variable called responseValue and that value will be dependent on which button the user has clicked.

Dragon follows a set number of rules to reflect which button has been clicked.

In this scenario Dragon will make the variable responseValue equal to the value of 1 when the OK button is clicked or alternatively make the same variable responseValue equal to the value of 2 if the Cancel button is clicked.

Now that our variable responseValue has a value we can now use an *If Then* statement in order to carry out an action dependent on what the value of that variable is.

The Line If responseValue = 1 Then MsgBox("You pressed the OK button.") performs a check that basically means, if the value of the variable responseValue is equal to 1 then display a Message Box with the prompt message "You pressed the OK button.".

The next line works on the same premise to deduce if the Cancel button has been clicked.

Table 8-7 shows a list of Message Box buttons and the values Dragon will return when they are clicked.

Table 8-7

Buttons	Value Returned
OK button	1
Cancel button	2
Abort button	3
Retry button	4
Ignore button	5
Yes button	6
No button	7

Refer to:

Chapter 8: If Then Statement

Setting the Focus on a Specific Message Box Button

Setting the focus on a specific button is sometimes a necessary requirement to protect users of your scripts from making hasty or wrong decisions.

As an example, let's say you have written a script that at some point reveals a Message Box that prompts the user to delete some data, your text would include "Are you sure?" with "Yes" or "No" buttons (see below).

```
Sub Main
  MsgBox("Are you sure?",vbYesNo)
End Sub
```

By default, Dragon will place the focus on the Yes button.

By setting the focus to the No button, this would force the user to manually switch to the Yes button in order to carry out the deletion, preventing those users who are trigger-happy on the Enter/Return key from deleting their data accidentally.

To set the focus to an alternative button, in this case the No button, we need to combine some Defined Symbols or add their values.

Our code above has the buttons parameter as vbYesNo. We need to add to this, the Defined Symbol vbDefaultButton2 which basically means set the focus to the second button in the Message Box. The code below demonstrates this:

```
Sub Main
  MsgBox("Are you sure?",vbYesNo + vbDefaultButton2)
End Sub
```

An alternative way of producing the same Message Box would be:

```
Sub Main
  MsgBox ("Are you sure?",260) ' 4 + 256
End Sub
```

The following example shows the code for producing a Message Box with the buttons "Abort", "Retry" and "Ignore". The focus will be to set to the "Ignore" button.

```
Sub Main
  MsgBox ("Focus is on Ignore",514) ' 2 + 512
End Sub
```

Below, is an alternative way of producing the same Message Box:

```
Sub Main
  MsgBox ("Focus is on Ignore",vbAbortRetryIgnore + vbDefaultButton3 )
End Sub
```

Finally, if you wish to include an icon of some sort, then the Defined Symbol of that icon would also need to be added to the value.

For example, to produce a Message Box with the buttons "Abort", "Retry" and "Ignore", include a question mark icon and have the focus set to the "Ignore" button. The following script will do this for you:

```
Sub Main
  MsgBox("Focus is on Ignore",vbAbortRetryIgnore + vbDefaultButton3 + vbQuestion )
End Sub
```

Below, is an alternative way of producing the same Message Box:

```
Sub Main
  MsgBox("Focus is on Ignore",546) ' 2 + 512 + 32
End Sub
```

Making sure your Message Box appears On Top

There is nothing more infuriating than sitting and waiting for a Message Box that seemingly does not appear. More often than not, the Message Box has indeed been activated but because there are other applications running in the foreground it cannot be seen. A quick check is to go down to the Windows taskbar and look for the highlighted Dragon icon.

When writing Dragon scripts that include Message Box pop-ups, there is a way to force them to be on top, regardless of any applications that are currently running. Let's explore how we can achieve this.

Suppose we want a simple Message Box to appear with the prompt text "All done." and include an exclamation icon. We could write the following code:

```
MsgBox("All done.",48)
```

You may recall from the section on "Message Box types", there are several defined symbols and their numerical values. The section on "Combining Defined Symbols and their values to produce alternative Message Boxes" shows how we can have combinations of these values and by adding certain values together, produce alternative Message Boxes.

In this scenario, so far, we have used the numerical value of "48" to produce the exclamation mark and by default Dragon would have added "0" to this amount to place the OK button.

Now, in order to make sure our Message Box pops up in front, we need to add another value to the "48". That value is "**4096**" which is the defined symbol "vbSystemModal". Therefore, our line of code would now be:

```
MsgBox("All done.", 4144)
```

Writing the code this way means we will get the same Message Box in look; and it will pop up on our screen regardless of other applications that are running.

SendKeys, SendDragonKeys & SendSystemKeys Statements

The *SendKeys* and *SendDragonKeys* statements are used in Advanced Scripting commands when you want your scripts to perform or emulate keyboard keystrokes. They are also used where there is a requirement to have text written out, for example, in word processing applications.

The *SendSystemKeys* statement is an alternative method that we use as a last resort when the *SendDragonKeys* and *SendKeys* statements do not work as required.

There are times when the SendDragonKeys and SendKeys statements do not appear to work; this could be due to the environment or software in which you are trying to execute the command. In such instances try the SendSystemKeys function, however, please note, you may need to change the second part of the command. For example, the line of code SendKeys "^a" would need to be changed to SendSystemKeys "{Ctrl+a}".

- **SendKeys & SendDragonKeys:** Is used for standard applications and are the fastest way to perform a task - They work through the application.
- **SendSystemKeys:** Is used for the operating system or non-standard applications. It works through the operating system - It is **slower but has a higher accuracy in performing tasks.**

Making use of the SendKeys Second Parameter

When creating your Advanced Scripts, if you intend to use the *SendKeys* statement to type out a large amount of text or the content of a variable which may contain several characters, you should make use of the *SendKeys* second parameter by adding the code ", 1" or ", true" (VBA) to the end of the line of code. This will force the running of the macro to pause until all the keys have been sent or typed out.

As an example, the following macro shows how we can ensure that the content of a variable is typed out before the beep sound is heard:

MyCommand Name: example send keys statement

Description: Example of using the SendKeys statement

Group: Dragon - A Step Further_Chapter_08

Availability: Global

Command Type: Advanced Scripting

Content:

```
Sub Main
    Dim someText As String
    someText = "The Quick Brown Fox Jumped Over The Lazy Lazy Lazy Lazy Dog"
    SendKeys someText, 1
    Beep
End Sub
```

Open a new Notepad or word processing application and try it by saying:
"example send keys statement"

By using the *SendKeys* second parameter you avoid the need to insert a *Wait* statement after the *SendKeys* line of code.

Experiment with the content of the variable someText and try removing the , 1 portion of the code to see and hear the difference.

The Second Parameter cannot be used with the SendDragonKeys statement.

 The SendKeys statement can send upto 128 characters (including spaces). An error will occur if there are more than 128 characters. Use the SendDragonKeys statement for a larger amount of characters.

Using both SendKeys and SendDragonKeys statements within an Advanced Script

Within an Advanced Script you can make use of both the *SendKeys* and *SendDragonKeys* statements, however, I would strongly advise that the *SendKeys* statements include the second parameter and to be safe, include a *Wait* statement after the *SendDragonKeys* statement. This will prevent undesirable results, especially where a *SendDragonKeys* statement immediately follows a *SendKeys* statement.

 For some developers, using the SendKeys command is the preferred choice as it is more consistent with other programming languages such as Visual Basic.

 When writing a line of code such as SendDragonKeys "{Ctrl+p}" for example. Do not use capital letters as part of the command apart from the modifier keys (such as the Shift, Alt etc.), i.e. the "p" is lowercase in this example.

Tables 8-8 and 8-9 list examples of Dragon script using the *SendDragonKeys*, *SendKeys* and *SendSystemKeys* commands, and the actions they will perform.

Dragon Script Performs Table

Table 8-8

Δ	- Can be used with SendKeys
Ω	- Can be used with SendDragonKeys
Ψ	- Can be used with SendSystemKeys

Dragon Script	Performs
SendKeys "{Enter}" ΔΩΨ	Press the Enter/Return key
SendKeys "{Del}" ΔΩΨ	Press the Delete key
SendKeys "{Backspace}" ΔΩΨ	Press the Backspace key
SendKeys "{Tab}" ΔΩΨ	Press the Tab key
SendKeys "{Space}" ΔΩΨ	Press the Space Bar
SendKeys "{Esc}" ΔΩΨ	Press the Escape key
SendKeys "{Ins}" ΔΩΨ	Press the Insert key
SendKeys "{F5}" ΔΩΨ	Press the F5 key ({F1}, {F2}, {F3},...{F16})
SendKeys "{Left}" ΔΩΨ	Press Left Arrow key
SendKeys "{Right}" ΔΩΨ	Press Right Arrow key
SendKeys "{Right 2}" ΔΩΨ	Press Right Arrow key 2 times
SendKeys "{Up}" ΔΩΨ	Press Up Arrow key
SendKeys "{Down}" ΔΩΨ	Press Down Arrow key
SendKeys "{Down 2}" ΔΩΨ	Press Down Arrow key 2 times
SendKeys "{Down 5}{Right 2}" ΔΩΨ	Press Down Arrow key 5 times and then Press Right Arrow key 2 times
SendKeys "{Home}" ΔΩΨ	Press Home key
SendKeys "{End}" ΔΩΨ	Press End key
SendKeys "{PgDn}" ΔΩΨ	Press PgDn key (Page down key)
SendKeys "{PgUp}" ΔΩΨ	Press PgUp key (Page up key)

Dragon Script	Performs
SendKeys "+a" Δ	Shift+a
SendKeys "%a" Δ	Alt+a
SendKeys "^a" Δ	Ctrl+a (Select All)
SendKeys "^c" Δ	Ctrl+c (Copy)
SendKeys "^x" Δ	Ctrl+x (Cut)
SendKeys "^v" Δ	Ctrl+v (Paste)
SendKeys "^b" Δ	Ctrl+b (Bold)
SendKeys "^u" Δ	Ctrl+u (Underline)
SendKeys "^i" Δ	Ctrl+i (Italics)
SendKeys "^i" & "^b" Δ	Ctrl+i & Ctrl b (Bold & italics)
SendKeys "^{Home}" Δ	Ctrl+Home
SendKeys "^{F3}" Δ	Ctrl+F3
SendKeys "^+{Enter}" Δ	Ctrl+Shift+Enter
SendKeys "^%b" Δ	Ctrl+Alt+B
SendKeys "+%1" Δ	Press Shift+Alt+1
SendKeys "%^+s" Δ	Hold down Alt, Ctrl & Shift keys and press S
SendKeys "~" Δ	(tilde) Press the Enter key
SendKeys "~~~" Δ	(3 tildes) Press the Enter key 3 times

SendDragonKeys "{Shift+a}" ΩΨ	Hold Shift key and press the "a" key
SendDragonKeys "{Ctrl+a}" ΩΨ	Hold Ctrl key and press the "a" key
SendDragonKeys "{Ctrl+Enter}" ΩΨ	Hold Ctrl key and press Enter
SendDragonKeys "{Alt+F4}" ΩΨ	Press Alt+F4
SendDragonKeys "{Alt+Space}{x}" ΩΨ	Hold Alt and Space bar keys and then press x
SendDragonKeys "{Ctrl+Right 3}" ΩΨ	Press Ctrl+Right Arrow 3 times

Dragon Script	Performs
SendDragonKeys "{Alt+o}f{Alt+f}"+"Courier New"+"{Enter}" ΩΨ	(In MS Word) Opens the Font window, selects fonts, types in Courier New and then presses the Enter key.
SendDragonKeys "{Alt+o}{f}{Alt+f}"+"Courier New"+"{Enter}" ΩΨ	Same as above.
SendDragonKeys "{Alt+o}f{Alt+f}"+ListVAR1+"{Enter}" ΩΨ	(In MS Word) Opens the Font window, selects fonts, inserts the value of the List variable ListVAR1 and then presses the Enter key.

SendDragonKeys "{Alt}" ΩΨ SendDragonKeys "{g}" ΩΨ SendDragonKeys "{i}" ΩΨ SendDragonKeys "{c}" ΩΨ	**If your command requires several individual key presses, use the more reliable option of placing each key press on an individual line.** Press Alt, press "g", Press "i", press "c" one at a time.

SendSystemKeys "{CapsLock}" Ψ	Press the Caps Lock key
SendSystemKeys "{NumLock}" Ψ	Press the Num Lock key
SendSystemKeys "{Alt+Tab}" Ψ	Hold Alt key and press Tab key
SendSystemKeys "{Alt+Esc}" Ψ	Hold Alt key and press Esc key
SendSystemKeys "{Ctrl+Esc}" Ψ	Press the Windows logo button
SendSystemKeys "{win}" Ψ	Press the windows key
SendSystemKeys "{win+Prtsc}" Ψ	Press the windows key+Prtsc
SendSystemKeys "{NumKey+}" Ψ	Press the Number Pad + key
SendSystemKeys "{NumKey/}" Ψ	Press the Number Pad / key

Do not include any spaces between the names of simultaneously pressed keys, such as Ctrl+Enter.

In applications such as MS Word, finding the shortcut keys to a specific menu and function can be achieved by pressing the "Alt" key to reveal a number of shaded characters (see Figure 8-8). Press the relevant character to navigate to a menu and its options, the options can also be accessed by pressing their relevant character.

Figure 8-8

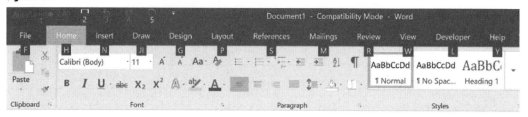

Including special characters such as quotations and parenthesis in your written text can sometimes yield undesirable results. Table 8-9 lists examples of Dragon script using *Send…* statements to write out text.

Dragon Script Writes Out Table

Table 8-9

Δ	- Can be used with SendKeys
Ω	- Can be used with SendDragonKeys
Ψ	- Can be used with SendSystemKeys

Dragon Script	Types out
SendKeys "Welcome to this Dragon guide" ΔΩΨ	Welcome to this Dragon guide
SendKeys "{""}" ΔΩΨ	" (double quotes)
SendKeys "{""}{""}" ΔΩΨ	"" (pair of double quotes)
SendKeys "He said {""}hello{""}" ΔΩΨ	He said "hello"
SendKeys "Mike & Jane" ΔΩΨ	Mike & Jane
SendKeys "<a href={""}*|ARCHIVE|*{""} target={""}_blank{""}>View this email in your browser</a>" ΔΩΨ	<a href="*|ARCHIVE|*" target="_blank">View this email in your browser</a>
SendKeys "Mike & " & myVariable ΔΩΨ	Mike & xxxx
SendKeys myVariable ΔΩΨ	xxxx
SendKeys Chr(35) ΔΩΨ	#

SendDragonKeys Chr(43) ΩΨ	+
SendDragonKeys Chr(123) & Chr(125) ΩΨ	{}
SendDragonKeys "{}" ΩΨ	{}

Dragon Script	Types out
SendDragonKeys "He said " & Chr(147) & "hello" & Chr(148) ΩΨ	He said "hello"
SendDragonKeys "line(s)" ΩΨ	Line(s)
SendDragonKeys "line" & Chr(40) & "s" & Chr(41) ΩΨ	Line(s)

SendKeys "normal " & "^b" & "bold " & "^b" & "^i" & "italic " & "^i" & "^u" & "underlined" & "^u",1 Δ	normal **bold** *italic* <u>underlined</u>

The "&" (ampersand) is used to join text and the contents of a variable in the same Send…Keys command line. The text to be written out is within quotes, the variable name is not within quotes. For example, SendDragonKeys "Hello Mr " & myVariable

In situations where a Send…Keys command statement is lengthy; a single statement can be continued on multiple lines using the "_" (underscore) at the end of each line except the last. This will improve the readability of the statement. Below is an example:

```
SendKeys WeekdayName(Weekday(Yesterday)) & " " _
MonthName(Month(Yesterday)) & " " _
Day(Yesterday) & " " & Year(Yesterday)
```

The Send…Keys instructions will work with ASCII characters. According to Nuance documentation, SendKeys cannot be used with characters that have a higher ASCII code than 127. It advises that for characters above this number, use the SendDragonKeys instruction instead. SendDragonKeys works for some characters that SendKeys does not work for.

Refer to:

Appendix: Popular Ascii Character Codes

Moving the Mouse Pointer and Mouse Button Clicks

The *SendKeys* statement can be used to move the mouse pointer to a specific point on the screen and carry out a mouse button action.

To perform a mouse action, the statement is made up of the following parameters:

```
SendKeys "mouseAction[,Xpos,Ypos]"
```

The **mouseAction** parameter is the mouse action that we want to perform.

The **Xpos, Ypos** parameters are optional and are used to place the Mouse Pointer in a specific position on the screen. If the (Xpos,Ypos) parameters are omitted then the previous mouse position is used.

A typical statement could be written as SendKeys "{ClickLeft 10,50}", where the mouseAction is to perform a Click of the mouse Left button at the screen pixel position 10,50.

 The Xpos, Ypos **values refer to the screen pixel location. Therefore, (0,0) is the upper left position of the screen.**

Table 8-10 provides a list of the *SendKey* mouse and click button statements that can be used.

Table 8-10

Dragon Script	Performs
SendKeys "{Move x,y}"	Moves the mouse pointer to the specified coordinates. However, I prefer to use the *MouseGrid* Function to position the Mouse Pointer.
SendKeys "{ClickLeft x,y}"	Move the Mouse Pointer to position x,y and Click the Left Mouse Button
SendKeys "{DoubleClickLeft x,y}"	Move the Mouse Pointer to position x,y and Double-Click the Left Mouse Button
SendKeys "{DownLeft x,y}"	Move the Mouse Pointer to position x,y and Hold-Down the Left Mouse Button
SendKeys "{UpLeft x,y}"	Move the Mouse Pointer to position x,y and Release the Left Mouse Button
SendKeys "{ClickRight x,y}"	Move the Mouse Pointer to position x,y and Click the Right Mouse Button
SendKeys "{DoubleClickRight x,y}"	Move the Mouse Pointer to position x,y and Double-Click the Right Mouse Button
SendKeys "{DownRight x,y}"	Move the Mouse Pointer to position x,y and Hold-Down the Right Mouse Button
SendKeys "{UpRight x,y}"	Move the Mouse Pointer to position x,y and Release the Right Mouse Button
SendKeys "{ClickMiddle x,y}"	Move the Mouse Pointer to position x,y and Click the Middle Mouse Button
SendKeys "{DoubleClickMiddle x,y}"	Move the Mouse Pointer to position x,y and Double-Click the Middle Mouse Button
SendKeys "{DownMiddle x,y}"	Move the Mouse Pointer to position x,y and Hold-Down the Middle Mouse Button
SendKeys "{UpMiddle x,y}"	Move the Mouse Pointer to position x,y and Release the Middle Mouse Button

Bear in mind that the screen pixel location and values will differ according to the end user's screen size and resolution.

Adjusting for Different Keyboards

It is important to bear in mind that when creating scripts that include keystroke commands, the outcome may differ depending on the end-user's PC, Laptop or keyboard setup. Function Key keystrokes can also be problematic, as again, a user may have changed their keyboard setup or hotkeys in applications such as MS Word.

To cater for such scenarios, when writing your advanced scripts, you can incorporate a symbolic keystroke instead of a fixed one, in doing so; you will make the process of catering to an end-user's choice a lot easier.

For example, let's imagine that a default function for an application is carried out by pressing the "F4" key. However, you have a few end-users who have setup their systems so that the function key "F8" is their preferred choice for that function.

Instead of writing the line of code as:

`SendDragonKeys "{F8}"` throughout your script.

We could do the following instead:

`preferredKey = "{F8}"`

`SendDragonKeys preferredKey` (This line is then placed throughout the script).

By writing your script this way, you save yourself the hassle of having to change every occurrence of a wrong `SendDragonKeys "{F8}"` throughout your whole script, specifically for any end user who prefers an alternative; you only need to change the line `preferredKey = "{F8}"` and the rest of your script would be fine.

Section 6: Ready to use Dragon commands

Chapter 9: Ready to use practical Dragon Macros

This chapter provides a number of useful Dragon voice commands that can be used with various applications.

In this section I am assuming that you have a grasp of Dragon script, application VBA and how to create Dragon commands of various types. Therefore, I will only comment on the key points that each macro demonstrates. References for related topics are provided for further reading.

The macros in this section go a small way to illustrate the potential of Dragon Professional and Dragon NaturallySpeaking, showing how Dragon can be used in collaboration with popular applications. The commands represent practical examples where Dragon automates repetitive tasks, increases your productivity and saves you valuable time.

At this point in time, Commands that require reference to Object Libraries have been created and tested using MS Word Office 365 (32 bit) and Mindjet MindManager 2018 (32 bit). The macros can be used with earlier versions of the applications; however, in order to make them work you may have to change to your version of Object References. Where necessary the following Object Libraries have been used:

- Microsoft Word 16.0 Object Library(8.7)
- Microsoft Excel 16.0 Object Library(1.9)
- Microsoft PowerPoint 16.0 Object Library(2.c)
- MindManager 18 Type Library(12.0)

Inserting a Custom Designed email Signature

Many of us include email signatures to end our emails. These can range from a simple line of text stating our contact details to more complex versions that include coloured text, font variations and logos.

This macro will create a custom email signature.

MyCommand Name: insert my company email signature

Description: Types out a custom designed email signature

Group: Dragon - A Step Further_Chapter_09

Availability: Global

Command Type: Auto-Text(Text and Graphics)

Content:

As can be seen in Figure 9-1.

Open a new email, Notepad or word processing application and try it by saying:

"insert my company email signature"

Figure 9-1

An example of an Auto-Text(Text and Graphics) command, which when run, produces an email signature consisting of formatted text and an image.

Discuss

A Dragon command of the type **Auto-Text(Text and Graphics)** is created. This will enable us to insert custom fonts, colours and images, which all goes towards creating the desired email signature.

Figure 9-1 shows that when we select the command type as Auto-Text(Text and Graphics), Dragon makes available several formatting options. The Content area is where we place the desired formatted text.

The (**Aa**) icon when clicked will reveal the Font window, enabling font selection, font size, colour and other formatting options. Simply highlight the text first, and then click on the (**Aa**) icon to make the necessary changes.

To place the logo into the Contents area, the image file must first be opened in a graphics application such as MS Paint. You will need to select the image and then use the copy command within the application, switch back to the MyCommands Editor window, place the cursor in the required position, right-click and select paste. Once pasted the image can be selected and resized.

If you have already formatted your text in a word processing application, copy the text from the application document and paste it in the Content area, it will maintain your formatted text as is. However, make sure the Check box "Plain Text" is not checked or you will lose all formatting and images.

Tab indents are achievable within the Content's text; however, to achieve this, you need to press Ctrl+Tab, as Tab on its own will move you out of the Content area.

Create Dragon commands of the type Auto-Text(Text and Graphics) when you want commands that will insert extensive amounts of text, for example, when sending out a standard letter or email, you might want a command that inserts a paragraph of text that you use regularly.

Refer to:

Chapter 1: Creating an Auto-Text(Text and Graphics) Command

Generate a Fillable Business Letter Template

The following voice command is an example of how we can generate a form with default text and include fields within that text that can be easily navigated.

These types of commands are ideal for business environments where standardised content is needed and helps to avoid potential human error.

Figure 9-2 shows an example document that has been generated and filled in by voice.

Figure 9-2

An example of a MS Word document generated and filled in by voice.

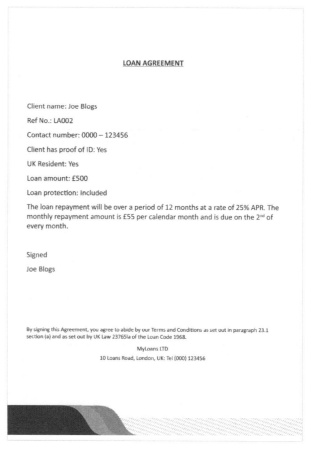

Creating an Auto-Text(Text and Graphics) command is the most effective way to produce such a form. We will name it and run it by saying *"create loan agreement"*

MyCommand Name: create loan agreement

Description: Produces text with fillable fields

Group: Dragon - A Step Further_Chapter_09

Availability: Global

Command Type: Auto-Text(Text and Graphics)

Content:

As can be seen in Figure 9-3.

Open a new Notepad or word processing application and try it by saying:

"create loan agreement"

Figure 9-3

An example of an Auto-Text(Text and Graphics) command which when run produces a block of formatted text and fields.

Discuss

When creating a command that involves producing a significant amount of text, creating an Auto-Text(Text and Graphics) command is the way to achieve your requirements and have the text instantly revealed.

Let's look at how this command is made up:

You will notice that the text held within the Content area consists of both text as well as what we call "Fields". These Fields are inserted so that when the command is run, we are able to insert a specific value for each of them or accept their default values.

A field is created by placing the cursor in the required position and clicking on the Insert Variable button. By default, Dragon will produce a field that has the words "default value" within it (**[default value]**).

We could have easily set up most of the fields to have the default value name, but you will find, especially with text that includes numerous fields, that when it comes to running the command, it may be confusing as to which field should contain what information. Therefore, I would suggest that you replace the [default value] fields with a name that is more appropriate to the data you want to fill it with, as can be seen with the fields [Telephone number], [Yes/No], [Included/Not included], [number of months], [percentage], [amount] and [day number].

When incorporating fields, it is a good idea to think about the name you wish to use for your fields and to name them according to either of these circumstances:

1. Do I want the field name to serve as a reminder of the values I should dictate into the field when the command is run? e.g. Loan protection: **[Included/Not included]**
2. Do I want the field name to be a default value? As more often than not, this will be the value inserted. e.g. UK Resident **[Yes]**

Bear in mind, all fields can be overwritten within the generated text.

The left ([) and right (]) square brackets that surround a field name are referred to as "Delimiters" and they mark the beginning and end of each field.

When the command is run, and the text is produced within a document, the inclusion of these fields within the content enables us to take advantage of several built-in Dragon commands:

If we say, "*next field*" Dragon will move the focus to the next field ready for us to dictate a value. By saying "*previous field*" focus will be moved to the previous field.

Once a field is focused, we can dictate a new value over the existing name (notice how the delimiters ([ ])are automatically removed). Or, in a situation where you have dictated all new values and only have the default field names remaining, we can say either "*accept defaults*" or "*clear variable delimiters*". These commands will automatically remove all remaining delimiters throughout the document.

The Content text and field variables can be formatted to a specific style by selecting the text and then clicking on the **(Aa)** icon in order to reveal the Fonts window. Justification, bullet points, bold, underlines and italic settings are also available by clicking on the icons in the MyCommands Editor window.

Towards the bottom right-hand corner of the MyCommands Editor window is the CheckBox labelled "Plain Text". If the CheckBox is checked (and the command is saved), all formatting will turn to plain text and the styling will be removed. When the command is run in a word processing application the text generated will be in the style as determined by the application.

Refer to:

Chapter 1: Creating an Auto-Text(Text and Graphics) Command

Filling Forms in MS Word

Working with forms in MS Word often involves having to navigate to various parts of a document in order to fill in the necessary information. This can be frustrating as it means constant mouse and keyboard action, especially when working with forms that are spread over several pages, as you look for that specific title or heading.

An ideal solution for this scenario is to create a voice command that when we say, "*move to* (whatever the title or heading is)", Dragon takes us to that heading and places the cursor after it, ready for us to dictate further information.

Figure 9-4 shows an example of a typical form.

Figure 9-4

An example of a MS Word document.

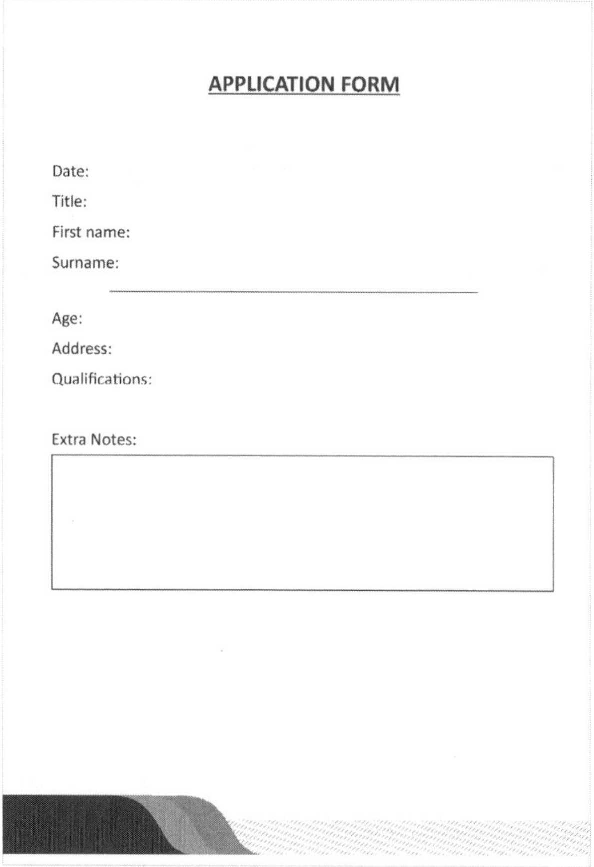

APPLICATION FORM

Date:
Title:
First name:
Surname:

Age:
Address:
Qualifications:

Extra Notes:

<**Word VBA Solution:** Needs Microsoft Word Object Library>

MyCommand Name: move to <dictation>

Name of List(s) used: <dictation>

List items:

any phrase

Description: finds specific text in a document

Group: Dragon - A Step Further_Chapter_09

Availability: Application-specific

Application: Microsoft Word

Command Type: Advanced Scripting

Content:

```
Sub Main
    Selection.Find.ClearFormatting
    Selection.Find.Replacement.ClearFormatting
    With Selection.Find
        .Text = ListVar1
        .Replacement.Text = ""
        .Forward = True
        .Wrap = wdFindContinue
        .Format = False
        .MatchCase = False
        .MatchWholeWord = False
        .MatchWildcards = False
        .MatchSoundsLike = False
        .MatchAllWordForms = False
    End With
    Selection.Find.Execute
    Selection.MoveRight Unit:=wdCharacter, Count:=2
    If ListVar1 = "extra notes" Then
        Selection.MoveDown Unit:=wdLine, Count:=1
        Selection.TypeText Text:=""
    Else
        Selection.TypeText Text:=" "
    End If
End Sub
```

Try it by saying:

"move to surname"

"move to address"

"move to qualifications"

"move to extra notes"

Discuss

To perform the requirements, we create a Dragon List type command using the in-built Dragon List called <dictation> to facilitate the Word VBA. This is the most powerful of the Dragon Lists as it enables the command to potentially respond to whatever the user dictates.

The line `Selection.MoveRight Unit:=wdCharacter, Count:=2` moves the cursor two-character spaces to the right of the selected heading and inserts a space after the colon to make ready for further dictation.

An *If Then* statement is used to make a slight adjustment to the procedure above when the variable `ListVar1` is equal to "extra notes", as it will also move the cursor position down one line to facilitate the population of the box below the heading "Extra notes".

Refer to:

Chapter 2: Object Library References

Chapter 4: The unique Dragon List named <dictation>

Chapter 8: If Then Statement

Create a Backup of the Current Word Document with the Date & Time in the Filename

When writing essays, reports or articles I often save draft copies as I go along. These draft copies are usually dated so that if I make a catastrophic mistake I can easily revert back to a previous version.

Performing a 'Save As' procedure, forces me to change the name of the document I am currently working on, when in fact, I want my current document to retain its name.

Rather than manually producing a copy of the current document and renaming it, this macro when run will automatically produce a copy of the document with the current date and time added to the original filename. The newly produced document will be saved in the same location as the current document and you will be able to continue editing in the original named document.

<Word VBA Solution: Needs Microsoft Word Object Library>

MyCommand Name: save dated word file

Description: Saves a version with the current Date and Time in the filename

Group: Dragon - A Step Further_Chapter_09

Availability: Application-specific

Application: Microsoft Word

Command Type: Advanced Scripting

Content:

```
Sub Main
'© www.dragonspeechtips.com
Dim currentDocPath_FileName As String
Dim currentDoc_FileName As String
Dim currentDocPath As String
Dim mySetBackUpFolder As String

currentDocPath_FileName = ActiveDocument.FullName
currentDoc_FileName = ActiveDocument.Name
currentDocPath = ActiveDocument.Path
mySetBackUpFolder = "C:\Users\...\myFiles_Folder"

On Error GoTo x:
'Get current Date & Time
saveNow = (Format(Now, "dd_mm_yyyy___hh-mm "))

'Backed up Filename and Path
currentFolder_File = currentDocPath & "\" & saveNow & currentDoc_FileName
mySetBackUpFolder_File = mySetBackUpFolder & "\" & saveNow & currentDoc_FileName

'Save the renamed backup
ActiveDocument.SaveAs2 FileName:=currentFolder_File, _
```

```
    FileFormat:=wdFormatXMLDocument, _
    CompatibilityMode:=Val(Application.Version)

'Save original
ActiveDocument.SaveAs2 FileName:=currentDocPath_FileName, _
    FileFormat:=wdFormatXMLDocument, _
    CompatibilityMode:=Val(Application.Version)

x: MsgBox ("ERROR! Please make sure of the following:" & _
   Chr$(13) & "That the Save path exists" & _
   Chr$(13) & "There are No special characters in the Date Format" & _
   Chr$(13) & Chr$(13) & _
   "",4160,"Error")

End Sub
```

Try it by saying:
"save dated word file"

Discuss

This procedure requires a few steps in order to carry out the objective:

- Store the name of the current (original) document.
- Get the current Date and Time.
- Save the document as a new filename with the date and time incorporated in the filename.
- Save the document again to its original name and location.

This macro uses the Dragon script function *Now* to gather the Date and Time at which the voice command is executed. The line saveNow = (Format(Now, "dd_mm_yyyy___hh-mm ")) is where the variable saveNow becomes equal to the current Date and Time in a format as determined by the dd_mm_yyyy___hh-mm portion of the code. It is this same portion of code that determines the format of how the Date and Time will be displayed in the filename (e.g. 02_05_2018___13-25 myFilename.docx).

 Feel free to change the format of the Date and Time. Refer to Chapter 8: Table of Date and Time Formatting Styles for assistance.

 Be careful not to include special characters such as colons (:), as filenames cannot include such characters.

Word VBA is then used to carry out the Save As procedure using the variable currentFolder_File to determine the file name and folder in which the file will be saved.

The dated version of the document will be saved in the same folder as the current document.

Alternative

If you wish to have all your backed-up versions of the document placed in a specific folder, then make the following changes to the script:

- Replace the portion of the script `C:\Users\...\myFiles_Folder` with your directory path to the specific folder.
- Replace the portion of the script `FileName:=currentFolder_File` with `FileName:=mySetBackUpFolder_File`

Refer to:

Chapter 2: Object Library References

Chapter 8: Changing the Display Format of Date & Time, On Error Instruction, MsgBox Function - Message Boxes

Export a MS Word Document as a PDF with a Hyperlinked Table of Contents

When creating a Word document containing a Table of Contents (TOC) that has been derived from the Heading Styles used. You may find it frustrating when attempting to save the document as a PDF, as the PDF produced does not contain links in the TOC to the various sections of the document.

Use this macro to export the current Word document as a PDF that contains Hyperlinks in the TOC to the Headings within the Word document.

<**Word VBA Solution:** Needs Microsoft Word Object Library>

MyCommand Name: export as book marked pdf

Description: Creates a book-marked PDF of the active Word document with a Table of Contents

Group: Dragon - A Step Further_Chapter_09

Availability: Application-specific

Application: Microsoft Word

Command Type: Advanced Scripting

Content:

```vba
Sub Main
'© www.dragonspeechtips.com
'Creates the PDF in the location and same name as the Word doc
On Error GoTo x:
With ActiveDocument
'Check if the document has a Table of Contents (TOC)
    If .TablesOfContents.Count < 1 Then 'No TOC
        'Create a TOC
        Set myRange = ActiveDocument.Range(0, 0)
        ActiveDocument.TablesOfContents.Add _
        Range:=myRange, _
        UseFields:=False, _
        UseHeadingStyles:=True, _
        LowerHeadingLevel:=3, _
        UpperHeadingLevel:=1, _
        UseHyperlinks:=True, _
        AddedStyles:="myStyleOne, myStyleTwo"
        Wait 1
        Selection.InsertBreak Type:=wdPageBreak 'Create Page Break
    End If
'Update any existing TOC
    For i = 1 To .TablesOfContents.Count
        ActiveDocument.TablesOfContents(i).Update
    Next i
End With
'Export the document as a book-marked PDF
ActiveDocument.ExportAsFixedFormat OutputFileName:= _
  Replace(ActiveDocument.FullName, ".docx", ".pdf"), _
  ExportFormat:=wdExportFormatPDF, OpenAfterExport:=False, _
  OptimizeFor:=wdExportOptimizeForPrint, _
```

```
    Range:=wdExportAllDocument, Item:=wdExportDocumentContent, _
    IncludeDocProps:=False, KeepIRM:=True, _
    CreateBookmarks:=wdExportCreateHeadingBookmarks, _
    DocStructureTags:=True, BitmapMissingFonts:=True, UseISO19005_1:=False
MsgBox("PDF has been created",4096)
Exit Sub
x: MsgBox("Error!, is the PDF already open?",4096)
End Sub
```

Try it by saying:
"export as book marked pdf"

Discuss

If your Word documents have the file name extension ".doc", you will need to change the portion of the script ".docx" to ".doc".

The line `On Error GoTo x:` is necessary to avoid the occurrence of an error in scenarios where the user runs the command, opens the PDF, and then runs the command again.

If an error does occur, the script moves to the portion of the script "x:" and produces a Message Box message.

The macro first checks to see if the document contains a Table of Contents (TOC), if it does not, it will use Word VBA to create one.

The line `Wait 1` will cause the script to pause for (1) second to give time for a TOC to be created. This time period can be adjusted, especially with larger documents and will enable the line of code `Selection.InsertBreak Type:=wdPageBreak` to create a page break in the correct place (immediately after the newly created TOC).

The macro then uses Word VBA to perform an update to the new or any existing TOC.

Next, the macro will use Word VBA to export the document as a book-marked PDF. The produced PDF file will be named and placed in the same file location as the active Word document.

Alternative

The portion of the code `OpenAfterExport:=False` means that the PDF will not open when created. You can change it to `OpenAfterExport:=True` so that the PDF automatically opens when created.

The portions of the code `LowerHeadingLevel:=3` and `UpperHeadingLevel:=1` determine the range (Heading Styles 1,2 & 3) of the built-in Header Styles that will be used to create the TOC.

The portion of the script `AddedStyles:="myStyleOne, myStyleTwo"` can be used to include any of your own custom styles within the TOC, replace `myStyleOne, myStyleTwo` with the names of your custom styles.

Refer to:

Chapter 2: Object Library References
Chapter 8: If Then Statement, On Error Instruction, MsgBox Function - Message Boxes, Wait

Insert Page Numbers in MS Word Starting at Page x

Writing essays and reports that require specific page numbering conventions can be a challenge.

Students are often faced with this scenario when handing in coursework as they may have to include title sheets and other university requirements as part of their documents.

Whether it's starting page numbers from a specific page within a document or removing page numbers from later pages, you will need to be familiar with creating and removing section breaks within MS Word.

This macro creates page numbers that start from a specific page.

As an example, you have a five-page document and you want the page numbering to start from page three (see Figure 9-5).

Figure 9-5

<**Word VBA Solution:** Needs Microsoft Word Object Library>

MyCommand Name: create my page numbering style

Description: insert page numbers starting at page x

Group: Dragon - A Step Further_Chapter_09

Availability: Application-specific

Application: Microsoft Word

Command Type: Advanced Scripting

Content:

```
Sub Main
'Start page numbers from a specific page of a MS Word document
'Run this macro on an open document
    userSelectedFromPage = 1
'In case of errors
    On Error GoTo NotValidInput
'Find out how many pages the document has
    numberOfPagesInDocument = Selection.Information(wdNumberOfPagesInDocument)
    'MsgBox "This document has " & numberOfPagesInDocument & " pages", vbInformation
'Ask user for the FROM page to start numbering
```

```
    ExecuteScript "SetRecognitionMode 3", 0
    Begin Dialog UserDialog 510,98,"Dialog Form - Input Box",.dialogfunc '
%GRID:10,7,1,1
        Text 10,7,120,21,"This document has ",.Text1
        Text 140,7,40,21,numberOfPagesInDocument,.Text2
        TextBox 10,49,110,21,.TextBox1
        OKButton 410,7,90,21
        CancelButton 410,35,90,21
        Text 170,7,90,14,"pages.",.Text3
        Text 10,28,380,14,"From which page number do you wish to start page
numbers?",.Text4
    End Dialog
  Dim dlg As UserDialog
  value_form_one=Dialog (dlg)
  userSelectedFromPage = dlg.TextBox1
  Select Case value_form_one
    Case 0 'Cancel button pressed
      ExecuteScript "SetRecognitionMode 0", 0
      Exit All 'Exit script
  End Select
  ExecuteScript "SetRecognitionMode 0", 0
'Check if user input page is larger than the number of pages in the document
    Select Case userSelectedFromPage
        Case Is > numberOfPagesInDocument
          MsgBox ("The number you entered is too high.")
          Exit Sub
        Case Is < 1
          MsgBox ("The number you entered is too low.")
          Exit Sub
    End Select
    MsgBox "We will start the page numbering from page " & userSelectedFromPage,
vbInformation
'Let's start the process
    GoTo Clear_All_Section_Breaks
    Return_From_Clear_All_Section_Breaks:
    GoTo Delete_Any_Existing_Page_Numbers
    Return_From_Delete_Any_Existing_Page_Numbers:
    'GoTo Insert_Page_Numbers
    Return_From_Insert_Page_Numbers:
'Part 01a Move insertion point to the top of the user selected from page.
    Selection.GoTo What:=wdGoToPage, Which:=wdGoToNext, Name:=userSelectedFromPage
'Part 01b Insert section page break.
    Selection.InsertBreak Type:=wdSectionBreakNextPage
'Part 02a Insert Footer page numbers starting from 1 in each of the sections.
    Dim oSec As Section
    Dim oFooter As HeaderFooter
    For Each oSec In ActiveDocument.Sections
        For Each oFooter In oSec.Footers
            oFooter.LinkToPrevious = False
            If oFooter.Exists Then
                oFooter.Range.Text = ""
                oFooter.Range.Fields.Add oFooter.Range, wdFieldPage, , False
                oFooter.PageNumbers.RestartNumberingAtSection = True
                oFooter.PageNumbers.StartingNumber = 1
```

```
                    'oFooter.Range.InsertBefore vbTab & "Page "
            End If
        Next oFooter
    Next oSec
'Part 02b Remove page numbers from section 01
    With ActiveDocument.Sections(1)
        .Headers(wdHeaderFooterPrimary).Range.Text = ""
        .Footers(wdHeaderFooterPrimary).Range.Text = ""
    End With
    Exit Sub
    Delete_Any_Existing_Page_Numbers:
        Dim objSect As Section
        Dim objHF As HeaderFooter
        Dim objPNum As PageNumber
        For Each objSect In ActiveDocument.Sections
            For Each objHF In objSect.Headers
                For Each objPNum In objHF.PageNumbers
                    objPNum.Delete
                Next
            Next
            For Each objHF In objSect.Footers
                For Each objPNum In objHF.PageNumbers
                    objPNum.Delete
                Next
            Next
        Next
    GoTo Return_From_Delete_Any_Existing_Page_Numbers
    Insert_Page_Numbers:
        With ActiveDocument.Sections(1)
            .Footers(wdHeaderFooterPrimary).PageNumbers.Add _
            PageNumberAlignment:=wdAlignPageNumberLeft, _
            FirstPage:=True
        End With
    GoTo Return_From_Insert_Page_Numbers
    Clear_All_Section_Breaks:
        Selection.Find.ClearFormatting
        Selection.Find.Replacement.ClearFormatting
            With Selection.Find
            .Text = "^b"
            .Replacement.Text = ""
            .Forward = True
            .Wrap = wdFindContinue
            .Format = False
            .MatchCase = False
            .MatchWholeWord = False
            .MatchByte = False
            .MatchAllWordForms = False
            .MatchSoundsLike = False
            .MatchWildcards = False
            .MatchFuzzy = False
            End With
        Selection.Find.Execute Replace:=wdReplaceAll
    GoTo Return_From_Clear_All_Section_Breaks
    NotValidInput:
```

```
        MsgBox ("You entered an invalid value! Only positive numbers please.")
End Sub
Rem See DialogFunc help topic for more information.
Private Function dialogfunc(DlgItem$, Action%, SuppValue&) As Boolean
    Select Case Action%
    Case 1 ' Dialog box initialization
    Case 2 ' Value changing or button pressed
      Rem dialogfunc = True ' Prevent button press from closing the dialog box
    Case 3 ' TextBox or ComboBox text changed
    Case 4 ' Focus changed
    Case 5 ' Idle
      Rem Wait .1 : dialogfunc = True ' Continue getting idle actions
DlgFocus("TextBox1")
    Case 6 ' Function key
    End Select
End Function
```

Try it by saying:
"create my page numbering style"

Discuss

This recipe starts off by using Word VBA to calculate the number of pages within the active document and stores the result in the variable numberOfPagesInDocument.

A Message Box is then generated, which displays the number of pages.

A Dialog Form styled as an Input Box is then used to ask the user from which page, page numbering should start. The required page number is then stored in the variable userSelectedFromPage.

A *Select Case* statement is used to check that the user's requested page number is within the range of the pages that are in the active document.

The rest of the script incorporates the user's request into Word VBA to produce the page numbers starting from the page requested by the user.

The *SetRecognitionMode* statement plays an important role because we require numerical values to be dictated by the user and this forces Dragon to interpret any spoken number as a numeral and not as a word.

Refer to:

Chapter 2: Object Library References

Chapter 5: Creating a Dialog Form in the style of a simple Input Box

Chapter 8: Exit Sub, MsgBox Function – Message Boxes, On Error Instruction, Select Case Function, SetRecognitionMode

Create a Backup of the Current Excel Workbook with Date & Time in the Filename

This macro is the MS Excel alternative of the macro "Create a Backup of the Current Word Document with the Date & Time in the Filename".

<Excel VBA Solution: Needs Microsoft Excel Object Library>

MyCommand Name: save dated excel file

Description: Saves a version with the current Date and Time in the filename

Group: Dragon - A Step Further_Chapter_09

Availability: Application-specific

Application: Microsoft Excel

Command Type: Advanced Scripting

Content:

```
Sub Main
'© www.dragonspeechtips.com
On Error GoTo x:
Dim objExcel As Excel.Application
Set objExcel = GetObject(, "Excel.Application")

Dim currentWbookPath_FileName As String
Dim currentWbook_FileName As String
Dim currentWbookPath As String
Dim mySetBackUpFolder As String

currentWbookPath_FileName = objExcel.ActiveWorkbook.FullName
currentWbook_FileName = objExcel.ActiveWorkbook.Name
currentWbookPath = objExcel.ActiveWorkbook.Path
mySetBackUpFolder = "C:\Users\...\myFiles_Folder"

'Get current Date & Time
saveNow = (Format(Now, "dd_mm_yyyy___hh-mm "))

'Backed up Filename and Path
currentFolder_File = currentWbookPath & "\" & saveNow & currentWbook_FileName
mySetBackUpFolder_File = mySetBackUpFolder & "\" & saveNow & currentWbook_FileName

Application.DisplayAlerts = False
'Save the renamed backup
objExcel.ActiveWorkbook.SaveCopyAs Filename:=currentFolder_File
Application.DisplayAlerts = True
GoTo cleanUp

x: MsgBox ("ERROR! Please make sure of the following:" & _
  Chr$(13) & "That the Save path exists" & _
  Chr$(13) & "There are No special characters in the Date Format" & _
  Chr$(13) & Chr$(13) & _
  "",4160,"Error")
cleanUP:
Set objExcel = Nothing
End Sub
```

Try it by saying:
"save dated excel file"

Discuss

This procedure does not require as many steps as the previous MS Word version as MS Excel has the built-in "Workbook.SaveCopyAs" VBA Method.

The macro uses the Dragon script function *Now* to gather the Date and Time at which the voice command is executed. The line `saveNow = (Format(Now, "dd_mm_yyyy___hh-mm "))` is where the variable `saveNow` becomes equal to the current Date and Time in a format as determined by the `dd_mm_yyyy___hh-mm` portion of the code.

The portion of the script `(Format(Now, "dd_mm_yyyy___hh-mm "))` determines the format as to how the Date and Time will be displayed in the filename (e.g. 02_05_2018___13-25 myFilename. xlsx). Feel free to change the format of the Date and Time. Refer to Chapter 8: Table of Date and Time Formatting Styles for assistance.

The line of code `objExcel.ActiveWorkbook.SaveCopyAs Filename:=currentFolder_File` saves a copy of the current Workbook using the variable `currentFolder_File` to determine the file name and folder in which the file will be saved.

 You can change the format of the Date and Time. Refer to Chapter 8: Table of Date and Time Formatting Styles.

 Be careful not to include special characters such as colons (:), as filenames cannot include such characters.

The dated version of the document will be saved in the same folder as the current document.

Alternative

If you wish to have all your backed-up versions of the document placed in a specific folder, then make the following changes to the script:

- Replace the portion of the script `C:\Users\...\myFiles_Folder` with your directory path to the specific folder.
- Replace the portion of the script `FileName:=currentFolder_File` with `FileName:=mySetBackUpFolder_File`

Refer to:

Chapter 2: Object Library References
Chapter 8: Changing the Display Format of Date & Time, On Error Instruction, MsgBox Function - Message Boxes

Renaming and Sorting MS Excel Worksheets

This command will allow a user to either rename the active worksheet or sort all worksheets within a workbook into alphabetical order.

<Excel VBA Solution: Needs Microsoft Excel Object Library>

MyCommand Name: <rename_or_sort_worksheets>

Name of List(s) used: <rename_or_sort_worksheets>

List items:

rename this sheet

sort the worksheets

Description: Rename or Sort Worksheets

Group: Dragon - A Step Further_Chapter_09

Availability: Application-specific

Application: Microsoft Excel

Command Type: Advanced Scripting

Content:

```
Sub Main
On Error GoTo X
Dim objExcel As Excel.Application
Set objExcel = GetObject(, "Excel.Application")

Select Case (ListVar1)
    Case "rename this sheet"
        GoTo renameWorksheet
    Case "sort the worksheets"
        GoTo sortWorksheets
End Select
Exit All

renameWorksheet:
    Begin Dialog UserDialog 460,63,"Dialog Form - Input Box",.dialogfunc '
%GRID:10,7,1,1
        Text 10,7,320,21,"Insert the new Worksheet Title ",.Text1
        TextBox 10,28,320,21,.TextBox1
        OKButton 350,7,90,21
        CancelButton 350,35,90,21
    End Dialog
    Dim dlg As UserDialog
    value_form_one=Dialog (dlg)
    userInput = dlg.TextBox1
    Select Case value_form_one
        Case 0 'Cancel button pressed
            Exit All 'Exit script
    End Select
```

```
    'Excel VBA required to change a Worksheet Title
    objExcel.ActiveSheet.Name = userInput
    Set objExcel = Nothing
    Exit Sub

sortWorksheets:
    'Declare Variables
    Dim CurrentSheetPos As Integer
    Dim PrevSheetPos As Integer
    'Set the starting counts and start looping
    For CurrentSheetPos = 1 To objExcel.Sheets.Count
        For PrevSheetPos = 1 To CurrentSheetPos - 1
            'Check Current Sheet against Previous Sheet
            If LCase(objExcel.Sheets(PrevSheetPos).Name) > _
            LCase(objExcel.Sheets(CurrentSheetPos).Name) Then
                objExcel.Sheets(CurrentSheetPos).Move _
                Before:=objExcel.Sheets(PrevSheetPos)
            End If
        Next PrevSheetPos
    Next CurrentSheetPos
    Set objExcel = Nothing
    Exit Sub

X: MsgBox ("Error!, please try again", 4096)
End Sub
Rem See DialogFunc help topic for more information.
Private Function dialogfunc(DlgItem$, Action%, SuppValue&) As Boolean
    Select Case Action%
    Case 5 ' Idle
      Rem Wait .1 : dialogfunc = True ' Continue getting idle actions
      DlgFocus("TextBox1")
    End Select
End Function
```

Select a worksheet and try it by saying:

"rename this sheet"

"sort the work sheets"

Discuss

For this macro a Dragon List command is created, which enables us to act upon the two phrases allowed to run the command. The variable ListVar1 will become equal to one of the two phrases.

A *Select Case* statement (Select Case (ListVar1)) is then used to determine which of the tasks the macro will carry out and then go to the associated portion of the script.

The line userInput = dlg.TextBox1 is where the variable userInput becomes equal to the value inserted into the generated Dialog Form (styled as an Input Box).

The line `objExcel.ActiveSheet.Name = userInput` is the Excel VBA code required to change the name of the active worksheet. It uses the value of the variable `userInput`, which is derived from the entry inserted into the Dialog Form.

The line `DlgFocus("TextBox1")` is placed within the "`Case 5`" area of the script in order to force the Dialog Form to appear above any running applications.

To sort the worksheets into alphabetical order, Excel VBA is used.

 When sorting alphabetically it is important to note that Excel sorts by text. Therefore, if you use numbers within your worksheet tab names you may achieve some unexpected results. For example, a worksheet titled "sheet9" will come after a worksheet titled "sheet10".

Refer to:

Chapter 2: Object Library References

Chapter 5: Creating a Dialog Form in the style of a simple Input Box

Chapter 8: Select Case Function

Export all Text from PowerPoint Slides to a Text File and Open the Text File in Word

There are times when viewing a PowerPoint presentation that it may be more convenient to review the text in a MS Word document.

Rather than spending time copying and pasting all the text from the slides into a new Word document. The following macro extracts all the text within a PowerPoint presentation and exports it to a newly created text file. It will then open the text file in MS Word.

<PowerPoint VBA Solution: Needs Microsoft PowerPoint Object Library>

MyCommand Name: extract all text and open in word

Description: Exports all text from all slides to a text file and open the file in MS Word

Group: Dragon - A Step Further_Chapter_09

Availability: Application-specific

Application: Microsoft PowerPoint

Command Type: Advanced Scripting

Content:

```
Sub Main
'© www.dragonspeechtips.com
    Dim PPApp As PowerPoint.Application
    Dim PPPres As PowerPoint.Presentation
    Dim PPSlide As PowerPoint.Slide
    Dim oShape As PowerPoint.Shape
    Set PPApp = GetObject(, "PowerPoint.Application")
    Set PPPres = PPApp.ActivePresentation
    Dim slideNum As Integer
    Dim shapeNum As Integer
    Dim destPath As String
    Dim fileName As String
    Dim createdFilename As String
    Dim userResponse As Integer

    destination_folder = "C:\Users...Path..to..folder\"
    fileName = "Exported_Text_from_PowerPoint.rtf"

'Checks if path exists
    If Right(destination_folder, 1) <> "\" Then
        destination_folder = destination_folder & "\"
    End If
    If Dir(destination_folder, vbDirectory) <> vbNullString Then
        'Do nothing
    Else
        MsgBox("The destination folder does not exist, please try again",4096)
        GoTo cleanUp
    End If
```

```
        createdFilename = destination_folder+fileName

Open createdFilename For Output As #1
With PPApp.ActivePresentation
        Print #1, "Text extracted from the file: " & .Name
        Print #1, "----------------------------"
        Print #1, ""
        Print #1, ""
    For slideNum = 1 To .Slides.Count
        Print #1, "Slide: " & slideNum
        With .Slides(slideNum)
            For shapeNum = 1 To .Shapes.Count
                With .Shapes(shapeNum)
                    If .HasTextFrame Then
                        Print #1, .TextFrame.TextRange.Text
                    End If
                End With
                Print #1, ""
            Next shapeNum
        End With
        Print #1, "======="
    Next slideNum
End With
Close #1
SetMicrophone 0
Beep
Wait 2
SetMicrophone 1
AppBringUp createdFilename

cleanUp:
    Set PPApp = Nothing
    Set PPPres = Nothing
    Set ActiveShape = Nothing
End Sub
```

Try it by saying:

"extract all text and open in word"

Discuss

Before running the script, change the destination folder path (C:\Users...Path..to..folder\) to a folder path on your PC.

The line of code destination_folder = "C:\Users...Path..to..folder\" is where we set the variable destination_folder equal to the directory path of the folder that will contain the created file.

The line of code fileName = "Exported_Text_from_PowerPoint.rtf" is the intended filename of the text file to be created. You will notice that the file extension is rtf, these types of files are usually opened in MS Word by default.

The line `createdFilename = destination_folder+fileName` is where the variable `createdFilename` becomes equal to the full path with filename.

Separating the file path (to the destination folder) from the filename enables us to check if the destination folder exists. In doing this, we avoid errors occurring if the folder does not exist.

The `Beep` function has been included in the script, so that we get an acknowledgement once the command has been carried out.

Finally, the line `AppBringUp createdFilename` can be interpreted as "double clicking" on the created text file and opens the file in the default application as determined by the settings in MS Windows.

Alternative

Changing the extension of the intended file name from `.rtf` to `.txt`, produces a file that when double clicked will be opened by the application Notepad.

> When running this script for a second time, you need to be aware that, if the created text file already exists in the same location, then that file, will be replaced with the new file.

Refer to:

Chapter 2: Object Library References
Chapter 8: Beep, If Then Statement, SetMicrophone, Wait

Display the Number of Words in the Selected Text in any Document

Applications such as "DragonPad", "Notepad" and "WordPad" do not contain a function to display a word count.

This macro will display a Message Box showing the number of words in the selected portion of text regardless of the application.

MyCommand Name: word count the selection

Description: Displays the number of words in selected text

Group: Dragon - A Step Further_Chapter_09

Availability: Global

Command Type: Advanced Scripting

Content:

```
Sub Main
SendDragonKeys "{Ctrl+c}" 'copy selection to clipboard
selectedText = Clipboard$() 'String becomes_equal To clipboard
numSpaces = 0 'Number of Spaces variable
spacePosition = InStr(selectedText, " ")
Do While spacePosition <> 0
  numSpaces = CStr(CLng(numSpaces)) +1
  spacePosition = CStr(CLng(spacePosition)) + 1
  spacePosition = InStr(spacePosition, selectedText, " ")
Loop
No_of_Words = CStr(CLng(numSpaces)) + 1
MsgBox ("The selection contains " & No_of_Words & " word(s)",4096)
End Sub
```

Highlight some written text in DragonPad, Notepad or WordPad and try it by saying:
"word count the selection"

Discuss

This macro examines the selected text and records the number of spaces within it. We can then calculate that the number of words in the text is equal to the number of spaces plus one. This is a tad crude as it relies on there being no extra space(s) in the selected text.

The script begins by using the line SendDragonKeys "{Ctrl+c}" to copy the selected text to the Clipboard.

The line selectedText = Clipboard$() copies the content of the Clipboard to the variable called selectedText. This now gives us the opportunity to examine the text that has been selected.

The variable numSpaces is set to zero and will eventually hold the number of spaces within the selected text.

Next, the command `spacePosition = InStr(selectedText, " ")`uses the *InStr* command to locate the position number in the selected text for the first occurrence of a space (" "). The variable `spacePosition` becomes equal to the position number.

We use a *Do While Loop* that will perform the statements between the lines `Do While spacePosition <> 0` and `Loop` repeatedly until the `spacePosition` variable becomes equal to zero (0).

Within the loop, we have an accumulative total for the number of spaces encountered, this value is stored in the variable `numSpaces`. The value of the variable `spacePosition` is incremented by one, the *InStr* command is then used to find the next occurence of a space. If no more spaces are found, the variable `spacePosition` will become equal to zero (0) and the script will then exit the *Do While Loop*.

The line `No_of_Words = CStr(CLng(numSpaces)) + 1` calculates the number of words by adding a value of one to the number of spaces found and stores the value in the variable `No_of_Words`.

Finally, we use the *MsgBox* command to reveal the number of words in the selected text.

 To perform calculations, we use the **CLng** and **CStr** functions when working with Integer and String values.

Refer to:

Chapter 8: Clipboard Function, CLng Function, CStr Function, Do While Loop, InStr Function, MsgBox Function – Message Boxes, SendDragonKeys, SendKeys & SendSystemKeys

Find a Topic by its Title Name in Mindjet MindManager

When working with large Mind Maps containing numerous Subtopics, it can often be frustrating looking for and selecting a specific Topic.

By dictating this command and including a Topic title, MindManager will instantly navigate to and apply focus to the requested Topic.

<MindManager VBA Solution: Needs Mindjet MindManager Object Library>

MyCommand Name: find the topic <dictation>

Name of List(s) used: <dictation>

List items:

any phrase

Description: finds, selects and applies focus to a specific topic by its title name

Group: Dragon - A Step Further_Chapter_09

Availability: Application-specific

Application: Mindjet MindManager

Command Type: Advanced Scripting

Content:

```
Sub Main
'Finds, selects and applies focus to the user requested topic title.
Dim MMapp As MindManager.Application
Set MMapp = New MindManager.Application

Dim topic_title As Topic
Dim userRequest As Variant
Dim notFound As Integer
notFound = 0

userRequest = ListVar1

'===== Search through all topics within the MindMap
For Each topic_title In MMapp.ActiveDocument.Range(mmRangeAllTopics)
  If LCase(topic_title.Title.Text) = LCase(userRequest) Then 'looks for a topic with the
title x, this is case sensitive
    topic_title.SelectOnly 'makes the topic become selected
    topic_title.Focus 'applies Focus to the topic
    notFound = notFound + 1
  Else
    'Do nothing
  End If
Next topic_title

If notFound = 0 Then MsgBox ("The Topic " & userRequest & " cannot be found. ",4096)
```

```
'cleanUp:
   Set MMapp = Nothing
End Sub
```

Open or create a Mind Map with topics and try it by saying:

"find the topic <topic title name>"

Discuss

MindManager includes its own Application VBA which we can take advantage of to create the command.

In this recipe we create a Dragon List type command using the built-in List called <dictation>. By doing so, we allow for any possible Topic title and enable the script to act on it.

The script searches through all the Topics within the Mind Map in a bid to find the Topic title that matches the user's choice.

An *If Then* statement is used to compare what is dictated against all the Topic titles within the Mind Map.

The *LCase* statement plays a major role within this script as it allows us to interpret the dictated title in lowercase. Equally, using *LCase* while searching through the Mind Map means that all the Topic titles are interpreted as lowercase. This is important; as searching for Topics, by default, is case sensitive. Therefore, by using the *LCase* statement we avoid the possibility of not finding our required Topic should there be a mismatch of case in the dictated and searched for titles.

Refer to:

Chapter 2: Object Library References
Chapter 4: The unique Dragon List named <dictation>
Chapter 8: If Then Statement, LCase and UCase Functions

Performing Mindjet MindManager Functions

The MindManager application offers a vast number of shortcut keys combinations to perform functions. As we all know, the ability to remember these combinations can be a bit of a headache. Rather than spending time trying to remember the keyboard shortcuts, use this macro instead to carry out several popular MindManager functions - just by dictating memorable voice commands.

MyCommand Name: <popular_mm_sc>

Name of List(s) used: <popular_mm_sc>

List items:

add callout

add subtopic

add topic

balance map

fit map

hide notes

show notes

Description: Popular Mindjet MindManager Keyboard Shortcuts

Group: Dragon - A Step Further_Chapter_09

Availability: Application-specific

Application: Mindjet MindManager

Command Type: Advanced Scripting

Content:

```
Sub Main
Select Case (ListVar1)
    Case "add topic"
        SendKeys "{Enter}" 'Press Enter key
    Case "add subtopic"
        SendKeys "{Ins}" 'Press Insert (INS) key
    Case "add callout"
        SendKeys "^+{Enter}" 'Ctrl+Shift+Enter
    Case "show notes"
        SendKeys "^t" 'Ctrl+T
    Case "hide notes"
        SendKeys "^t" 'Ctrl+T
    Case "balance map"
        SendDragonKeys "{Ctrl+Alt+b}" 'Ctrl+Alt+B
    Case "fit map"
        SendKeys "^{F5}" 'Ctrl+F5
End Select
End Sub
```

Try it by saying:

"add topic"

"add subtopic"

"show notes"

...

Discuss

To avoid making numerous commands to perform various functions, a Dragon List command is created, whereby, the List named <mm_functions_sc> holds all the voice command options we would like to include.

As usual the variable ListVar1 is populated with the dictated request and a *Case* statement is used to instruct Dragon to perform the *SendKeys* function (keyboard shortcut) relating to the request.

When looking for shortcut keys combinations in MindManager, most of them can be observed by positioning your mouse over the intended function.

MindManager is a part of the Windows family of applications that goes a long way to providing keyboard control to access all functionalities. By pressing the Alt key, you will see several highlighted letters and numbers appear under the menus. If you know the menu that contains the function you wish to use, you can press the relative letters or numbers to navigate your way to that function. By noting down the keys pressed you can easily create a command to do the same.

Refer to:

Chapter 4: Dragon List Commands

Chapter 8: Select Case Function, SendDragonKeys, SendKeys & SendSystemKeys

Performing Sonocent Audio Notetaker Functions

Sonocent Audio Notetaker has several keyboard shortcuts within the application. However, for some, remembering these keyboard combinations can be quite a chore. Creating memorable voice commands instead will undoubtedly make your life a lot easier. This macro enables you to carry out several popular Audio Notetaker functions by voice.

MyCommand Name: <popular_sonocent_functions>

Name of List(s) used: <popular_sonocent_functions>

List items:

%f{e}{a}\export audio as album

%f{e}{t}\export text and images

%f{i}{i}\import images

%f{i}{s}\import slides or pdfs

%o{l}\trim silence

%o{r}\remove section break

^{Enter}\insert section break

^m\merge chunks

^n\new project

^s\save project

^t\split chunk

^w\close project

Description: Sonocent Audio Notetaker functions

Group: Dragon - A Step Further_Chapter_09

Availability: Application-specific

Application: Audio Notetaker 5.3

Command Type: Advanced Scripting

Content:

```
Sub Main
SendKeys Mid(ListVar1, 1,InStr(ListVar1, "\")-1),1
End Sub
```

Open the Sonocent Audio Notetaker application and try it by saying:

"new project"

"split chunk"

...

Discuss

This script takes advantage of the flexibility that a Dragon Written\Spoken words List gives us. By populating the List with all the voice options and their associated keyboard shortcuts means that the main body of the command needs only one line of code.

Refer to:

Chapter 4: Dragon Written\Spoken words List
Chapter 8: SendDragonKeys, SendKeys & SendSystemKeys

Section 7: Appendix

Appendix

Send Keys Step Dialog Box Table

Table A-1 lists the codes that the Send Keys Step supports when creating Step-by-Step commands.

Table A-1

Key	Code
ADD	{ADD}
APPLICATIONS	{APPLICATIONS} or {APPS}
BACKSPACE	{BACKSPACE} or {BS}
BREAK	{BREAK}
CANCEL	{CANCEL}
CAPS LOCK	{CAPSLOCK}
CLEAR	{CLEAR}
DECIMAL	{DECIMAL}
DELETE or DEL	{DELETE} or {DEL}
DIVIDE	{DIVIDE}
DOWN ARROW	{DOWN}
END	{END}
ENTER	{ENTER}
ESC	{ESCAPE} or {ESC}
EXECUTE	{EXECUTE} or {EXEC}
F1-F24	{F1} through {F24}
HELP	{HELP}
HOME	{HOME}
INSERT	{INSERT}
LBUTTON	{LBUTTON} or {LBTN}

Key	Code
LEFT ARROW	{LEFT}
MBUTTON	{MBUTTON} or {MBTN}
MULTIPLY	{MULTIPLY}
NUMPAD0	{NUMPAD0} or {NP0}
NUMPAD1	{NUMPAD1} or {NP1}
NUMPAD2	{NUMPAD2} or {NP2}
NUMPAD3	{NUMPAD3} or {NP3}
NUMPAD4	{NUMPAD4} or {NP4}
NUMPAD5	{NUMPAD5} or {NP5}
NUMPAD6	{NUMPAD6} or {NP6}
NUMPAD7	{NUMPAD7} or {NP7}
NUMPAD8	{NUMPAD8} or {NP8}
NUMPAD9	{NUMPAD9} or {NP9}
PAGE DOWN	{PGDN}
PAGE UP	{PGUP}
PRINT	{PRINT}
RBUTTON	{RBUTTON} or {RBTN}
RETURN	{RETURN}
RIGHT ARROW	{RIGHT}
SCROLL LOCK	{SCROLLLOCK}
SELECT	{SELECT}
SEPARATOR	{SEPARATOR}
SNAPSHOT	{SNAPSHOT}
SPACE	{SPACE}
SUBTRACT	{SUBTRACT}
TAB	{TAB}

Key	Code
UP ARROW	{UP}
WINDOWS	{WINDOWS} or {WIN}

SHIFT	+
CTRL	^
ALT	%

Repeating key sequences:

Key sequences can be repeated by adding a number in the brackets. For example, to have the Enter key pressed three times, use {ENTER 3}. Make sure there is a space between the key name and the number.

Popular Ascii Character Codes

Table A-2 lists several useful Ascii character codes.

Table A-2

Chr(9)	horizontal tab
Chr(10)	new line
Chr(13)	carriage return
Chr(32)	Space

Chr(33)	!	Chr(41)	)	Chr(59)	;	Chr(93)	]
Chr(34)	"	Chr(42)	*	Chr(60)	<	Chr(94)	^
Chr(35)	#	Chr(43)	+	Chr(61)	=	Chr(95)	_
Chr(36)	$	Chr(44)	,	Chr(62)	>	Chr(96)	`
Chr(37)	%	Chr(45)	-	Chr(63)	?	Chr(123)	{
Chr(38)	&	Chr(46)	.	Chr(64)	@	Chr(124)		
Chr(39)	`	Chr(47)	/	Chr(91)	[	Chr(125)	}
Chr(40)	(	Chr(58)	:	Chr(92)	\	Chr(126)	~

Chr(145)	'
Chr(146)	'
Chr(147)	"
Chr(148)	"

Useful Built-in Dragon Commands

Dragon NaturallySpeaking and Dragon Professional are packed with a large number of built-in commands covering a wide range of applications.

A comprehensive list of useful built-in Dragon commands for MS Office, Google Chrome and other applications can be found at this book's companion site at - www.dragonspeechtips.com/

Here are a few to get you going…

Styling Text

Say "*Change font colour to red*" - Changes the selected text to the colour red.

Say "*Change font to times new roman*" - Changes the font of the selected text to "Times New Roman".

Say "*Change the style to heading 1*" - Changes the selected text to the style named "Heading 1".

Types of Text

Hyphenated Words

Say "*<word> hyphen <word>*" – Produces hyphenated words, for example, "director-general"

Compound Words

Say "*<word> no space <word>*" – Produces compound words, for example, "spacewalk"

Hearing Your Text

Say "*read that*" – Reads out the selected word(s) or reads out the word adjacent to the cursor.

Say "*read the selection*" – Reads out the selected words or reads out the word adjacent to the cursor.

Say "*read the paragraph*" – Reads out the current or selected paragraph.

Miscellaneous

Say "*Insert 3 by 4 table*" – Creates 3 columns by 4 rows table.

Say "*Set background to yellow*" – Changes the background colour of the document to "Yellow".

Navigation and Pressing Keys

Say "*Press spacebar*" - Presses the keyboard Space Bar

Say "*Press enter (return)*" - Presses the keyboard Enter (Return) key

Say "*Press Tab key*" - Presses the keyboard Tab key

Say "*Click OK*" - Clicks the "OK" button when a window containing an OK button is active.

Say "*Move down 4*" - Moves the cursor down 4 lines

Say "*Press <left/right/up/down> arrow*" - Moves the cursor one-character left, right, up or down.

Useful Links

A list of useful built-in Dragon commands for MS Office and other applications can be found at this book's companion site at – www.dragonspeechtips.com/

For a list of MS Word WDColor Enumeration codes and their values visit the Microsoft site at the following URL – https://docs.microsoft.com/en-us/office/vba/api/word.wdcolor

For a list of MS Excel chart type codes visit the Microsoft site at the following URL - https://msdn.microsoft.com/en-us/VBA/Excel-VBA/articles/xlcharttype-enumeration-excel

For a list of MS PowerPoint (VBA) Shapes and their numerical values visit the Microsoft site at the following URL - https://docs.microsoft.com/en-us/office/vba/api/Office.MsoAutoShapeType

For a list of MS PowerPoint (VBA) Slide layout types and their values visit the Microsoft site at the following URL - https://docs.microsoft.com/en-us/office/vba/api/powerpoint.ppslidelayout

For a list of MS Publisher (VBA) alignment values and descriptions visit the Microsoft site at the following URL - https://msdn.microsoft.com/en-us/vba/publisher-vba/articles/shaperange-align-method-publisher

For a list of MS Publisher (VBA) Shapes visit the Microsoft site at the following URL - https://msdn.microsoft.com/en-us/vba/publisher-vba/articles/pbshapetype-enumeration-publisher

For a useful list of Ascii code characters visit - https://www.branah.com/ascii-converter

Index

N

O

Printed in Great Britain
by Amazon